SAGEBRUSH COLLABORATION

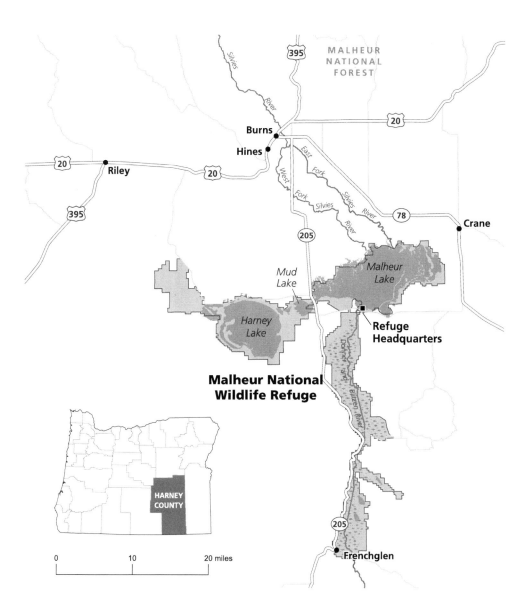

Cartography by InfoGraphics Lab, Department of Geography, University of Oregon.

Sagebrush Collaboration

How Harney County Defeated the
Takeover of the Malheur National Wildlife Refuge

PETER WALKER

Oregon State University Press   Corvallis

Library of Congress Cataloging-in-Publication Data

Names: Walker, Peter (Peter Abel), author.
Title: Sagebrush collaboration : how Harney County defeated the takeover of
    the Malheur National Wildlife Refuge / Peter Walker.
Description: Corvallis : Oregon State University Press, 2018. | Includes
    bibliographical references and index.
Identifiers: LCCN 2018016273 (print) | LCCN 2018039999 (ebook) |
    ISBN 9780870719509 (e-book) | ISBN 9780870719493 | ISBN
    9780870719493 (original trade pbk.; alk. paper)
Subjects: LCSH: Militia movements—United States. | Malheur National
    Wildlife Refuge (Or.) | Land use, Rural—West (U.S.) | Radicalism—
    United States. | Government, Resistance to—United States.
Classification: LCC HN90.R3 (ebook) | LCC HN90.R3 .W357 2018 (print) |
    DDC 303.48/40973—dc23
LC record available at https://lccn.loc.gov/2018016273

All photographs by the author unless otherwise noted.

Oregon State University
OSU Press

Oregon State University Press
121 The Valley Library
Corvallis OR 97331-4501
541-737-3166 • fax 541-737-3170
www.osupress.oregonstate.edu

Contents

Militia Go Home

The sight of a sign nailed to a power pole on a main street in Burns was my first clue that something wasn't right in our town.

Although retired as ranchers, my husband and I continue the pattern of vacationing in October and November after the crops are in and before it is time to feed cattle hay for the winter. I was unaware of what had been happening in my community in the late fall months of 2015. Sunday, December 6, 2015, I was on my way home from church. Conversation there had been our usual friendly banter. No mention of anything unusual. What did this threatening sign mean?

MILITIA GO HOME. The message was roughly scrawled in black paint.

Who put up the sign? This is out of place in Burns. Should I drive around the block and take it down? I'd need a hammer or a crowbar, I decided. Oh well. Some stupid joke. Somebody will take it down.

As the days went by, I noticed some odd letters to the editor in the local newspaper and advertising of events featuring speakers about the Constitution—and flyers in store windows advertising meetings at various coffee shops and at the fairgrounds. As a history buff, I thought the talks on the Constitution would be interesting but didn't plan on attending. I have trouble hearing in public meetings and get more satisfaction from reading or visiting in small groups. The local newspaper was only hinting that something was astir. The local radio station had been off the air since November. So, I turned to social media to see what I could find out. It was like opening Pandora's box.

There was talk of forming a committee of safety made up of self-appointed Harney County citizens to take the place of county government and a protest rally for the Hammonds scheduled for January 2, 2016. The news about the Hammonds returning to prison to finish a mandatory minimum sentence for arson on public lands was upsetting to many in the community.

As a journalist—fourteen years a regional correspondent for the *Oregonian* and eighteen years as reporter and editor of the *Burns Times-Herald*, I knew the Hammonds and their history, had read most of the court case documents and rulings, and had reported on many public land issues and environmental concerns. I was aware of the controversy about the men being resentenced after a sympathetic judge ignored the sentencing guidelines and gave the two men a fraction of the prison time required by the mandatory minimum sentence rule.

Like many others in our community, I felt the resentencing was unfair. Unfair to send the men back to prison after they had already served the original sentence, paid a massive fine, and been stripped of grazing rights and returned to their ranching life. The judge made the mistake. The judge is the one who did not follow the rules. The Hammonds had accepted a plea bargain and had agreed not to appeal their sentence. It seemed unfair for the government to appeal the sentence prosecutors did not like and send the Hammonds back to prison. Thinking it was unfair didn't change the mandatory minimum sentence laws or the facts of the Hammonds' long confrontational relationship with the US Department of Fish and Wildlife, the Malheur National Wildlife Refuge, and the Bureau of Land Management. Nor did thinking the resentencing was unfair change a jury's guilty verdicts.

I'd heard the stories of the death threats that had been made, the excuse that lightning storms gave start to additional fires, and stories of cutting boundary fences, trespassing cattle, and the feud over the waterhole the refuge would no longer allow the Hammonds to use. My opinion was that there was right and wrong on both sides of the controversy and a whole lot of questionable behavior. Correspondence between the Hammonds and the refuge management shows deep frustration all around.

As a news reporter, I had seen documentation of the problems faced by ranchers, public land managers, and environmentalists. I'd also been a part of reporting the controversial and divisive issues and the efforts to collaborate, to mend ideological differences, and to find courses of action that would serve a variety of interests and practice good management, allow ranching to survive, and protect the environment too.

After retirement, as a community member, I had served on the education committee for the High Desert Partnership. Even though my husband and I have never been permittees for public grazing, limiting our production to private lands, I have concern for the environment and for the agricultural way of life. Use of public lands is a big part of that.

I watched the live-streamed video of the protest march for the Hammonds and the subsequent takeover of the refuge. I remained glued to my computer screen to watch live-streamed news videos, videos of meetings, newspaper and radio and television coverage, as well as the constant barrage of words from the Bundy bunch and their compatriots, constitutionalists, patriots, Oath Keepers, this group and that group, elected officials, and the many, many emotional sentiments from those who thought the movement was a strike for citizens' rights and those who thought it was a step to anarchy.

I saw my community ripped and torn. Feelings raw. Friends against friends. Family members against family members. I heard many untrue statements, and misinformation and unreasonable criticism. It was heart-breaking, worrisome, and, yes, struck a little terror that an awful episode could occur if things got out of hand. I was outraged when I saw trenches dug through the area designated as a gravesite for the bones of Paiute ancestors. I had been present, as a reporter, for the solemn ceremony the Burns Paiute Tribe held to dedicate the site as a final resting place for the ancestors whose remains had been uncovered by receding Malheur Lake waters after the flooding in the 1980s.

As I write this, we have suffered further shock or elation, depending on one's point of view. The citizenry of Harney County rebuffed by roughly a 70 percent majority a recall election against its government's leader, and those elected to county offices in the primary election were those who had opposed the occupation.

In October 2016, the first seven accused of breaking the law by occupying the refuge were found not guilty of conspiring to impede government workers by a federal district court jury after the controversial removal and replacement of one juror from the deadlocked panel.

In November 2016, Donald Trump was elected president. Harney County cast 4,082 ballots from 4,749 eligible voters; 75.4 percent voted for the Republican candidate; 17.7 percent voted for Democrat Hillary Clinton; and 6.9 percent for other parties. Nonpartisan sheriff David Ward, who faced both praise and criticism for his handling of the occupation and who refused to give in to the occupation demands while working for a peaceful resolution, retained his position with 58 percent of the vote.

What does this mean for my isolated, rural, frontier ranching community of ten thousand square miles with seven thousand people and 75 percent of the land publicly owned?

Some believe Harney County, of all places in the West, was a most unlikely location to succeed in a takeover of public lands and local government. Although some welcomed the brashness of the Bundy movement to wrest control, most did not agree with the tactics.

However, concern over the economy of rural America runs deep in Harney County. Government management of public lands and environmental pressures on land use issues weigh heavily on a small population in a very large space. The historical roots of those who live here go deep into a land they love and a way of life they love—whether they engage in the agricultural way of life or have taken jobs with the public land agencies.

Peter Walker explores the phenomenon of the dichotomy of provincialism and progressivism in a community that is independent to a fault, doesn't like change, respects education, and strives for excellence and quality against high odds.

His exploration generates questions that remain to be answered: Why was the Bundy revolution doomed to fail, for the majority's part, in Harney County? And, for the majority's part, is it a contradiction that a decidedly conservative political approach to land management, and economic and social issues, is favored? In light of what has transpired since the occupation, did Bundy fail? Will the movement of a very radical approach to government thwart the collaboration efforts that have become a trademark for Harney County? Can the Harney County community heal and move forward?

Pauline Braymen
Burns, Oregon, December 2017

Preface

On Sunday morning, January 3, 2016, as I woke up, I listened to Oregon Public Broadcasting on the radio. In my usual pre-coffee fog, at first I did not realize the importance of what was being said. I noted with interest the radio announcer's description of a protest rally in Burns, Oregon,[1] on behalf of rancher Dwight Hammond and his son Steven Hammond, who had been convicted of arson on federal land. The rally in Burns was notable to me because in 2008 I had spent some time in Harney County for an earlier book project, and I had come away with an impression that the community is quiet and conservative, not a place where I would expect a big street protest. As the radio announcer continued, my puzzlement shifted to disbelief:

> But then, one radical faction split off. A group of armed men headed to the headquarters of the Malheur National Wildlife Refuge, south of town. Locals reported seeing a half dozen or so trucks enter the area. The occupiers draped an American flag over the welcome sign outside the refuge headquarters and they blocked the road with a pickup truck. Several of the men who occupied the refuge were involved in the standoff in 2014 on Cliven Bundy's ranch in Nevada. Ammon Bundy, Cliven's son, is the group's spokesperson. [Bundy's voice:] "We stand in defense and when the time is right we will begin to defend the people of Harney County in using the land and the resources. . . . If [law enforcement officers] come and try to force that issue, then they make it about a building and about a facility, and lives could be lost because of that."[2]

Armed militiamen and a commandeered US Fish and Wildlife Service truck controlled the entrance to the Malheur National Wildlife Refuge headquarters.

If I had my coffee, I might have spit it out. *Ammon Bundy* is in Harney
County, Oregon; and he did *what*? I recalled the Bundy family clearly from
their armed standoff in Nevada in 2014 over a cattle roundup. I scrambled to
my computer to find out what was happening. As I was reading an account
of the takeover of the Malheur National Wildlife Refuge on the *Oregonian*'s
website, I received a voicemail from Oregon Public Broadcasting. As a
scholar in the field of natural resource governance, I was on a list of people
to call at such times to explain what was happening. I did not return the
call, as I had nothing to offer as to how or why this could be happening—
above all in Harney County, which had become something of a poster child
for collaborative land use problem-solving.

Just a few years earlier the Malheur National Wildlife Refuge had
completed an extraordinary collaborative process—the Malheur
Comprehensive Conservation Plan—which was celebrated as a model
of collaborative, community-based decision-making on federal lands. So,
Ammon Bundy proposed to "defend the people of Harney County" from
what? And what was the cause that he was prepared to defend to the point
that "lives could be lost"?

After a few days of watching over the internet as the takeover of the Malheur National Wildlife Refuge unfolded, I realized that something of historic importance was happening. In the American West, the "Sagebrush Rebellion" had been simmering for decades, but nothing of this magnitude had happened before. I knew that whatever happened, this escalation of the Sagebrush Rebellion would be important. How it was resolved would be important. How the community responded would be important. Whether Harney County's deep investment in collaborative problem-solving at places like the Malheur National Wildlife Refuge would survive would be important.

I halfway joked that if Ammon Bundy had to take over the Malheur National Wildlife Refuge, I was grateful that he did it during my research sabbatical. I dropped my other research projects and drove the approximately three hundred miles of snow-packed roads from my home in Eugene, Oregon, to Burns. Almost two years later, on December 18, 2017, while on one of my by-then-uncountable trips to Burns, I sent an email to editor Mary Braun at Oregon State University Press with my first complete draft of this book.

By then, Burns bore little resemblance to the way it had looked two years earlier. When I arrived in Burns on January 9, 2016, the streets were packed with vehicles—many with out-of-state license plates. Every motel had a No Vacancy sign. Press vehicles with satellite dishes were double-parked downtown because every parking space was filled. Reporters from all over the world stood on street corners with TV cameras and lights and microphones doing interviews.

More unsettling, men wearing camouflage with military-type insignia and carrying large, modern handguns and sometimes rifles stood in parking lots outside supermarkets and motels—especially at the Silver Spur Motel, where, by exceptional good luck, I was able to get a room after a cancellation. Pickup trucks in the Silver Spur parking lot were packed literally to their ceilings with supplies—in what appeared not unlike preparation for a war. The intentions of the armed outsiders were unknown; the potential for armed confrontation seemed very real.

The worst-case scenarios did not come to pass, and, two years later, life in Burns and Harney County had mostly returned to normal. In 2017 and early

2018, Harney County citizens were as busy as ever—or more so—working together to plan how to resolve natural resource problems through peaceful, collaborative means. Having received an explicit invitation, backed by force, to host a new, heavily armed Sagebrush Rebellion, the community had declined it and returned to its proven collaborative methods. Harney County chose sagebrush collaboration. This book attempts to explain how and why Harney County made that choice.

Above all, I observed that Harney County is a community that thinks deliberately about how to be a great community. One of my interviewees memorably said that Harney County is all about "full contact citizenship." I was reminded of that statement in September 2017 at the Harney County Fair, where I noted a sign that read, "Before you complain, have you volunteered?" It was quintessential Harney County. That attitude of encouraging civic engagement paid off handsomely when tough times came. The community emerged bruised but still very much a community. It is a community that weathered a storm unlike almost anything any other American community has experienced and, in some ways, came out stronger.

These observations, while specific to Harney County, may have value as the nation faces a more restless rural future. On January 8, 2018, charges against the main leaders of the 2014 armed standoff in Bunkerville, Nevada, in 2014, were dropped after prosecutors in Las Vegas mishandled evidence. On October 27, 2016, a federal court in Portland, Oregon, had acquitted some of the same individuals for leading the takeover of the Malheur National Wildlife Refuge after a baffling failure by prosecutors to persuade a jury of the group's conspiracy to impede federal workers at the refuge, which seemed obvious to many, including myself, who directly witnessed the event. The Bundy family emerged as triumphant folk heroes to anti-federal-government activists. They immediately promised to keep fighting.[3]

The majority of Harney County residents, who saw the Bundys and their supporters not as heroes but as misguided and threatening invaders, were deeply disappointed by the absence of accountability for the trauma inflicted on their community. Many were also deeply disappointed by the lack of opportunity through the legal system to tell their story—the story of their "subjective" experience that was literally disallowed as evidence in court. This book represents my effort to tell that story. I tell it to advise that such antigovernment activism can inflict profound disturbance on communities, and to show how one community successfully stood against it.

First, a few words about words. This book was written in response to events that took place in Harney County, Oregon, near the end of 2015 and at the beginning of 2016. The press and much of the world often described those events as the "Oregon standoff." I found that description misleading because the vast majority of individuals involved brought their dispute to Oregon from other places and involved a political agenda with a national scope. One might more accurately call it the "mostly-not-Oregon standoff."

Because that phrasing is awkward, in this book I use two terms throughout: (1) the "Bundy occupation of Harney County" (or just the "Bundy occupation"); and (2) the "takeover of the Malheur National Wildlife Refuge" (or just the "Malheur Refuge takeover," or "Malheur takeover"). The Bundy occupation refers to the period from the beginning of November 2015 when Ammon Bundy and Ryan Payne arrived in Harney County to a period roughly in the middle of 2016 when the last few outside "militia" (see below) mostly left the county. I use the term "Malheur Refuge takeover" to emphasize that the Malheur Refuge was not passively "occupied"; it was actively taken over. The Malheur takeover began on January 2, 2016, when the Malheur Refuge was seized by armed outsiders and ended with the arrests of the last four militia "holdouts" on February 11, 2016.

The word "militia," in turn, is problematic, but I use it for one main reason: it is the word most people in Harney County used to describe the groups from outside Harney County who came to support the Bundy occupation. The word militia has historical meanings that are not consistent with the kinds of groups that came to the Bundy occupation. Also, in scholarly literature the word "militia" generally applies to the period of antigovernment activism in the 1990s, as distinct from the so-called patriot movement of the late 2000s and 2010s. Some residents of Harney County chafed at the appropriation of the word "patriot" by a movement they saw as not patriotic, and chose instead to use the word "militia." Partly out of respect for that local choice, I use the term "militia" throughout this book to describe the outsiders who came to Harney County to support the

Bundy occupation, with the exception of chapter 2, where the scholarly distinctions between the 1990s "militia" and the later "patriot" movements are discussed.

In conducting research for this book, I recorded more than one hundred interviews with key figures in the story, and I attended dozens of community meetings. All quotes and extracts in this book that do not have a specific source citation are direct transcriptions of my recordings and notes.

To all Harney County citizens, I offer my sincerest respect and esteem. I spent many days after January 2, 2016, in Harney County, and your remarkable community is now woven into my own life story. You live in a very special place, and it has been my privilege to visit your home.

The people who shared their ideas with me and went out of their way to help make this book possible are almost too numerous to list. A partial listing includes the following; the rest of you know who you are: Mel Aikens, Sue Arbuthnot, Mike Arnold, Chelsey Ballot, Keith and Katie Baltzor, Gretchen Bates, Ken and Debbie Bentz, Jim Bishop, Dennis Brownridge, Ammon Bundy, Son Burns, Carla Burnside, Forrest Cameron, Christy Cheyne, Derick Clark, Stacy and Elaine Davies, Patty Dorroh, John Dougherty, Joe Mike Dully, Andy and Vena Dunbar, Duane Ehmer, Brent Fenty, LaVoy Finicum, William C. Fisher, Isabelle Fleuraud, Scott and Nellie Franklin, Steve Grasty, Paul Gray, Erik and Réglisse Hamerlynck, Peter Harkema, Robin Harkless, John Helmer, Candy Henderson, Dennis Jenkins, Alan Johnson, Dustin Johnson, Kevin Johnson, Sharon Johnson, Chad Karges, Terry Keim, Jarvis Kennedy, Georgia King, Earl Kisler, Ian Kullgren, Craig and Lori LaFollette, Beverly LaFollette, Nancy Langston, Paul Larsen, Esther Lev, Jeff Mackay, Mark Owens, Gary and Georgia Marshall, Taylor McKinnon, Hipolito Medrano, Gary Miller, Karen Moon, Linda Neale, Dan Nichols, George and Holly Orr, Fred Otley, Mark Owens, Stephanie Radinovich, Skip Renchler, Bill Robbins, Dag Robinson, Charlotte Rodrique, Jeff Rose, Rick Roy, Pete Runnels, Bob Sallinger, Daniel Schiell, Suzanne Settle, Tom and Pat Sharp, Brenda Smith, BJ Soper, Jack Southworth, Kieran Suckling, Spencer Sunshine, Bruce Taylor, Buck and Linda Taylor, Diane Teeman, Jeanette Vinson, Dave Ward, Richard Wilhelm, Nancy Willard, Les Zaitz. Special thanks go to my editor Mary

Elizabeth Braun and our peer reviewers for exceptionally meticulous and constructive input; and to Janet Braymen for providing me with a home-away-from-home in Harney County.

Above all, I thank the person who was my constant adviser and friend, Harney County rancher Pauline Braymen. Pauline's sage advice and seemingly bottomless well of knowledge about Harney County is infused into almost every part of this book. Any errors that somehow got past Pauline, however, are entirely my own.

This project was made possible in part by support from the University of Oregon's Oregon Humanities Center, and the University of Oregon Vice President's Office for Research and Innovation. The map at the beginning of this book was generously provided by Alethea Steingisser and the InfoGraphics Lab in the Department of Geography at the University of Oregon.

|

Occupation

Even for someone born in the West and accustomed to its open spaces, at first the sense of emptiness and isolation on the road to Harney County is startling. Heading east from the small city of Bend, Oregon, on Highway 20, one drives 130 miles through a landscape with few obvious signs of human presence. The high desert stretches out, mostly treeless, to the horizon—an ocean of sagebrush. One can feel surprised and even unsettled in a landscape with mile after mile of open space, possibly without seeing a single human being.

The sense of emptiness is deceiving. The high desert tells many stories, some spectacular and impossible to miss, others that are equally remarkable but call for a closer look and a careful eye. The region is known for its vast migrations of birds and for its overwhelming springtime explosions of wildflowers. Looking closely, however, one can also see an abundance of subtler life. Mule deer and pronghorn antelope in dozens blend their colors into the brown hills. Hawks and eagles soar overhead and occasionally dive headlong to the ground, swooping back up with unlucky gophers, squirrels, or chipmunks in their talons. Small rivers and marshes are home to beavers, muskrat, and otters. At night owls fly, coyotes sing, and jackrabbits seem to emerge from the soil itself.

Harney County first makes itself known only with a sign at the side of Highway 20—"Welcome to Harney County We Honor Veterans." In all directions from the sign the high desert sagebrush goes on otherwise uninterrupted. With 10,226 square miles, Harney County is roughly the same total area as the state of Massachusetts, with one one-thousandth the population—7,292 in 2016.[1] With a county-wide average of only 0.71 persons per square mile, almost 60 percent live within urban boundaries—the rest on sparsely scattered farm and ranch homesteads barely visible from the main roads, if at all. From the county border to the first towns, it is common to see no human beings.

When it reappears, the urban landscape can seem startling. As one drives east on Highway 20 over a low rise near the Bureau of Land Management office, the twin towns of Hines and Burns appear like an island of human habitation in the desert—with tidy residential streets, schools, a library, a courthouse, big-box stores, and chain restaurants. In short, towns that look much like any other small American community. In the ocean of sagebrush, the members of this island of a little more than 4,200 people are born, grow up, marry, have families and dreams, struggles and conflicts, and make important achievements, like those of other small towns.

Yet almost no small town anywhere in America has experienced anything like the events of late 2015 and early 2016. The armed seizure of the nearby headquarters of the Malheur National Wildlife Refuge became a focus of national and international fascination for much of January and February 2016. Like the region's well-known explosions of waterfowl and springtime flowers, news of these events was almost impossible to miss. Yet there was also much that required a more careful eye—stories that were equally important and remarkable but required getting off the main road and looking closely into the subtler spaces that make up a community.

Prelude

On November 5, 2015, Harney County sheriff David Ward received a phone call. On the phone was Ammon Bundy, owner of a truck fleet service in Arizona. Originally from Bunkerville, Nevada, Bundy informed Sheriff Ward that he was in the sheriff's town of Burns, Oregon, to discuss father-and-son ranchers Dwight and Steven Hammond, who had recently been resentenced to prison for arson on federal land.

Sheriff Ward knew the Bundy family name. In April 2014, Ammon Bundy's father, Cliven, led hundreds of protestors in Bunkerville, Nevada, in an armed confrontation against law enforcement officers who attempted to impound Bundy's cattle on federal land because of his twenty-year refusal to renew his Bureau of Land Management (BLM) grazing contract and pay associated fees. Outside supporters of the Bundys pointed guns in the direction of the law enforcement officers, who backed down rather than risk a bloodbath. When the Bundy family made its appearance in Harney County in 2015, Cliven Bundy and his armed supporters had not been arrested for their actions in Nevada, and his cows continued to illegally graze on federal land. Cliven Bundy and several hundred armed, self-described "patriots" appeared to have successfully faced down the most powerful government on Earth. Rule of law appeared suspended at gunpoint. Sheriff Ward said the Bundy history "made me feel a little bit nervous about why these guys were in my community, and what they were truly up to."[2]

Sheriff Ward met with Ammon Bundy a few hours after the phone call. Bundy stated that it was his belief that the Hammonds were victims of injustice by the federal government and demanded that Sheriff Ward shield the Hammonds from arrest. Bundy's demands quickly escalated to what the sheriff viewed as pointed threats.[3] With Bundy at the time was Ryan Payne, an Iraq War veteran and Montana militiaman originally from Southern California who helped lead the 2014 armed confrontation in Nevada between Cliven Bundy and federal workers. Payne was known in the militia[4] community for his exceptionally extreme, violent views.[5] Ward described an air of intimidation that set in almost immediately during the meeting, emanating largely from Payne:

> It was made pretty clear to me that if I went along with their game plan, their agenda, everything would be all right. When I stated that I couldn't tolerate bloodshed in our community, Mr. Payne indicated that as long as I went along with their game plan—which was to tell the federal court system that they had no authority over citizens in Harney County—[violence] could be avoided. There was a lot of saber-rattling and ultimatums that were handed out. . . . If I didn't do my job according to what they thought it was, they would bring thousands of people to town and do that job for me.[6]

Ward later recalled, "I told them they were welcome to protest, to use their rights within the boundaries of the law, . . . but I could not have what happened in Bunkerville, Nevada, happen in Harney County, Oregon."[7] When it became clear to Bundy and Payne that Ward would not go along with their "game plan," Ward recalled that Bundy became agitated and Payne threatened to bring thousands of additional armed supporters into the county. Payne pointedly noted that he could not necessarily control what these armed outsiders might do.

In the weeks leading up to the armed takeover[8] of the Malheur National Wildlife Refuge, Ryan Payne proved that his threats were no idle words. Sheriff Ward received thousands of emails and phone calls that included obscenities, insults, and threats. Ward was warned that by not shielding the Hammonds from federal arrest, he was in violation of the US Constitution, and he could be brought before a "citizens grand jury" for treason and hanged. Bundy supporters, some armed, staked out Ward's home, stalked his family, and verbally confronted his elderly parents. Ward's wife found her car tire slashed and temporarily left the community. Ward, who served as a US Army combat medic in Somalia and Afghanistan, observed that he had never felt such a need to "look over my shoulder," even in his military service. The intense threats and antagonism from Payne led Ward to believe that, eventually, "either I'd have to kill him or he'd have to kill me."[9]

Following a "call to action" by Ammon Bundy, the local 911 dispatch line was flooded with threats and attempts to intimidate Ward. Bundy declared he would marshal a citizen's army to force local authorities to act according to Bundy's views of the US Constitution. In effect, Bundy declared his intent to overthrow the democratically elected county government by armed force, with or without the support of the majority of the community or its leaders.

To make Bundy's point, on November 19, Bundy and Payne returned to the sheriff's office with a group of ten armed individuals that the sheriff identified as representing six militia groups.[10] The Harney County Sheriff's Department had only five armed officers (the sheriff, a lieutenant, and three deputies). The ten individuals represented regional and national militia. The purpose of the meeting appeared to be to reiterate Bundy and Payne's demand that the sheriff must shield the Hammonds from federal arrest. This time, however, Bundy and Payne brought with them leaders of groups that could in fact mobilize thousands of militants.

Between the first meeting on November 5 and the second meeting on November 19, Sheriff Ward reviewed the Hammonds' case in depth and became convinced that the Hammonds had received due process in accordance with the law and the US Constitution. Ward informed the visitors and provided them with documentation supporting his conclusions. Ward stated flatly that it was his duty under law to enforce the court order and he would do so. When Bundy and his group realized that Ward still would not embrace their plan to block federal authority and shield the Hammonds, they warned that if the Hammonds spent one more day in jail there would be "extreme civil unrest."[11]

Bundy and his supporters formally stated their demands in a notice for "redress of grievance" submitted in the name of "We the People" and twelve militia and political groups on December 11, 2015. The letter, hand-delivered to Sheriff Dave Ward's office in the Harney County Courthouse, was addressed to Sheriff Ward and two county commissioners but not to Judge Steve Grasty. In the document, Bundy demanded that the Harney County government "immediately assemble an independent Evidential Hearing Board (EHB) comprised of the people of Harney County in accordance with Common Law principals [sic]" to hear alleged evidence that Dwight and Steven Hammond were not afforded their rights to due process. The document went on to demand that the "Hammond family be protected from reporting to federal prison until all allegations can be determined," and concluded by indicating that failure to respond within five days would indicate Harney County leaders' unwillingness to do their duty. County judge Steve Grasty, the county's top elected official, later noted that he was not addressed in the notice,[12] and it was unclear how to respond to "We the People of the United States."[13] Sheriff Ward had already stated that the Hammonds received due process and that he would not shield them from federal arrest. When the county did not respond, Bundy said he therefore had no choice but to "stand" for the Hammonds.

Bundy's "stand," like many twenty-first-century political struggles, unfolded largely at first on the internet. Sheriff Ward described Bundy's use of social media as a "weapon."[14] Even before Ammon Bundy and Ryan

Payne met with Sheriff Ward on November 5, entries were posted on the Bundy Ranch blog complaining of alleged "incomprehensible injustices" by federal courts against the Hammond family, along with a warning that "the incarceration of the Hammond family will spawn serious civil unrest."[15] After the meeting between Bundy and Ward on November 5, numerous new posts and videos were released by the Bundys and their supporters with the apparent intent to pressure Sheriff Ward to shield the Hammonds from federal authorities. Ammon Bundy posted a lengthy statement titled "Facts and Events in the Hammond Case."[16] Right-wing internet talk-show host Pete Santilli, who would later play a key role in the Bundy occupation, posted videos with provocative titles such as "BLM Terrorizes Oregon Family."[17] The Bundy family blog denounced the federal government for allegedly declaring the Hammonds as "terrorists,"[18] even though the federal prosecutor in charge of the case emphatically denied that the government ever used that word to describe the Hammonds.[19] Sheriff Ward complained that the statements by Bundy and his supporters on social media were simply untrue,[20] but Ward's efforts to refute the Bundys' version of events in the Hammond case only intensified threats against him:

> As soon as they realized that I was not going to embrace their agenda, my office began getting flooded with phone calls and emails. . . . It literally shut our dispatch center down to the point that we couldn't fully provide the emergency services needed. . . . They put [sheriff's department] contact numbers out [on social media] and encouraged people to call in and express their dissatisfaction with my stance. Another thing we got was emails, many of them laced with profanity and insults. Threats started coming after I put out information to show that what was being spread on social media [about the Hammonds] was untrue. . . . [I] cleared up a significant amount of misinformation that had been put out on the internet. Mr. Bundy's response to that was to put out a video onto social media claiming that federal agents had contacted the Hammonds' attorneys and threatened to have the Hammonds killed.[21]

After the November 19 meeting, the local harassment—including threats to Sheriff Ward's life and intimidation of his family—continued and intensified. The militia initiated surveillance of other local law enforcement officers and their families, and on December 7, Ryan Payne came to the sheriff's office while Ward was away and demanded that Ward's second-in-command, Lieutenant Brian Needham, must remove Ward "by any means necessary." [22] Needham refused. Meanwhile, the goal of Bundy's social media war appeared to shift from pressuring Ward to calling for a mass influx of Bundy supporters into Harney County. By the end of December, Bundy's pleas reached fever pitch. On December 30, right-wing internet activist Pete Santilli re-posted a video by Ammon Bundy with the title "BREAKING ALERT ALL CALL TO ALL MILITIAS! AND PATRIOTS!" (emphasis original).[23] In the video, Bundy, his usual soft-spoken style rising in pitch and volume, called for supporters to come to a rally on January 2, 2016, ostensibly to support the Hammonds:

> I'm asking you to come to Burns on January 2 to make a stand. I feel that this is every bit and in many ways more important than the Bundy Ranch [stand-off in 2014]. I know that the abuses that [the Hammonds] have endured is much greater than even the Bundy family. This is something that can't be ignored. It has to happen now. We cannot allow these violations to be so blatant and do nothing and expect that we will not be accountable for it. We will be accountable if we do not stand. I'm asking you now to come to Burns and defend this family, and defend [Harney] county because it's not just the Hammonds that are being affected by this [alleged federal tyranny]. They have put this whole county in oppression. . . . It is time that we make a stand and I'm asking you to do that.

In late November and throughout December 2015, hundreds of videos and blog entries were posted, most with similar alarming titles and tone. Sheriff Ward later observed, "Everything they put on social media was intended to provoke an emotional response,"[24] much of it outlandish and wholly fabricated. On December 5, Ammon Bundy published a video on his personal YouTube channel titled "BLM Destroying Ranches by Fire."[25] The video claimed federal Bureau of Land Management workers were intentionally setting fires in Frenchglen (near the Malheur National Wildlife Refuge) to burn ranchers' homes, destroy their livestock, and drive ranchers off their land. BLM staff and local ranchers not aligned with the Bundys adamantly insist that the video was a flat-out lie,[26] but it was re-posted by numerous far-right activists such as Gavin Seim, who changed the title to "Feds Burning Cows ALIVE, Torching Homes, Imprisoning Ranchers!"[27] (emphasis original). Seim's post, like many others, included contact information for Sheriff Ward so viewers could express their anger.

Although Bundy's social media campaign was specific about alleged acts of government "tyranny" and "oppression," the exact nature of the "stand" that he proposed to take on January 2, 2016, was vague. Residents of the community were skeptical that Bundy and his supporters would go to so much effort merely to hold a "peaceful rally," as Bundy claimed. Even Bundy's supporters considered the purpose of the event on January 2 to be unclear. Right-wing activist Gavin Seim wrote to Bundy on December 30 asking whether the event would be a rally or a "call to action." Bundy replied cryptically, "I would never show up to a rally without my arms."[28] The Bundys' true goals remained unknown—and worrying to many members of the community. Jeff Rose, the district manager of the Burns Bureau of Land Management, described believing that "at multiple occasions, we were a heartbeat away from gunfire. . . . It was so tense, and so close to a bad thing, a really bad thing."[29] One local business owner who was born and raised in Burns, and is a close personal friend of local law enforcement officers, observed,

> Thanksgiving had a dark cloud hanging over it. We knew something was happening. You could just feel it, the tension in the community. And at Christmas. I started to feel angry, because I thought, yeah, there's the [Bundy protest] parade [on January 2], but what next? . . . I thought honestly something awful would happen in town during that parade, but I didn't think they would go take over buildings. Not in my wildest dreams. I thought it could get ugly downtown. All of those people were open-carry [guns]. . . . Law enforcement officers were told that their lives were expendable. . . . It was hideous. . . . It was terrifying to not know what was going to happen next. I felt like I was going to barf every day until it ended. It was so awful to live here at that time. I was afraid that there was going to be a revolution in our town. . . . We would be taken over and the people who didn't agree [with Bundy] would be rounded up.[30]

The idea of an entire American community being taken captive did not seem far-fetched to many who lived in Burns in November and December 2015. In very real ways, the town *was* held captive. Sheriff Ward, who had the most direct contact with Ammon Bundy and Ryan Payne, believed at first that the militia would try to take over the sheriff's office and county courthouse. As the January 2, 2016, protest rally drew closer, however, the intimidation became more widespread. Residents noticed a substantial increase in the number of outsiders in town, many driving vehicles with out-of-state license plates and openly carrying guns. In Harney County, most residents own guns themselves, but carrying weapons openly is not normal and many consider it rude. Yet, when residents went to the Safeway supermarket, Rite Aid drug store, or the Big R feed store, they encountered strangers openly armed and often wearing camouflage and militia-style insignia. Armed strangers confronted local residents in stores and on the street asking their views of the Hammonds. The purpose of this questioning appeared to be to raise local support for the Hammonds, but it was widely perceived as intimidation. A resident who posted a sign in front of his house with the words "GO HOME BUNDYS!!" was confronted by Ryan Payne, who walked past a No Trespassing sign to, in his words, "educate" the resident.[31] Some groups, such as federal employees and members of the Burns Paiute Tribe,[32] appeared specifically targeted.

Certain local motels became known as centers of militia activity, with entire parking lots full of mostly out-of-state license plates on vehicles bearing Confederate flags and antigovernment slogans. Occupier Jon Ritzheimer's pickup truck, frequently seen in Burns, bore the words "FUCK ISLAM" on the back window of the cab—open hate speech unfamiliar and offensive to many in the community. Some of these vehicles drove slowly and ominously past, or parked in front of, the homes of law enforcement and government personnel and their families—some of whom left or were evacuated from the county because of concerns of violence or kidnapping. Some parents would not allow their children to go to school unaccompanied. Law-abiding citizens who had never before carried a gun in town did so.

Some residents became aware that Ammon Bundy and Ryan Payne had rented houses and were living in Burns. A sense that the town had been taken over by outsiders with a violent history, an intimidating attitude, and unknown intentions set in. One resident later recalled, "I felt like we were hostages in our own town."[33] For a time, the quiet town of Burns as locals had always known it became something else. The community was on edge. The town filled with outsiders. Guns were visible and loaded. Almost everyone believed that something big was about to happen.

Adding credibility to concerns that the outside militia might attempt to take over the community, in mid-December 2015 Ammon Bundy and his supporters established a kind of parallel county government. Bundy and Ryan Payne, with assistance from Oregon militia leader BJ Soper and Georgia militia member Jason Patrick, held a public meeting in Burns on December 15 calling for the formation of a Harney County Committee of Safety. Ryan Payne explained to an audience of about thirty-five to forty local residents[34] that committees of safety existed as "civil bodies politic" in prerevolutionary America for mutual aid in case of natural or civil emergency, and also to protect against perceived political oppression. Payne gave an example of a committee of safety created in 1689 by Boston militia dissatisfied with the government of the British Crown that imprisoned a colonial governor. In another example, from 1774, Payne stated that committees of safety in western Massachusetts sent armed militia to force the resignation of judges who supported British rule. Drawing comparisons between the tyranny of British colonial rule and the failure of the state and county governments to protect the Hammond family, Bundy—at times choking up and wiping tears—pleaded with local residents: "It is time to form a committee of safety because our current government is not even attempting to do its job [to protect the Hammonds] and form a committee of safety here among the people and begin to enforce the Constitution. That's what we're calling for."[35]

At the conclusion of the meeting, Bundy asked for a vote of those assembled in the room on whether they wished to form a committee of safety. By Bundy's count, 80 percent of those in attendance supported the idea, and none spoke against it. Seven local residents, including a rancher, a retired fire chief, and a tax preparer, were elected to form the committee. Bundy observed that opposition to the Hammonds' pending incarceration must be led by local people, and that the job of a committee of safety would be to oversee the militia that, Bundy assured, would come from all over the country to help protect the Hammonds. After assuring local residents that they too would be subjected to the kind of "tyranny" that was allegedly inflicted on the Hammonds, the goal of "standing with" the Hammonds seemed to be assumed to be the first task of the new Harney County Committee of Safety. Although Bundy stated that actions should be taken by the committee, he quickly established a website for the group himself and drafted a strongly worded letter to Sheriff Ward that he issued in the name of the committee on behalf of the people of Harney County.[36]

The Harney County Committee of Safety continued to operate long after the occupation of the Malheur National Wildlife Refuge ended, and much of the division and sense of betrayal in the community before, during, and after the takeover centered on the committee.[37] Yet, even the Committee of Safety itself appeared divided, and certainly felt betrayed by Ammon Bundy: the committee drafted a letter that denounced the takeover because Bundy had taken "aggressive action" without the committee's knowledge or any other local approval. The takeover "created huge distrust" for the committee and the community.[38] On January 8, 2016, Committee of Safety member Melodi Molt publicly read a draft letter from the Committee of Safety to Ammon Bundy, complaining that Bundy acted without consulting the committee: "We approved of most of your message, but disapprove of your unilateral method of occupation." Molt said Bundy's point had been made, and he should leave in a "peaceful and honorable fashion."[39]

Takeover

On Saturday, January 2, 2016, the sun in Burns, Oregon, was bright but the temperature peaked at only 15°F (and dropped at night to –18°F). Standing in the Safeway supermarket parking lot in the center of Burns were approximately three hundred people in heavy coats, hats, and scarves. Some held signs declaring support for the Hammond family, or opposition to the federal government. Many clutched American flags and cups of hot coffee. Many also openly carried firearms. By the estimates of local law enforcement, only fifty or sixty were from the community,[40] with the rest being members of militia groups from all over the country—the most numerous from Idaho and other western states, as well many from Central and Southern Oregon.

The rally for the Hammond family was announced weeks ahead, and many local residents and law enforcement officers braced for possible violence. Until almost the end, however, nothing dramatic happened. Dwight and Steven Hammond, fearing that association with militia activities could destroy their chances for clemency, declined to march in the rally and announced their intent to report to prison on January 4, 2016, as required, turning down offers of protection by the militia.[41] When the Hammonds' refusal of protection was announced by militia leaders at the rally, one person in the crowd yelled out, "What are we here for?" A militia leader replied, "The community. This community is scared."[42] Another militia leader claimed that because many local residents were federal employees, the community was afraid to express their frustrations with the government and needed support from the militia to make their frustrations heard.

While many in the local community and even the leaders of some national militia groups feared violence and stayed away from the rally, almost no one knew what was about to unfold. One man, however, was quietly giving hints. After the militia leaders' speeches ended and people were waiting to begin the march, Ammon Bundy said to those in attendance, "We will be continuing the stand after the rally at the Malheur National Wildlife Refuge. I want everybody to know to go to the Malheur National Wildlife Refuge."[43] As a celebrity anti-federal activist because of his participation in the April 2014 armed standoff with Bureau of Land Management agents at his father's ranch in Nevada, Ammon Bundy drew intense media attention. In front of cameras, Bundy spoke only about his support for the Hammonds and the Constitution. Off camera, the soft-spoken Bundy's hints seemed almost lost in the noisy crowd, and the rally proceeded as planned. Protesters marched several blocks to the sheriff's office (where the participants tossed pennies to symbolize their view that the sheriff was a "sellout"), and then another few blocks to the Hammonds' home, where participants gave Dwight and his wife Susie Hammond hugs and flowers. Protesters then marched back to the Safeway parking lot.

The Safeway supermarket is often considered the heart of Burns and Harney County, and it was from there that Harney County and the nation learned that something almost without parallel in modern American history was unfolding. Before departing the rally, Ammon Bundy told a

Portland television reporter[44] that "a hard stand is happening today." Bundy declined the reporter's requests to elaborate, but in militia culture a "hard stand" is understood to mean armed civil disobedience—a clear signal that Bundy planned more than just a protest march. Standing in the Safeway parking lot, where protestors remained talking about the events, internet talk show host Pete Santilli, while live-streaming, revealed Bundy's "hard stand":

> There's a group of individuals right now at the Malheur Wildlife Refuge. There is a federal building [the refuge headquarters] that a group of individuals is going to take over. . . . There is a group of individuals that want to take a stand at that building. . . . Ammon Bundy is down there, LaVoy Finicum is down there.

According to later trial testimony by Walter "Butch" Eaton, who was the only known Harney County resident to participate in the initial takeover[45] (albeit "accidentally"[46]), Bundy and about ten others, most of them armed, used military-style tactics to seize the headquarters buildings (which had no staff present), and then blew a horn to signal that the site was secured. With winter daylight waning, temperatures dipping well below zero, and the thirty miles of road between Burns and the headquarters of the Malheur National Wildlife Refuge covered in hazardous snow and ice, the throng of reporters that would quickly become a fixture at the occupied refuge headquarters would not arrive until the next morning. Fittingly, for a political action that took place largely through social media, one of the first reports to emerge that evening was a video from Ammon Bundy, posted on Facebook:

> We have basically taken over the Malheur National Wildlife Refuge. This will become a base for Patriots from all over the country to come and be housed here, and live here. We're planning to stay here for several years. While we're here what we're going to be doing is freeing these lands up and letting the ranchers get back to ranching, getting the miners back to mining, the loggers back to logging. They can do it under the protection of the people and not be afraid of this tyranny that's been set upon them. What will happen is Harney County will be able to thrive again. At one time [Harney County] was the

Militia spokesman LaVoy Finicum (January 12, 2016). Militia members renamed the Malheur Refuge head-quarters as the "Harney County Resource Center."

Anti-militia counter-protesters at the Narrows, near the entrance to the Malheur National Wildlife Refuge (January 19, 2016).

wealthiest county in the state, now they're the poorest county in the state. We will reverse that in just a few years by freeing up their land and resources. We're doing this for the people. We're doing this so the people can have their land and resources back where they belong. It's really that simple. We're the point of the spear that's going to bring confidence and strength to the rest of the people. We're calling on people to come out here and stand. . . . They need to bring their arms to the Malheur National Wildlife Refuge.[47]

The events that unfolded over the next forty-one days made headline news across the world. At 11:00 the following morning, a media ritual was set in place that made icons[48] of the men with cowboy hats, camouflage, guns, flags, tattoos, and military-style insignia who espoused radical political ideologies while standing at the entry to a frozen bird sanctuary in one of the most remote places in the country. Each morning at that time, Bundy or another occupation leader such as LaVoy Finicum stood before dozens of jostling journalists, a row of TV cameras, and banks of microphones to declare their goal to "assist Harney County to claim their rights" against "unconstitutional" government actions. The occupiers publicly disavowed any plan for violent action, despite the presence of many prominently displayed firearms.[49] Over the next weeks, the number of occupiers would grow from about a dozen to roughly fifty individuals from all regions of the country. For more than three weeks, law enforcement had no visible presence, and journalists and assorted observers including myself took advantage of the mostly welcoming approach of the occupiers, who invited visitors in to hear their views. Environmentalist counter-protesters maintained a steady presence that attracted less media attention but successfully aggravated militia occupiers.

Thirty miles away in Burns, the anxiety that began with the increasing militia presence two months earlier intensified. While the geographic focus of activity partly shifted from the town to the refuge, the number of outsiders coming in to Burns dramatically increased. Outside militia in Burns grew from perhaps a few dozen in November 2015 to an estimated three hundred at peak periods in January 2016.[50] Almost overnight, fleets of press vehicles filled with reporters from around the world crammed into every available parking space in the tiny downtown. Additional law enforcement officers, including uniformed deputies from other counties all over the state as well as plainclothes agents in unmarked-but-obvious federal vehicles, arrived. In local motels and restaurants, reporters, law enforcement officers, and armed militia packed every available room and table, often sleeping and dining mere inches from each other.

A sense of tension intensified. Individuals from outside the community, often with military-type long guns and handguns openly carried, were visible throughout town. Local schools temporarily closed for safety, based on concerns by law enforcement that even a single unstable individual among the many armed outsiders coming into the community might choose to make a violent statement. Similarly, there were concerns that the courthouse and airport, which were sealed off as law enforcement command centers, might attract violent actions. During the forty-one-day takeover, armed militia members repeatedly challenged law enforcement officers. Sheriff Ward recalled that militia members committed traffic violations with the apparent intent of provoking confrontations with law enforcement. Employees of the Malheur National Wildlife Refuge and other federal facilities reported being harassed in Burns, and refuge manager Chad Karges, who became refuge manager in 2015, as well as federal prosecutors, later testified in court that occupiers at the Malheur Refuge threatened to kidnap federal employees. The employees were evacuated for their safety.[51]

Meanwhile, the refuge itself remained outwardly peaceful, with no law enforcement visible—just a steady stream of journalists and assorted civilian visitors. However, the activities of the occupiers at the refuge were a source of special alarm for one group: the Burns Paiute Tribe. Burns Paiute then tribal chair Charlotte Rodrique recalled that, years earlier, floods had exposed tribal remains, which the tribe and the US Fish and Wildlife Service reburied at the refuge, so Rodrique knew where they were. She also knew the Bundy occupiers were excavating and road-building in areas very close to the reburial sites.[52] In addition, a video was posted online of occupier LaVoy Finicum handling tribal artifacts—a matter of extreme sensitivity for the tribe. Rodrique complained, however, that anything the tribe did to push back against the Bundy group seemed only to draw more attention to the occupiers. The tribe struggled to not engage the Bundys despite extreme anger and frustration.

Back in Burns, some local residents argued about which were more intimidating—militia or federal agents. Almost everyone, however, was on edge. Above all, no one knew how the volatile situation might end. The sense of uncertainty resulted in part from the seeming confusion among the leaders of the takeover themselves about their goals. At first, Ammon Bundy and his supporters said the rally on January 2, 2016, was to support the Hammonds. After the takeover, Bundy's stated goal shifted to giving the Malheur National Wildlife Refuge "back" to "ranchers, loggers, and miners"—a demand based on fundamental misunderstanding or misrepresentation of the history of the refuge[53] and almost completely ignoring the claims of the Burns Paiute Tribe—from whom the federal government had unambiguously "taken" land. In private, the occupiers spoke of leading a revolution to establish a "federal-free" county. Meanwhile, Ammon Bundy's brother Ryan stated that if the community asked the occupiers to leave, they would. That statement was quickly retracted, and Ammon Bundy publicly declared that the takeover would last for years. With each shift in the occupiers' stated goals, much of the community expressed palpable exasperation.

Harney County sheriff Dave Ward expressed his desire for a peaceful closure and regret at the loss of LaVoy Finicum (January 27, 2016).

In the end, none of Bundy's stated goals were realized. The takeover of Harney County and the Malheur National Wildlife Refuge did raise awareness of Bundy's views (this book, for instance, would not have been written otherwise). Yet, in their stated goals (freeing the Hammonds; giving "back" the refuge to "ranchers, loggers, and miners"; establishing federal-free "constitutional" governance of land), the occupiers failed. The "several years" of occupation that Ammon Bundy promised ended in forty-one days.

Sheriff Dave Ward later explained that law enforcement strategically allowed the occupiers to become complacent—traveling freely to and from town, shopping, eating in restaurants, attending church, and speaking at meetings.[54] On January 26, the waiting strategy by law enforcement paid off. All the main leaders of the takeover set out in two vehicles to speak at a meeting in the town of John Day, in neighboring Grant County, about a hundred miles north by Highway 395, a narrow, isolated forest road. Oregon State Police officers, assisted by the Federal Bureau of Investigation and local law enforcement, arrested eight occupiers. Another occupier, LaVoy Finicum, was killed by Oregon State Police officers in a confrontation after Finicum attempted to evade arrest. That evening most of the remaining occupiers fled the refuge. On February 11, four holdouts were arrested after dramatic marathon negotiations with the FBI. For all intents and purposes, the active part of the takeover ended on January 26 on Highway 395—ironically, on federal land (the Malheur National Forest, which Ryan Bundy once demanded be relinquished from federal control[55]).

To anyone following the story in January and February 2016, these events were almost impossible to miss. Yet there was also much that remained only superficially understood. If the painful events of that time are to yield constructive lessons, a closer look behind the headlines is essential. A closer look begins, like the takeover of the Malheur National Wildlife Refuge itself, with the story of the Hammonds.

Hammonds

For those who followed media coverage of the occupation of the Malheur National Wildlife Refuge, the story of the Hammond family may seem familiar, but it is also likely incomplete. The Hammonds were the lightning rod for the occupation of the Malheur National Wildlife Refuge, but they were not an entirely unifying presence in the community—a fact that had bearing on the occupation's failure.

Much of the Hammonds' story is well known: on October 7, 2015, Harney County rancher Dwight Hammond and his son Steven Hammond were resentenced by a federal judge to five years in prison for arson on federal land, with credit for time served. In June 2012, both Hammonds were convicted of setting fire to 139 acres of BLM land in 2001 to destroy evidence of their illegal deer hunting. The Hammonds argued unsuccessfully that they set fire to their own property to destroy invasive plants and the fire spilled onto BLM land. The jury also convicted Steven Hammond of arson for illegally using the cover of a lightning storm in August 2006 to start "backfires" to protect his winter feed stores. Steven Hammond started the fires during a burn ban that was in effect because of dangerous drought conditions, without permission or notifying the BLM, endangering the lives of BLM firefighters camped nearby.[56] By law, arson on federal land carries a mandatory minimum sentence of five years, but a judge instead sentenced Dwight Hammond to three months and Steven Hammond to a year and a day, which they served. Federal prosecutors appealed the sentences, and the Ninth Circuit Court of Appeals ordered the Hammonds to be resentenced to comply with mandatory minimum sentencing laws. The US Supreme Court declined the Hammonds' request to review the case, and the chief US district judge resentenced the Hammonds to serve the remainder of the five-year mandatory sentence. They reported to prison on January 4, 2016.[57]

After the Hammonds were resentenced in October 2015, they were in contact with the Bundy family. By late October, Ammon Bundy and Ryan Payne were in Harney County, holding meetings with the Hammonds at the Hammond family's home in Burns.[58] It was not the first time the Hammonds had had a brush with the law: in 1994, Dwight and Steven Hammond were arrested over a dispute about a fence on the Malheur National Wildlife Refuge. After then US Representative Bob Smith confronted then US Secretary of the Interior Bruce Babbitt about the case, the charges were dropped.[59] Knowing of the Bundy family's seemingly successful standoff against federal authorities in 2014, the Hammonds presumably hoped the Bundys could pressure the government to drop charges against them once again.

For the Bundys, the Hammond family appeared to be an ideal vehicle to further their goal of facing down the federal government and forcing the handover of federal lands. Bundy judged correctly that many people in Harney County would be sympathetic to the Hammonds' situation. What Ammon Bundy, Ryan Payne, and other leaders of the occupation,

Dwight and Steven Hammond were first arrested in a confrontation with Malheur National Wildlife Refuge Staff in August 1994.

as well as much of the media, did not understand, however, was that the Hammonds' history made them a flawed vehicle for a revolution. Although much of the community strongly supported the Hammonds, this support was tempered by knowledge that—as Dwight Hammond himself publicly stated—"I'm no angel."[60]

When the Hammonds squared off with the law in 1994, much of the community initially stood strongly behind the Hammonds, but the family's actions changed how some in the community viewed them. The Malheur Refuge, which exists to protect migratory birds, was under orders to eliminate conflicting uses including cattle grazing and watering. Refuge staff tried to build a fence along the survey line of its property boundary, shutting the Hammonds' cattle out of a waterhole that the Hammonds had long used but, according to the refuge, had no legal right to. The Hammonds cut the new fence to allow their cattle passage. The Hammonds were arrested when Dwight Hammond parked a large Caterpillar earthmover on the fence boundary to prevent refuge staff from rebuilding the fence. Hammond dug the blade of the Caterpillar into the ground, almost hitting a refuge employee, and disabled the machine to prevent it from being moved. Meanwhile, Steven Hammond reportedly shouted obscenities at the refuge employees (Langston 2003, 123).

For those in the county who remembered 1994, the events surrounding the Hammonds in 2016 would seem like déjà vu: after the Hammonds were arrested in August 1994, almost five hundred people, mainly from the "wise use" movement, came to Burns to angrily protest what they considered federal abuse of the Hammond family.[61] Wise use leader Chuck Cushman published names, photos, and phone numbers of refuge employees, some of whom received threatening calls at home.[62] National media, including CNN television, covered the Hammonds' 1994 dispute in depth, calling Dwight Hammond a "martyr to many in the land rights movement."[63]

Refuge staff, however, saw the Hammonds as no heroes. US Fish and Wildlife Service correspondence, sworn court testimony, and numerous public statements by employees indicate a long-standing pattern of threats and harassment by the Hammonds against Malheur National Wildlife Refuge staff. In a sworn court affidavit, US Fish and Wildlife Service law enforcement agent Earl M. Kisler, who arrested Dwight Hammond in 1994, stated that Hammond repeatedly threatened to kill refuge manager Forrest Cameron and his assistant Dan Walsworth.[64] Following the arrest of Dwight Hammond in 1994, his wife Susie told the *Oregonian* that the refuge had verbally intimidated her husband, but acknowledged that the intimidation "was from both sides."[65] One former refuge employee who was present during the 1994 fence altercation stated that Dwight Hammond pointed at him and said to refuge manager Forrest Cameron, "His blood will spill over this fence." Dwight Hammond then pointed at Cameron and said, "Then I'm coming for you."[66] On another occasion, Dwight Hammond said that if he did not get his way at his next meeting with the refuge staff, they should call the sheriff and an undertaker.[67]

In 2017, former Malheur National Wildlife Refuge manager Forrest Cameron confirmed press accounts that the Hammonds had made extreme violent threats against him, his family, and his staff:

> My wife would take these phone calls, it was terribly vulgar language. They said they were going to wrap my son in barbed wire and throw him down a well. They said they knew exactly which rooms my kids slept in, in Burns. There were death threats to my wife and two other staff members and their wives. . . . At the refuge headquarters, one of the Hammonds said they would tear my head off and shit down the hole. One of the Hammonds told my deputy manager, Dan Walsworth, they were going to "put a chain around his neck and drag him behind a pickup."[68]

When a CNN reporter asked Dwight Hammond whether accusations of such threats were true, Hammond did not deny making the threats, but replied, "I've said I'm willing to die. Maybe they're willing to die."[69]

By 2016, patience with the Hammonds was wearing thin for some in the community. One local rancher who knew the Hammonds since they moved from California to Harney County in 1964 observed, "The Hammonds have been antigovernment since the day they were born."[70] The community, however, had moved toward collaborative approaches, and the Hammonds' confrontational attitude seemed increasingly out of sync.[71] Meanwhile, some in the community had become aware of the truth in Dwight Hammond's statement that he was "no angel." Burns is a small community where secrets are short-lived. Some knew, for example, of an incident in 2004 when, according to a sheriff's office report, Steven Hammond took coarse sandpaper to the chest of his sixteen-year-old nephew, Dusty Hammond, to remove initials the boy had carved into his own skin. A sheriff's department investigation described a pattern of systematic extremely harsh punishments against Dusty.[72]

Yet, the Hammonds were prominent members of the community, widely seen as good ranchers and generous and civic-minded citizens— active in the Cattlemen's and Cattlewomen's Associations, for example, and generous contributors to local charitable causes. Some neighbors in Burns described the Hammonds as friendly and helpful. Until the 2016 takeover of the Malheur National Wildlife Refuge put the national spotlight on the Hammonds and their history received closer scrutiny, many in the community, especially those who live in town, far from the Malheur Refuge and the Hammonds' ranch near Diamond, say they were not aware of the family's antagonistic behavior toward federal employees. When information about the Hammonds' actions became more widely known, some questioned its truthfulness. Others expressed disappointment with the Hammonds: federal employees are members of the community, and by 2016, threats and intimidation against community members were considered to be not the Harney County way.

To outsiders, the enigmas surrounding the Hammonds were often lost. Outside militia held up the Hammonds as heroes victimized by government tyranny. The Hammonds even attracted sympathy from some liberals who had long railed against mandatory minimum sentencing laws, bringing a measure of agreement between left and right.[73] Although government prosecutors never called the Hammonds "terrorists,"[74] the law that required the Hammonds to serve minimum five-year sentences bore the Orwellian name "Antiterrorism and Effective Death Penalty Act of 1996"—a label that caused much concern for both conservatives and liberals in public discussions of the Hammonds' case. Media reports used terms such as "absurdly harsh," and a public narrative emerged about mildly scofflaw ranchers subjected to excessive punishment under a law designed to address terrorism—seemingly unjust in an age of mass shootings and major terrorist acts.

Some in the community, however, understood that the Hammonds' convictions represented a long-term pattern of confrontation, and that the Hammonds willingly accepted the five-year sentences to avoid possible convictions on more serious outstanding charges. On June 17, 2010, a grand jury indicted the Hammonds on nineteen charges, including conspiracy to commit arson, five counts of arson, four counts of depredation of government property by means of fire, four counts of illegal operation of an aircraft, four counts of threatening to assault federal officers, and one count of witness tampering.[75] The federal government possessed detailed witness testimony and photographic and forensic evidence supporting the charges.[76] On May 16, 2012, a superseding indictment combined charges into a single count of conspiracy to commit arson and other illegal acts, seven counts of destruction of government property, and one count of witness tampering.[77] On June 21, 2012, after only a few hours of deliberation, a jury released a partial verdict finding Dwight Hammond guilty of one count of destruction of government property by means of fire[78] and Steven Hammond guilty of two counts of destruction of government property.[79] The jury acquitted the Hammonds of the other charges except the most serious charge—conspiracy—on which the jury remained undecided. The judge ordered the jury to continue deliberating on the conspiracy charge, which carried a maximum sentence of twenty years and an additional mandatory minimum of five years.

While the jury deliberated, the parties reached an oral agreement in which the Hammonds accepted the verdicts on destruction of property returned up to that point and waived their rights to appeal the sentences in order to "bring this matter to a close." The district court accepted the agreement and dismissed the outstanding conspiracy charge.[80] The Hammonds were fully informed that the mandated five-year minimum sentences would be applied to their convictions up to that point.[81] Given that some in the community knew of the Hammonds' history of threats against federal employees and that the Hammonds deliberately made a deal accepting the five-year sentences to avoid possible conviction on the more serious outstanding conspiracy charge, the outcome felt closer to justice than was perceived by many outsiders.

Ammon Bundy, however, never indicated awareness that the Hammonds were anything other than, in his view, purely innocent victims of a federal legal system run amok. When Bundy came to Harney County in late 2015, he represented the Hammonds as perfect symbols of federal "abuse." Bundy made the Hammonds into his cause, justifying "direct action." If the alleged "extreme injustice" against the Hammonds continued, "it will certainly happen to other families," Bundy warned. He insisted that Harney County must "take a stand."[82] Bundy appeared to assume the community of Harney County would be uniformly outraged about the fate of the Hammonds and would unify in their defense—behind him. A few in the community did support the Bundy occupation as a way to stand with the Hammonds. Others, however, were put off by the aggressive behavior of the Hammonds. Most of all, nearly everyone in the community disliked an outsider such as Bundy, apparently with his own "agenda," coming in and claiming to speak for the community, regardless of where they stood on the Hammonds.

In the end, the refusal of the majority in the community to embrace Bundy and the Malheur takeover indicated that considerable empathy for the Hammonds among many local residents was not enough to draw most in the community to Bundy's side. For many in Harney County, both the Hammonds as symbols of Bundy's movement and the movement itself were flawed. It was no coincidence that the Bundy leadership was arrested en route to neighboring Grant County, where they perceived a possibly more effective vehicle for their movement in the person of Grant County's "constitutional" sheriff, Glenn Palmer.[83]

In Harney County, in keeping with the community's character, local divisions regarding the Hammonds were mostly kept private. The Bundys' takeover of the Malheur National Wildlife Refuge, in contrast, ripped the community apart so deeply that the divisions were painfully displayed for the world to see.

Division

Speaking from a windowless, painted-cinderblock room in the Multnomah County jail five weeks after his arrest, Ammon Bundy (wearing blue jail scrubs and a pocket Constitution) insisted to a Portland TV news reporter that "by far the majority of the people [in Harney County] supported us.... I would challenge anybody who says Harney County was not behind us."[84] At a minimum, Bundy's statement represented deafness to hundreds of community members who had told him personally, loudly, and repeatedly that they wanted him to go home. At a Harney County community meeting on January 19, 2016, hundreds of local citizens chanted directly to Bundy himself, "Go home! Go home! Go home!" One local resident, for example, demanded directly to Bundy that he should "get the hell out of my yard. Look what you did to this county."[85] Bundy's jailhouse recollections were correct that he received substantial moral and material support from some members of the Harney County community, but his assertion that the "by far the

Harney County then judge Steve Grasty told Ammon Bundy that Grasty would personally escort Bundy out of the county (January 19, 2016).

majority" supported him appeared to knowingly disregard the many opposing voices that he had personally heard. In the aftermath of the Bundy occupation the community was, without dispute by almost anyone other than Bundy, deeply divided by his actions.

Reflecting an absence of public opinion research and the journalistic tendency to treat opposing sides as equal, the world outside Harney County seemed to perceive that Harney County citizens supporting and opposing the Bundy occupation and ideology were roughly equal in number. Each side claimed to represent the majority.[86] The only available quantitative measures—local elections that took place later—indicated that the great majority opposed the Bundy ideology.

The first measure of the political legacy of the Bundy occupation in Harney County came with the 2016 primary election on May 17. In an unusually large field of eight candidates for a single county commissioner's seat, the top three candidates (with a combined total of 79.26 percent of the vote) were all viewed as Bundy opponents, while the bottom five candidates (for a combined 20.48 percent of the vote, with eight write-in votes) were viewed as Bundy sympathizers. In the same election, strongly anti-Bundy county commissioner Pete Runnels was elected county judge with an outright majority of 52.98 percent against three opponents all considered Bundy sympathizers. In arguably the closest to a pure referendum on the Bundy legacy, on June 28, 2016, a recall election against county judge

When Ammon Bundy came to a community meeting at Burns High School, a local resident told him to "go to jail where you belong" (January 19, 2016).

At a community meeting in the Burns High School gym, Ammon Bundy remained stone-faced as residents stood and chanted "Go home! Go home!" (January 19, 2016).

Steve Grasty (ostensibly because of Grasty's denial of Bundy's request to hold a meeting in a county building) failed by 29.66 percent to 70.34 percent. On November 8, 2016, Sheriff Dave Ward, Ammon Bundy's most visible opponent, won a second term against a candidate widely perceived as sympathetic to local "militia" (though the candidate denied militia sympathies), by 58.62 percent to 41.25 percent (with five write-in votes). Despite Ammon Bundy's claims to represent the people of Harney County, the majority of Harney County's voters did not appear to agree.

Whatever else the numbers might mean, there was no question that the divisions in the community during the Bundy occupation were often wrenchingly painful, and left enduring scars. A lifelong resident later recalled that a childhood friend who sympathized with the outsiders took to parking in the driveways of government employees and stalking their families. Some Bundy sympathizers tried to have other community members fired for not supporting the militia. Neighbors began to look differently at neighbors, uncertain where they stood. A sense of betrayal set in that lifelong friends—and even family members—could adopt such a hard stance:

> It's [a sense of] betrayal. When you've got friends that you've known for years, maybe you grew up with them, you've broken bread with them, attend church with them, and [then] a group of strangers show up in town shouting a bunch of obnoxious stuff that you clearly haven't seen here and [some locals] take their word over the word of people you know you can trust? . . . There's a level of betrayal there that's hard to get over. There are people here in town I know were mixed up with the occupation. I find it easier to forgive them than it is to look at my own relative. I think, [my relative] should have known just from the fact that I'm on one side of the line and I knew enough about it—he should have known the other side of the line was wrong. It drove a wedge that's going to take some time to get over. You look down the street and you see some guy and you think, "That no-good SOB." That's on both sides.[87]

The community had been divided ever since the outside militia began arriving in noticeably large numbers in November 2015, but the takeover of the Malheur National Wildlife Refuge on January 2, 2016, forced these divisions into public view. On January 6, 2016 (four days after the takeover), residents held the first of three community-wide meetings. The chilly Harney County Fairgrounds Memorial Building was standing-room only, with about 750 residents in bulky winter coats and scarves crammed into every available folding chair. Reporters and camera crews stood along the walls as armed law enforcement officers looked on. When Harney County sheriff Dave Ward entered, he received an immediate standing ovation as he spoke of the need for unity:

> This community is a united family unit. You don't get to come here from elsewhere and tell us how we're going to live our lives [loud cheers and

applause].... What's going on down at the wildlife refuge, it's unfortunate. ... There's been some things going on in our community—maybe it was our visitors, maybe it wasn't—our deputies followed home, families followed around, somebody flattened my wife's tire. She packed up and left town.... They followed my parents. My dad's 78 years old, my mom's 74 years old, both of them have heart problems and pacemakers. You're [the Bundys] not invited to come here and intimidate people.... So I'm here to ask that regardless of what side of the fence you're on, Harney County, we need to mend those fences with our friends and neighbors and put on a united front and ask these folks out here at the refuge to pack up and go home. Work out your issues elsewhere and let us get back to our lives. We're going to work on solutions to the problems we face here in Harney County amongst ourselves. [Applause] I'm just going to go ahead and ask you. How many citizens of Harney County do we have in here? [Show of hands] Now I'm going to ask for the same show of hands. How many people want to work this out peacefully and would like these folks to go home?[88]

Nearly every visible hand in the room shot up, at first giving an impression of nearly unified opposition to the armed takeover of the Malheur Wildlife Refuge by outsiders. The sheriff exclaimed, "God bless you Harney County!" Quickly, however, it became apparent that the nearly unanimous community opposition to the refuge takeover did not necessarily mean rejection of the concerns and ideology that the occupation was perceived to represent. In public comments following the sheriff's speech, Mr. Kim Rollins, a thirty-year resident and local building contractor who later led a recall petition against Judge Steve Grasty, argued that Sheriff Ward's straw poll of community opinion was misleading:

I have a lot of respect for those men out there doing something that I don't agree with. Brave, brave men standing up for our rights. Sheriff, I came [to speak] because you had a straw poll earlier. First you asked the question, "Do we want this to end peacefully?" My hand went up. But then you added to that, "Do we want them to go home?" And my position on this is, not necessarily. Those people have brought us a voice. I don't necessarily want them to go home, because I want to hear what they have to say so that I may consider it. They have the same rights as we do, rights of free speech, etcetera, and those rights don't stop, or shouldn't stop, when we cross a county line or a state line. I don't agree with what they did at the refuge, but I'm willing to listen to what those people have to say so that I may consider it.[89]

After Rollins' speech, loud and boisterous applause erupted—an early indication that although many in the community wanted nothing to do with the armed takeover of the wildlife refuge, there was also a substantial portion of the community who rejected Bundy's methods but was sympathetic to his political message. At the same community meeting, it also quickly became clear that both of the emerging sides surrounding the Bundy presence held their views passionately.

Many members of the ranching community in particular—those with the most knowledge of the federal land management issues that Bundy cited to justify his rebellion—simply did not accept the argument. Many ranchers in the county had observed substantial improvements over recent decades in relations between ranchers and federal land managers. Bundy appeared unable to conceive that rural, resource-dependent, staunchly conservative Harney County might not overwhelmingly share his view of the federal government as an irredeemable "tyranny" that must be overthrown by armed force. The possibility that the majority of the community was satisfied with the innovative, collaborative methods they had crafted to cope with their often very substantial frustrations with federal rules seemed to have never crossed Bundy's mind.

Had Bundy chosen to look into the question of how well nonviolent, collaborative methods of resolving land management issues were working in Harney County (he did not), he might have consulted multigeneration rancher Georgia Marshall. In further public comments following the sheriff's speech at the county fairgrounds, Marshall spoke eloquently, passionately, and with memorable grit of the many achievements of the county in resolving difficult resource management issues through collaboration, and of her anger at having outsiders come in and tell her community to dismiss those accomplishments:

I'm a rancher. I have a BLM permit, several allotments. I have a [Malheur National Wildlife] Refuge permit. I've gone through numerous [refuge] managers and range [conservationists], both BLM and on the refuge. I've seen the progress that we've made in this community compared to the shit we went through years ago when you could not stand and talk to a manager, you could not stand and talk to a range [conservationist]. But now we have been making some progress. . . . We have an organization here that stands up for us across the board. It's called the High Desert Partnership. You may not know a lot about it, but it's working damned hard for all of us. It takes the time to listen across the board to what we all have to say as a community, as environmentalists, as agencies, as business owners, and educators. We are the poster child of the ranching community, the environmental community, the government community, when they see what's happening here in Harney County.[90]

Although the community meeting on January 6, 2016, provided an opportunity to recognize the community's successes in collaborative problem-solving, it also exposed rifts in the community that remained long after the Bundy occupation. As some lifelong members of the community explained, there had always been tensions in the community, as there are in any community, but on important issues that required working together, divisions tended to be put aside in favor of working together, and friendships tended to bounce back with time.

With the onset of the Bundy occupation, in many cases relationships seemed to be stretched beyond the breaking point. Fault lines included where one stood on the presence of the Bundy militia; the presence of law enforcement agents; the armed takeover of the wildlife refuge; and the Bundy ideology itself. There emerged two major factions: those sympathetic to the ideology, though not necessarily the methods, of the Bundy occupiers, and those adamantly opposed to all-things-Bundy. Community members became identified as either "pro-Bundy" or "anti-Bundy," with seemingly few in between. These divisions remained as one of the most important and lasting impacts of the Bundy occupation.

Supporters of the Bundy occupation often recognized the disruptive nature of these divisions but argued that they had awakened the community to an important political message. Bundy supporters also argued that the divisions were not created by the Bundy occupation but had already existed beneath the surface. The truth in the latter point became painfully clear from early on. On January 19, 2016, Harney County held its third community meeting—this time in the Burns High School gym. About twenty minutes into the meeting, Ammon Bundy and an armed contingent of his militia supporters unexpectedly entered the meeting and sat down, saying nothing, among the community. With Bundy observing silently from the bleachers, the acrimony in the room amplified many times over. Most of the angry words spoken were about Bundy, perceived injustice to the Hammond family, or the takeover of the Malheur Refuge. Some clearly used the opportunity to air old grievances.

In an intensely raw exchange, a young woman who had received criticism on social media for being a "Bundy supporter" stood in tears clutching a microphone while directing comments to her former high school teacher sitting a few seats away:

> I have to applaud the courage of [teacher's name] here, to tell me to my face that I've never been very bright, after he was my teacher in high school. [Sarcastically:] That was awesome. Do not presume to know where I stand [on the Bundys]. . . . I am not necessarily a Bundy supporter, . . . [and] putting each other down, especially your former students, is not ok.

The teacher then took the microphone:

> I told [the former student] that I was wrong. In a moment of anger, I said something I shouldn't have. And that is a perfect example of what is going on in this community. Over the last two months Ammon Bundy and his tribe have brought a lot of anguish to this community. [A voice in the audience interjects: "An awakening!"] It may be an awakening. It may be something that needs to be discussed. But it needs to be discussed through the proper channels. It needs to be discussed through the community as a group, not as Bundy lovers, anti-Bundy lovers, or anything else. It needs to be discussed as a community.

In apparent response to the previous heated exchange, another man stood up and spoke directly to Ammon Bundy, angrily jabbing his finger:

> My name is [. . .]. If anybody wants to know where I live, I'm the one with the upside down American flag on Highway 20. That's a sign of distress. . . . Mr. Bundy, I agree with you one hundred percent, we have way too much

government. But . . . get the hell out of my yard! [loud applause] Look at what you've done to this community. Are you happy that you did this to the community? Stand up, man, I'm asking you a question! [Bundy remained seated and stone-faced.]

Unity

That evening of January 19, 2016, at the Burns High School gym, was the only occasion during the Bundy occupation when a cross section of the community, almost every local official, and the Bundy leadership met face-to-face. The dramatic exchanges were predictable; but to an outsider one of the more remarkable impressions that evening were the many heart-felt expressions of concern about the divisions that Bundy's presence had caused. In the midst of division and crisis, "pro-Bundy" and "anti-Bundy" residents were united in alarm at seeing their tight-knit community seemingly tearing itself apart. With the community, county leaders, law enforcement, and Ammon Bundy himself watching, a local woman stood at the top of the high school bleachers and warned Bundy supporters and opponents alike of the dangers in allowing the passions of the moment to create permanent scars:

> Why is it now that the entire nation is watching our every move that we decide to tear each other down? We've gone to school together, our kids learn and play together, we attend the same community functions together. We've broken bread, prayed, lost friends and family together. . . . It doesn't matter which side of the [Bundy] fence you stand on, but how you compose yourself during this time will follow you forever. Our community needs to focus on changing and healing. Neither will be accomplished if the malice that's at the heart of the great Harney County divide is not addressed. Choose wisely the way you express your opinion, because doing so in a manner that is hurtful, slanderous, or just plain nasty will be your burden to carry after the cameras leave.

Similar concerns were strongly voiced in many other forums as well. In an editorial published near the beginning of the occupation, *Burns*

Times-Herald reporter Samantha White defended solidarity in her community:

> As a local reporter, you'd think I'd be chomping at the bit to cover the story that's been making headlines across the nation. You'd think I'd be pointing my camera and tape recorder in the face of every man, woman, and child in Harney County in order to get "the scoop." You'd think I'd be thrilled to watch a sensational scene unfold in my own backyard. But that's simply not the case. . . . I hope Harney County will be remembered for its people. Like the sagebrush that blankets the landscape, our people are strong and resilient. Accustomed to working with limited resources and short supplies, we are resourceful, creative, and innovative. Geographically isolated, we are forced to depend on each other, work collaboratively, and solve our problems by communicating with one another. This is a community that takes care of its people, whether it's organizing a spaghetti feed to raise money to purchase a new projector for the local movie theater, collecting clothing for a family who lost everything in a house fire, or pulling over to assist a stranded motorist with a flat tire or dead battery. This is a place where time moves slower, and everyone waves as they pass each other on the street. Sure, Harney County has its problems. . . . But those of us who are fortunate enough to call this place our home have always had the will to figure out a way.[91]

After allowing Ammon Bundy to publish a lengthy letter to the editor before the Malheur takeover, White and the *Burns Times-Herald* staff felt that Bundy's subsequent requests to the newspaper were not honest, and even vaguely threatening. Consequently, unlike almost every other news organization in the region, the newspaper declined to give Ammon Bundy and other outside occupiers a platform to espouse divisive views. The *Burns Times-Herald* did give extensive coverage to local views of the occupation, but chose not go to the refuge and allow Bundy more opportunities to spread his divisive message. More than a year after the occupation ended, White observed that the occupation "did bring about suspicions and divisions that are taking time to heal," but "I continue to be amazed by the resiliency of this community."[92] A Harney County native and granddaughter of a former Harney County judge, White also reiterated what she had told outside reporters: that a community so geographically isolated

Burns Paiute Council then member Jarvis Kennedy speaks forcefully against the militia occupation.

and interdependent cannot remain divided. White asked, "Do we want to give up generations of love between our neighbors and our friends because of this? No. Heck no."[93]

One group of neighbors and friends that played a particularly important role in promoting unity was the Burns Paiute Tribe. Historically all of what is today the Malheur National Wildlife Refuge was Paiute territory, and the refuge headquarters was a winter camp for the tribe, with many burials. Paiute Tribal Council then chairwoman Charlotte Rodrique spoke publicly and eloquently of what the tribe considered the disrespectful approach of the Bundy occupiers to the refuge, its land, and the artifacts kept at the headquarters. Rodrique observed that the federal government is required to protect Native rights.[94] When the Bundys took over the refuge head-quarters, members of the tribe were among the most adamant and outspo-ken opponents. Burns Paiute Tribal Council member Jarvis Kennedy said early on, "[The Bundys] just need to get the hell out of here."[95] In response to the Bundys' statement that the refuge should be returned to its "rightful owners," Rodrique pointed out that the Burns Paiute are the only federally recognized tribe in Oregon that never legally ceded any land[96]—it was merely taken by force.

Yet the tribe also turned down offers of aid from other Native American communities, believing that bringing in additional angry Native people could only further escalate a volatile situation and possibly lead to violence. Similarly, members of the tribe chose to avoid going to the occupied refuge, believing their presence could trigger confrontation. The tribe held back some of their more passionate members for the same reason—despite a deep anger at the Bundy occupiers' disrespect.

Instead, the tribe prayed for everyone involved, including the occupiers. Tribal Council member Jarvis Kennedy was among those who held a traditional vigil on a high peak to guard the peace for all in the community. Kennedy was later awarded the Man of the Year Award for 2016 by the Harney County Chamber of Commerce for his strong and patient leadership during the occupation. Many noted that a silver lining of the occupation was that it brought the tribe and the non-Native community, whose relationship had at times been difficult owing to a painful past and lingering racism, closer together than ever before.

Perhaps surprisingly, another source of unity was social media. As many observers (including Sheriff Dave Ward) noted with alarm, during the Bundy occupation social media channeled and amplified many divisive remarks. At the same time, some in the community used social media to build solidarity. Even those who agreed with Ammon Bundy's political ideology generally resented having an outsider claim to speak for the community. In a county where it can take two to three hours to drive from one small town to another even in summer on dry roads, social media is a vital tool for communicating and organizing—and it was put to use repeatedly during the Bundy occupation to coordinate events expressing unity.

In particular, much of Harney County's population relies heavily on Facebook, and during the Bundy occupation many new Facebook groups were created for the specific purpose of organizing resistance (and some existing pages were overtaken by discussion of little else). An example was a group called "WE are Harney County Support Rally. YOU Are Not Our Voice"—a closed group (only approved members can read posts) that had about three hundred members by late January 2016. The group organized one of the seminal events of the Bundy occupation: the February 1, 2016, rally in front of the Harney County Courthouse, to defend county leaders and local and outside law enforcement and to demand that the remaining militia groups associated with Bundy occupation go home (in early February the Bundy leadership had been arrested, but four "holdouts" still occupied the Malheur Refuge, and many militia remained in Burns).

Following the arrests of the Bundy leadership and the alleged "assassination" of occupier LaVoy Finicum on January 26, 2016, many outside militia and local supporters turned their anger on Harney County's leadership. On social media, militia threats and calls for the overthrow of Harney County's leaders grew. A focal point of militia anger was the role of county judge Steve Grasty, who had earlier denied Bundy and his supporters' request to use a county building to hold a meeting (Grasty cited safety concerns, saying he could not allow individuals who were at the time engaging in what were believed to be criminal acts to use the building). Local anxiety grew that militia groups would attempt to enter the Harney County Courthouse and seize Judge Grasty or other officials and put them on trial in a so-called common-law court. On social media, militia accused Grasty of "treason" and asked pointedly, what is the punishment for treason? Concern came to a head on February 1, 2016. Militia groups had planned a noon demonstration. By 11:30 a.m., local supporters of the county's leaders and law enforcement formed a human barricade on the steps in front of the courthouse, defiantly holding signs and chanting to the militia, "WE are Harney County, YOU are not our voice."

In all, about five hundred people gathered, with an estimated two hundred on the militia side (many from outside the community) and three hundred mostly local people standing in defense of the county leaders.[97] Militia protesters held signs and yelled slogans declaring "Grasty and [Sheriff] Ward have blood on there [sic] hands," "Rest in peace LaVoy," "Ambushed and assassinated," and "End government tyranny." Pro-Harney County government counter-protesters held signs and shouted "Militia go home!" "It's not your place to tell us who our elected leaders are," "Rancher with my own voice," and "WE are Harney County! Everyone else G.T.F.O." (get the fuck out). Many on the militia side openly carried firearms. With the two sides physically intermingling, intense yelling went on for four

Militia supporters and opponents face off in front of the Harney County Courthouse (February 1, 2016).

Mostly nonlocal militiamen protest the death of LaVoy Finicum (February 1, 2016).

On the streets of Burns, nonlocal militiamen openly display their firearms (February 1, 2016).

At the militia face-off on February 1, 2016, local residents express their commitment to community, collaboration, and getting the militia out.

A Paiute woman offers a humorous reminder of who the "rightful owners" of the Malheur Refuge might be (February 1, 2016).

Local residents express their wishes to nonlocal militiamen in their community (February 1, 2016).

hours as local police stood by patiently, intervening only to separate particularly intense arguments.

Eventually, exhaustion and frigid temperatures dispersed the crowd without incident, but a clear statement had been made. On social media, militia activists expressed surprise at the large turnout of local support for county leaders. Some insisted the pro-Harney County government counter-protesters were paid actors. Other militia and anti-federal activists such as "constitutional" sheriff Richard Mack and anti-federal-government speaker KrisAnne Hall, however, seemed to take the community's statement as an indication that Harney County was beyond redemption, and refocused their attention elsewhere. To a considerable extent, the pro-Harney County government counter-protesters' demand for militia to "go home" worked.

Ten days later, the three-month saga that began with the arrival of Ammon Bundy and Ryan Payne in Harney County in early November finally ended. After the leaders were arrested and most occupiers fled, four holdouts remained at "Camp Finicum," a ramshackle cluster of tents and vehicles erected at the refuge headquarters parking lot—near trenches the occupiers had dug for human waste, very close to Paiute burial sites. On February 11, 2016, Sean and Sandy Anderson, Jeff Banta, and David Fry surrendered to the FBI after a night of intensely emotional negotiations that was live-streamed by pro-Bundy internet talk-show host Gavin Seim. At times the holdouts seemed to veer toward suicidal violence. Seeming to reach a point of exhaustion, three surrendered; then the last holdout, David Fry, stated his intent to surrender if all law enforcement officers shouted, "Hallelujah." They did. Fry smoked a cigarette, ate a cookie, and surrendered. The physical takeover of the Malheur National Wildlife Refuge was over.

As discussed in the following chapter, however, the political movement that the occupation of Harney County represented was far from over, for the community or the nation. The ideological forces that precipitated the occupation long pre-dated the events of late 2015 and early 2016, and would remain long after. Harney County residents understood the challenge, and set out to do what they had done in the face of adversity many times before—build community. At the initiative of a single Harney County

The morning after the final four militia members surrendered, a recent latrine trench and garbage were visible at "Camp Finicum" near the Malheur Refuge entrance (February 12, 2016).

citizen and with help from the Harney County Chamber of Commerce, the county launched a campaign to display orange ribbons to signify unity. Scars remained and the county would never be quite the same; but driving through Burns and Hines came to resemble driving through a field of orange flowers, not unlike the wildflowers that blossom in the springtime desert.

2

Rebellion

In 2014, Americans got some startling lessons in the political philosophy of extremists willing to confront the federal government with deadly force. Since 1993, Nevada rancher Cliven Bundy had refused to renew his Bureau of Land Management grazing contract under new terms to protect the threatened desert tortoise. Bundy continued to illegally graze his cattle on public land without a contract, accruing over $1 million in fines. Meanwhile, by 1998, all other ranchers in the area had sold their grazing contracts, which were then retired. Bundy then allowed his cattle to expand onto the other ranchers' former allotments, giving him more land and cattle than when he grazed legally.[1] In the same year, a US district court issued an injunction to stop Bundy's illegal grazing, but he continued.[2] In late March 2014, following a repeated court order in 2013,[3] the BLM served notice that Bundy must remove his cattle from public land or they would be impounded. Bundy refused.

On April 5, 2014, the BLM began to round up Bundy's cows. Bundy posted a video call to action on social media, and within days press accounts estimated Bundy's supporters, including armed "patriots," at several hundred to a thousand. On April 12, after several days of small skirmishes, the confrontation between armed protesters and federal agents came to a head. Law enforcement officers and heavily armed "patriots" alike reported that the situation could have easily turned violent.[4] Internet images of "patriots" in sniper positions with rifles pointed toward law enforcement officers circulated widely. Reporter Jim Urquhart of Reuters reported that one "patriot," with his rifle pointed in the direction of federal agents, stated, "I've got a clear shot at four of them."[5] Fearing a bloodbath, the BLM withdrew, and the Bundy cattle were released. Ammon Bundy crowed that "We sent [the government] packing," and "The war has just begun."[6]

Bundy supporters were ecstatic at the apparent victory of "patriots" over "tyrannical" federal government. Supporters included conservative media and politicians, such as Fox News celebrity Sean Hannity, Kentucky's US senator Rand Paul, and Nevada's US senator Dean Heller. Cliven Bundy relished the media attention and seized every opportunity to expound on his philosophy. However, with news cameras rolling and the loquacious Bundy in full pontification mode, the inflammatory ideology that emerged from his mouth soon sent some supporters scrambling for cover. As reported by the *New York Times*, Bundy stated:

> I want to tell you one more thing I know about the Negro. . . . They abort their young children, they put their young men in jail, because they never learned how to pick cotton. And I've often wondered, are they better off as slaves, picking cotton and having a family life and doing things, or are they better off under government subsidy? They didn't get no more freedom. They got less freedom.[7]

Cliven Bundy even went so far as to suggest that in the struggle to prevent (in his view) dictatorship and communism, nonwhites are enemies:

> There's one thing that's on my mind, though, through this whole [standoff with the BLM]. You look around and we're all basically white people. Where's our colored brothers? Where's our Mexican brothers? Where's our Chinese, where are they? They're just as much American as we are, and they're not with us. If they're not with us, they're going to be against us.[8]

The Bundy family denied Cliven Bundy is a racist, but to anyone familiar with the history of America's extreme political right, the racialized language is immediately recognizable (Levitas 2002; Neiwert 1999; Aho 2016). Although Cliven Bundy's "Negro" comments caused the greatest public outcry, his views on governance and the Constitution also raised eyebrows. To almost any reporter who would stand still long enough, Bundy explained his view that, under the US Constitution, Nevada is a "sovereign state" and that the United States government has no authority over land within its boundaries. Thus, in explaining his refusal to renew his contract or pay fees to graze on public land, Bundy said the problem was not the money—he had even tried to pay grazing fees to the county. The problem was that the bills came from the federal government, and "I don't recognize [the federal government] having any jurisdiction or authority over this land, and I do not have a contract with the United States government."[9] In an interview with ABC News/KTNV, Bundy stated, "I abide by all Nevada state law, but I don't recognize the United States government as even existing."[10]

The beliefs the Bundys represented are far from isolated or unique. By 2016 they could be said to have been reflected to a considerable degree in the national political landscape. The Bundys spoke incessantly of representing "We the people," but their view of "the people" was narrowly confined to people like themselves. When a rancher in Harney County pointed out that a birdwatcher in Portland, Oregon (a relatively diverse, liberal city), has as much right as ranchers to decide how public land should be used, Ammon Bundy dismissed the comment as "hypothetical."[11]

Similarly, the Bundys dismissed Native American rights. Ryan Bundy, for example, stated, "We also recognize that the Native Americans had the claim to the land, but they lost that claim. There are things to learn from cultures of the past, but the current culture is the most important."[12] Bundy ignored the fact that the land was brutally taken from the Paiute (not somehow "lost"). In asserting with no explanation that the "current culture," which is dominated by white ranchers and farmers, is "most important," Bundy privileged one group over another. The Bundys also persistently claimed that the United States is a republic, not a democracy[13] (see Mulloy 2004)—a claim consistent with "patriot" ideology that justifies the preservation of rights for some white Americans against the democratic will of a pluralistic nation.[14] Similar ideas were echoed in the presidential election of 2016 in overtly anti-immigrant ideologies with racial overtones, as well as a general notion of returning to a time when the pluralism of America could be ignored, to the benefit of a narrow "most important" segment of society.

Federalism

The core political ideology represented by the Bundy family can be viewed in the context of a debate as old as the founding of the nation, one famously expressed by the competition between Alexander Hamilton, who supported a strong central government, and Thomas Jefferson, who deeply distrusted centralized power (Holloway 2015). Throughout America's experiment with the federalist model, the question of the appropriate balance of power between the national government and state and local governments has been highly contentious. The Bundy ideology departs, however, from most other modern expressions of states' rights–oriented federalism[15] in its open embrace of armed confrontation—up to and including potentially lethal confrontations with federal authorities.

The most extreme expressions of today's federalist ideology, which advocates for a radically minimalized role of national government, have roots in the racialized politics of the Reconstruction-era southern states following the Civil War. With the military victory of the United States over the Confederacy in 1865, much of the work of keeping the peace and enforcing law in the former Confederate states fell to the United States Army. Occupation of southern states by the United States military caused seething anger among defeated white southern populations. In response, southern politicians sponsored the Posse Comitatus Act of 1878, which prohibited the United States from enforcing domestic policy using federal troops. The act derived its name from the English concept of posse comitatus (Latin for "power of the county"), in which sheriffs can conscript local able-bodied men to capture fugitives and enforce laws (often abbreviated simply as "posse," the stuff of Hollywood westerns).

The intent and outcome of the Posse Comitatus Act was less benign, however, than a mere shift toward an idealistic Jeffersonian vision of limited central authority and strong local governance. With federal troops removed, county sheriffs in the southern states effectively became the sole and supreme law of the land. Local law enforcement came to reflect the bloodied but unbowed racist southern power structure at the time. Jim Crow laws, segregation, and extralegal intimidation and violence by the Ku Klux Klan flourished. Through posse comitatus, an angry, racist, and unrepentant white southern ruling class maintained, if not sovereignty, autonomy from the United States government.

Posse comitatus in the nineteenth century became the inspiration and root of many of the anti-federal government ideologies and movements that thrive today. President Eisenhower's deployment of federal troops in Arkansas to force school desegregation in 1957 so enraged California-based white supremacist Christian Identity minister William Potter Gale that he formed a new movement to oppose similar "overreach" of federal authority. Gale, a World War II lieutenant colonel, insurance salesman, and rabid anti-Semite (who was himself half-Jewish; Levitas 2002) named his movement after the nineteenth-century law—posse comitatus. In a flurry of documents and recordings self-published in the early 1970s, Gale reiterated the core posse comitatus belief that the county sheriff is the supreme law of the land, with the right and duty to stand against federal laws that the sheriff deemed unconstitutional. County residents, too, had the authority and duty to form a posse of "sovereign citizens" to enforce the Constitution as they interpreted it. Gale wrote that if the sheriff failed to uphold the Constitution, "He shall be removed by the Posse to the most populated intersection of streets in the township and at noon hung by the neck, the body remaining until sundown as an example to those who would subvert the law."[16]

Investigative journalist JJ MacNab, who reports on antigovernment extremists for *Forbes* magazine, states that Gale "fabricated" these legal theories, which were then passed from generation to generation, largely in rural communities, becoming the precursor to the modern "sovereign citizen" movement.[17] Self-described sovereign citizens maintain that the current United States government is in violation of the Constitution and therefore has no legal right to exist, and they are therefore not subject to its laws. The Southern Poverty Law Center estimates that three hundred thousand people in the United States subscribe to sovereign citizen theory to some degree, and one hundred thousand of them are considered "hard core."[18]

The most extreme sovereign citizens maintain that it is their right and duty to resist authority up to the point of lethal force. Individuals associated with the sovereign citizen movement have been involved in some of the most violent acts of domestic terrorism in the United States. Timothy

McVeigh and Terry Nichols, the convicted perpetrators of the 1995 bombing of the Alfred P. Murrah Federal Building in Oklahoma City that killed 168 people, including 19 children, were both associated with the movement. Sovereign citizens today are involved with numerous crimes, including shootings and murders of law enforcement officers. JJ MacNab identified seventy-eight individuals—law enforcement, civilians, and others—killed by sovereign citizens between March 2000 and February 2017.[19] The FBI has identified sovereign citizens as a top threat to law enforcement.[20]

William Potter Gale's posse comitatus also reemerged in recent years in the form of "constitutional" sheriffs who subscribe to Gale's notion that the sheriff is the highest law enforcement official in the land, with the right and duty to prohibit what they perceive as unconstitutional federal activities within their counties. This idea was the basis of the formation of the Constitutional Sheriffs and Peace Officers Association by former Arizona sheriff Richard Mack. According to the CSPOA, the county sheriff is "the first line of defense in preserving the constitutional rights of a citizen," whose power "even supersedes the powers of the President."[21] CSPOA supported the Bundy family in the 2014 Bunkerville standoff, where the group's founder Richard Mack strategized to put women at the front of the protest so that, "if they're going to start shooting, it's going to be women that are going to be televised all across the world getting shot by these rogue federal officers."[22] Mack was also present in Burns, Oregon, when Ammon Bundy seized the Malheur National Wildlife Refuge in 2016. Mack did not participate in the takeover and stated that he did not support it, but he held a public meeting in Burns declaring that Harney County sheriff Dave Ward "did not do his job"—referring to Ward's refusal to comply with the Bundys' demand that he shield local ranchers Dwight and Steven Hammond from a federal arrest.[23]

Also present in Burns, Oregon, during the Malheur takeover were groups that represent much of America's modern "patriot" movement. The modern "patriot" movement can be traced to the tragedies at Waco, Texas, and Ruby Ridge, Idaho, in the 1990s (Sunshine 2016).[24] "Patriot" group memberships surged during the Obama presidency. "Patriot" groups are diverse in their ideologies but tend to share a number of core beliefs, including support for transferring federal lands to local control, unrestricted gun ownership, and opposition to federal regulations and immigration (especially from Islamic regions). Many advocate "nullification" of federal laws believed unconstitutional (an idea that traces directly back to opposition to federal control in southern states in the Civil War era), and "coordination"—the idea that federal agencies must comply with local land use decisions (Sunshine 2016, 7).

The "patriot" groups present and active in Burns, Oregon, during the takeover of the Malheur National Wildlife Refuge included Three Percenters[25], Oath Keepers, and the Pacific Patriots Network (PPN). Some of these groups, including the PPN and the Oath Keepers, explicitly rejected the Bundys' takeover of the Malheur Refuge. Oath Keepers published an article calling the takeover a "clinically retarded maneuver."[26] While the "patriots" and the Bundy group did not share the same tactics, their goals—fighting what they consider unconstitutional "tyranny"—are similar. Although most of the "patriots" appeared to have no direct ties to resource-based livelihoods on public land, they appeared to adopt at least parts of the Bundys' anti-federal-lands ideology. At the January 2, 2016, rally for the Hammonds in Burns, Idaho Three Percenters leader Brooke Agresta warned, for example, "If I hear any one of you say 'federal' land today I'll rip your head off."[27] Mostly, however, "patriots" seemed to find the Bundys' willingness to confront federal authorities with force for a seemingly patriotic cause irresistible. Some members of Oath Keepers, for example, eventually supported the Bundy occupation despite opposition from the Oath Keepers' leadership. The Bundys, in turn, found in the "patriots" useful muscle (MacNab forthcoming).

The Bundy takeover of the Malheur Refuge also received support from a group calling itself the Coalition of Western States (COWS). Although not a "patriot" group per se, COWS is described by investigative journalist John Sepulvado as "the political arm of the militant movement."[28] COWS consists of western state legislators whose goal is to "restore management of public lands to the States where it Constitutionally belongs."[29] The group was established after the Bundys' 2014 standoff with the Bureau of Land Management to keep the anti-federal government momentum going. The group includes several members who were present and active in the 2014 Bunkerville standoff and are friends of the Bundy family, including

Washington state representative Matt Shea and then Nevada state assemblywoman Michele Fiore. COWS encouraged support for the Bundys during the occupation, and afterward helped some to flee the refuge and the last four to peacefully surrender.

During the occupation, COWS members met with Harney County judge Steve Grasty, the district attorney, a deputy sheriff, and an FBI agent and passed the information they gathered on to the occupiers.[30] Responding to a question on its Facebook page, a COWS spokesperson confirmed that its members are "associated with" the American Lands Council,[31] a major anti-federal-lands activist organization funded in part by Americans for Prosperity, the influential advocacy group representing billionaire anti-federal-government activists Charles and David Koch (Mayer 2016).

Probably the most important motivation behind the Bundy family's anti-federal-government activism, however, came from their association with hard-right Mormon theology (Sunshine 2016), especially the ideas of theologian W. Cleon Skousen. An FBI agent, police chief, and professor at Brigham Young University, Skousen emerged in the 1950s as an anticommunist crusader and conspiracy theorist. Skousen, along with Ezra Taft Benson (a fellow far-right John Birch Society supporter and president of the Church of Jesus Christ Latter Day Saints), accused President Dwight Eisenhower of being a communist "tool."[32] Skousen was a vocal and widely cited advocate for the principle of "original intent" in interpreting the US Constitution, from which he concluded that the contemporary United States government had grown in power vastly beyond the Founders' original vision. For Skousen, Benson, and others in the Mormon hard-right, big government is akin to the work of Satan—it is not only a political matter, but literally an article of faith.[33]

Skousen promoted the belief that the US Constitution is divinely inspired, and went further to claim that all law—including the Constitution—must be measured against "natural law," or God's law; that religion is necessary for the governance of a free people; and (citing John Locke) that a government that takes away property should be altered or abolished to restore liberty (Skousen 2007). Skousen was a prolific writer. Some of his writings proved still more controversial, including the suggestion that slavery was beneficial to African Americans (Skousen 1985). Although Skousen, who died in 2006, did not specifically address the issue of federal public lands, his anti-federal-government, "theo-constitutionalist"[34] ideology became influential in the emerging anti-federal-public lands movement.[35] In the 1990s, Cliven Bundy and his neighbor Keith Nay compiled their beliefs (in what became known as the "Nay Book"[36]) on how "defense" of the Constitution and property rights is a duty under Mormon scripture. These observations appear consistent with the views of Benson, Skousen, and other hard-right Mormons.

Although interpretation of Mormon faith was central to Skousen's beliefs, his more eccentric beliefs were deeply controversial within the Mormon Church. Skousen and the Bundy family also had that in common. The Bundys' 2016 takeover of the Malheur National Wildlife Refuge was strongly denounced by the main church in Salt Lake City.[37] In mainstream Mormonism, when "Salt Lake" issues a public edict, the faithful comply.[38] The Bundys' political-religious beliefs, in contrast, appear to be aligned with a fringe "Skousenite"[39] splinter group.

The Center for Biological Diversity, an environmental organization that has repeatedly clashed with the Bundy family over their disregard for rules to safeguard the threatened desert tortoise, has researched links between Cleon Skousen and the Bundys. Among their findings are that the version of the US Constitution that almost always appeared in the Bundys' pockets was edited by Cleon Skousen and published by the National Center for Constitutional Studies, which Skousen cofounded with ultraconservative businessman Bert Smith. Bert Smith[40] (who called Cliven Bundy "a hero" and supported the 2014 Bunkerville standoff), paid for the distribution of the Skousen-edited Constitutions that appeared at the Bundy takeover of the Malheur Refuge; and many of Cliven Bundy's most controversial public statements, including the claims that slavery was good for African Americans and that the federal government has no constitutional right to own land outside Washington, DC, almost directly parallel Skousen's writings. Also, some of Ammon Bundy's children attended the Skousen-based Heritage Academy high school, headed by Earl Taylor Jr., who is also president of the National Center for Constitutional Studies founded by Cleon Skousen and Bert Smith.[41]

The Bundy family's conflicts with the federal government aligned substantially with posse comitatus, "constitutional" sheriffs, the "patriot" movement, and hard-right Mormonism, but their focus on land use and defending the rights of ranchers also placed them in the tradition of the Sagebrush Rebellion that had simmered in the American West since at least the 1970s, and in important respects even since the founding of the federal public lands system at the turn of the twentieth century.[42]

Setting the Bundy occupation in historical context, Phil Brick, professor of politics at Whitman College, observed that in 1911, after President Theodore Roosevelt established the system of national forests, there was a rebellion against the forest reserves: "Foresters, loggers, did not want to pay for the use of federal lands they had been using for free." In 1911, the US Supreme Court[43] tested the constitutionality of the Forest Reserve Act of 1891. The argument was, as the Bundys would argue more than one hundred years later, that the federal government does not have the right under the Constitution to own and regulate access to land. The loggers lost the case, but "there were continual legal challenges."[44]

Opposition to federal government control of public lands simmered for many decades, and tensions flared again particularly intensely in the 1970s, when a spate of new federal environmental regulations began to be felt on the ground.[45] Yet again, the argument was made that the federal government exceeded its legitimate constitutional authority and severely undermined the rights and livelihoods of ranchers, loggers, miners, and others who depend on the land to make a living. The movement sought regulatory rollbacks and, ultimately, the transfer of federal lands to the states. The 1970s Sagebrush Rebellion ebbed in the 1980s under President Ronald Reagan, who called himself a Sagebrush Rebel and whose interior secretary, James Watt, supported the movement's goals.[46] However, few of the goals were actually met, leaving continued anger, which erupted again as the "wise use" movement in the 1990s, and coming to a head when then president Bill Clinton designated the Grand Staircase-Escalante National Monument in Utah.

The Bundys were not the first or only family to become the face of activist ranchers in opposition to, in their view, overreaching federal authority. Since the 1980s, the most prominent activist ranchers had been the Hage family, headed by Wayne Hage Sr. and then Wayne Hage Jr., after his father's death in 2006. The Hage family fought in court for decades against charges that they illegally ran cattle without a permit on federal land, claiming that under the principle of prior appropriation their water rights gave them a property right on the federal grazing lands that make up most of their Pine Creek Ranch in central Nevada. After decades, the US Supreme Court issued a final rejection of the Hages' argument in 2016.[47] However, the Hage family's battle against the federal government, and in particular Wayne Hage Sr.'s book *Storm over Rangelands* (1989), made their struggle into a rallying cry for opponents of federal control of public lands in the West.

With the end of the Hage family's legal battle in the same year that Ammon Bundy seized the national spotlight with his claims of federal "tyranny" against ranchers, it might be thought that the Bundy family became the new face of anti-federal rancher activism. With the arguable exception of spokesman LaVoy Finicum, however, none of the occupiers at the Malheur National Wildlife Refuge were themselves ranchers. The armed occupiers at the Malheur National Wildlife Refuge were mostly anti-federal-government "patriots," seemingly rallying behind the symbolic banner of the Sagebrush Rebellion. The Bundys' anti-federal goals also aligned closely with the broader anti-federal and anti-environmental agenda of extraordinarily deep-pocketed ultra-libertarian activists (Mayer 2016). If the Bundys were the new face of the Sagebrush Rebellion, their apparent merger with the "patriot" movement and alignment with super-rich ultra-libertarian activists would seem to have taken the movement in a more radical—indeed revolutionary—and violent direction.[48]

Revolution

Highway 78 from Burns to the town of Crane, Oregon, is twenty-nine miles of dead-flat road. In daylight with good weather, the farm fields on either side of the highway allow an uninterrupted view of a vast robin's-egg-blue sky. On the night of January 18, 2016, the sky was completely dark. Car headlights refracted off freezing fog in confusing patterns, making the flat but curving, icy road almost invisible and treacherous. From Burns, the first lights visible were the Crystal Crane Hot Springs resort. The resort's parking lot was completely covered with ice and pickup trucks. Inside the resort, a warm, well-lit dining hall with a rustic Western décor was filled with about thirty Harney County ranchers, a few small press crews, and me.

Heading the meeting were the leaders of the then-ongoing occupation of the Malheur National Wildlife Refuge: Ammon Bundy, Ryan Bundy, Ryan Payne, and LaVoy Finicum, along with Blaine Cooper, Sean and Sandy Anderson, and Ammon Bundy's burly bodyguard Brian Cavalier (aka Booda, or Fluffy Unicorn). The immediate purpose of the meeting was to enlist Harney County ranchers to pledge to repudiate their federal grazing contracts at a ceremony the following Saturday. The presentation was well organized and delivered, complete with a PowerPoint slide show and soundtrack. Oregon Public Broadcasting reporter Conrad Wilson described the event as "not unlike a pitch for a timeshare."[49] Ultimately, however, the "pitch" was for something far more extraordinary. The meeting was the Bundys' clearest and most comprehensive explanation of their ideology and the ultimate purpose of the occupation: to launch a revolution against the federal government.

To the general public, the Bundys insisted that the occupation was about freeing the Hammonds and transferring Malheur National Wildlife Refuge land to Harney County. In a CNN interview, Ammon Bundy stated that "we're going to stay here until we've secured the [refuge] land and the resources back to the people of Harney County, where they can get back to ranching, back to logging, get back to using these lands without feeling fear and intimidation—that's our goal."[50] However, as the occupation of the refuge dragged out through most of the month of January despite repeated requests by local law enforcement and the community for the occupiers to leave, doubt set in among many local residents about the true agenda of the occupiers. Many concluded that the occupation was not really about the Hammonds, and few seemed convinced that handing over the Malheur Refuge to local ownership was realistic or even desirable. While the occupiers' stated goals met with skepticism, the actual goals remained murky. In the intimate space of the Crystal Crane Hot Springs resort, however, with mostly local ranchers present, the occupiers unveiled a very clear—and radical—vision.

Contrary to public perceptions and the occupiers' prior statements, the Bundy vision is not based solely or even primarily on the Constitution.

Ammon Bundy, and followers, lecture Harney County ranchers on his views of the Constitution (January 18, 2016).

There is no question the occupation leaders were staunch defenders of their distinctive interpretations of the Constitution, but the arguments that the occupiers presented in Crane went beyond their iconic "pocket constitutions."[51] Legal scholars expressed exasperation at the unconventional interpretations of the Constitution offered by the Bundys, noting, in particular, that the US Supreme Court has ruled repeatedly that under the Property Clause (Article IV, Section 3, Clause 2) the federal government does have constitutional authority to own land outside Washington, DC— contrary to the Bundys' assertion of the primacy of the Enclave Clause.[52] Even Ammon Bundy's own one-time attorney, Mike Arnold, stated that unless there is a "massive catastrophe where [President Trump] has to appoint four other justices, or maybe three other justices that have a complete 'originalist' point of view," a "revolutionary" reinterpretation of the Enclave Clause in the way the Bundys see it is unlikely.[53]

What few outsiders grasped was that the occupiers simply did not care what scholars or practitioners—even the US Supreme Court—say about the Constitution. In the occupiers' views, the only true authority on the

Constitution is God, as expressed in principles they describe as "natural law." When challenged by one local rancher during the Crane meeting, Ryan Bundy flatly insisted that it is the job of an unspecified "We the People" to interpret the Constitution, not the Supreme Court—a direct contradiction of any plausible reading of Article III of the Constitution. Thus, the Bundys not only offered highly idiosyncratic interpretations of particular sections of the Constitution, but also were willing to ignore other parts of the Constitution that did not fit their views. In defending this apparent pick-and-choose approach, Ryan Bundy explained that the Constitution is "a written expression of Natural Law,"[54] making moot any other basis for interpretation. Where the written Constitution and natural law are at odds, natural law prevails. Moreover, the Bundys appeared confident that they themselves were rightful ministers of natural law. Though the Bundys did not say so explicitly, by claiming to know better than others the meanings of natural law (and thus the Constitution), they implicitly claimed to speak for God.

For three hours, the leaders of the occupation, taking turns, presented their ideas to the Harney County ranchers in the room—many of whom shared a sense of frustration with federal government policies but were skeptical of the Bundys' ideology and solutions. After briefly reviewing his complaints regarding the Hammonds, Ammon Bundy began the meeting with an introduction to his view of natural law as applied to property:

> When it comes to property, The Lord has natural laws in which we can very clearly understand whose is what, and not fight about it. . . . There are two primary rules. The first one is prior appropriation. The doctrine of first in time, first in right. Which means whoever got there first, they had the right to claim it.[55] . . . The second part is . . . you have to beneficially use it. That's the doctrine of use it or lose it. . . . What law book did you read that out of? It's just natural. We understand it, it's inside us. We don't have to fight, we all agree and understand that. That's Natural Law.

Crucially, according to Bundy, under natural law the legitimate role of government is extremely limited, and mostly it should exist at the county rather than federal or state level. When government exceeds its rightful limits under natural law, it becomes illegitimate:

At the occupied Malheur Refuge, religious motivations for the militia takeover were widely evident.

The purpose of government is to assist the individual in claiming, using, and defending their rights. . . . Claiming, that's why we record our property in the County Recorder's office. . . . The second part of government is to assist the individual in using their rights. That's why we have, like, roads. County roads. They help us use our property. . . . Government should not be there to try to restrict you from using your rights. . . . They're supposed to encourage you to use [your property] so you can benefit from it, so you can pursue happiness with it. So you can profit from it. So you can do what you want to do with it. . . . And then, the third function of government is to assist the individual in defending [their property]. Like, the county sheriff. . . . Whenever government is performing something that doesn't have to do with you claiming, using, and defending [your rights], then government has stepped outside the purpose of which you need government for . . . they've exceeded their authority.

Bundy went on to state that federal government is necessary, but its functions must be restricted to a few tasks specifically enumerated in the

Constitution: "[Federal] authority is national defense, international trade, border security . . . a few other little responsibilities that made sense for them, like running a post office."

With regard to land, Ammon Bundy went on to present an interpretation of the Constitution that allows for only extremely limited federal ownership. Specifically, Ammon Bundy claimed that the Property Clause of the Constitution (Article IV, Section 3, Clause 2[56]) requires the federal government to transfer almost all land to the former territories upon statehood:

> The federal government has to dispose of [land], they can't hang onto it. They have to dispose of it. . . . [At statehood, land] goes completely out of [the federal government's] hands and now it becomes the people's. No longer does the federal government make all needful rules and regulations.

According to Bundy, after statehood the federal government can only own land for a few very specific purposes that are specifically enumerated in the Constitution, and then only with express permission from the states. Almost every journalist or close observer of the Bundy occupation memorized Article I, Section 8, Clause 17 of the Constitution (the Enclave Clause), which Bundy and the other occupiers recited like a mantra:[57]

> What [the Founders] did there, is they just established that Congress has a right over Washington, DC. Ten square miles [sic],[58] . . . and that would become the seat of the federal government . . . . To have land inside a state, [the federal government] has to have consent from the state legislatures. And they have to purchase it. . . . Then, they can only use it for the erection of forts, magazines, arsenals, dockyards, and other needful buildings. So, they can only use it for the purposes of national defense, . . . international trade, . . . and other needful buildings like post offices or a courthouse. Basically, for these enumerated purposes. . . . They can't use it for anything that's not listed in the Constitution.

Therein lies what Bundy called the "nitty-gritty," where the federal government has, in his view, exceeded its constitutional authority as intended by the Founders, who were in Bundy's view guided by God and natural law. Expressing a conspiratorial view shared by other far-right thinkers, including some "mainstream" libertarians (Mayer 2016), this "overreach" is not merely incidental but is an intentional power grab by a predatory government intent on consolidating power and wealth:

> The Founders were very, very worried about the federal government controlling the land and resources. Because they knew, as Thomas Jefferson said, if the federal government was able to come down into the states and control land and resources it would put the state and the people in economic depression, put the states into undue obedience. . . .
>
> The government knows exactly where wealth comes from. They're not ignorant to these natural laws. They also know, just like the way claiming, using and defending [land] maintains rights, that's also the way you take [land]. What did the federal government do? They came down into the states in the '30s, '40s, and '50s, and they began to claim . . . all the land that wasn't used. Literally, that's just what they did, they put their signs all over, they did surveys, put their stamp on it. They began to say it's [government land] even though ranchers own the grass, miners own the mineral rights, and so on [according to natural law]. They began to say, "We own the real estate so we own all the rights." And they transferred the rights that the ranchers own . . . to themselves. So now what we're doing is we're paying a permit or a lease for our own forefathers' rights.

Turning to the immediate goal of the meeting, Bundy made the case for ranchers to repudiate their federal government grazing contracts, to get "their" land "back." Bundy claimed grazing contracts are a legal trick the federal government uses to gain control over land and forage that belong to ranchers:

> They [the federal government] don't have constitutional authority to be leasing the land to you. It's yours to begin with. The People's to begin with. The only way they get authority over you is because you signed a [grazing] contract, so if you violate that contract they pull you up into federal court and they say, "See, you agreed you would do this," and they prosecute you. That's contractual law, not constitutional law. By signing the contract, you're giving up your rights.

Ryan Bundy, a louder and more forceful speaker than his brother, then took over the presentation. Getting straight to the immediate goal of the evening's meeting, Ryan Bundy urged Harney County ranchers to break their federal grazing contracts:

> Your forefathers established those [grazing] rights by beneficial use and prior appropriation. They do not belong to BLM , they belong to you. So why would you ask permission from them? The way to fix this problem . . . is you cannot believe you are asking them for permission. You are not leasing anything from them. You've got to use [the land] as though it is your own because it is. And you've got to defend it. The way you've got to claim this is, right now you've got [grazing] contracts with the federal government. That's the only way they have power over you. . . . So if you want to clear yourselves of this unconstitutional mess and claim the rights that you truly already own and use them the way you should, you need to take that contract and tear it up and tell them that you're never signing another one again.

Appearing arranged to ratchet up the emotional impact, the presentation was then taken over by the only rancher among the occupiers, LaVoy Finicum. Looking every bit the part in slim jeans, boots, plaid shirt, dungaree jacket, and a cream-colored cowboy hat, Finicum appealed to ranchers in the room in terms that went beyond mere land management. Finicum, his voice rising as if delivering a fiery sermon, spoke of a grand struggle for freedom against tyranny:

> I'm here making a plea to you, you ranchers here, I'm asking you on this Saturday to take action. We're having a signing ceremony. We have a rancher coming clear from New Mexico to lend courage and strength. He's going to come here to the Harney County Resource Center[59] [and] in front of media he's going to . . . cancel his [US Forest Service grazing] contract. . . . That's the crossing of the stream. That is when you say . . . [you've become] a free rancher grazing on your free grass. I've done it. Cliven Bundy has done it. On Saturday, it's going to double[60] and we'd like to see it multiple [sic]. . . . We invite you to be there, maybe you'll catch the spirit at the moment, or maybe you will now. Now is the day. Now is the time. Are you going to wait for tomorrow? . . . When will you stand up, if not now? . . . You must be willing to put everything on the table for freedom. If you are not willing to put every- thing on the table for freedom, are you worthy to have freedom? . . . Our

Founding Fathers laid everything on the line. Their lives. Their sacred honor. Their fortune. We have been the beneficiaries of these great sacrifices. . . . This day has come again. . . . Will you have the courage to stand up there and cancel that [grazing] agreement between you and the federal government? . . . I promise you, if you stand, others will stand with you. If you stand, God will stand with you. But God cannot stand with you if you do not stand. . . . I beg of you here in Harney County, stand.

LaVoy Finicum gave the most passionate and eloquent address of the evening, but the still-more-dramatic—and chilling—speech was delivered in a soft monotone by Ammon Bundy's top lieutenant, Montana militiaman Ryan Payne. While the Bundy brothers and LaVoy Finicum had focused on persuading ranchers to tear up their federal government grazing contracts, Ryan Payne (the only featured speaker of the evening not wearing a cowboy hat) made it clear that the occupation was the "point of the spear" for something much bigger: a second American Revolution. The idea of a second American Revolution is common and widely discussed among "patriot" groups. The "patriot" community buzzed with speculation about whether the Bundy confrontations in Nevada and Oregon would be the events that "kick off" the second revolution.[61] To the Harney County ranchers at the Crystal Crane Hot Springs resort that evening, Payne made it clear that a second American Revolution was precisely the goal. Payne argued that the current American government had exceeded its constitutional authority, stating, "Anything that's not in the Constitution, the government is not allowed to do." Payne stated that once a government turns away from the Constitution, it can never be righted and must be overthrown. Using an example common in sovereign citizen ideology, Payne said,

You don't lawfully have to have a driver's license, because you have the right to travel freely. You have a right to own a vehicle—you have the right to own private property. And you have the right to travel wherever you want to in that private property. . . . But an officer will pull you over and he'll ask you for your license. If you don't produce it, he's going to try to arrest you. He won't just write you a ticket. And now I tell him, "Well, Sir, according to the Constitution, I don't have to have a license to travel." It's not that [the

Constitution] says you don't have to have a license; it's that it doesn't say you have to have a license. It doesn't give the government the authority to tell you [that] you have to have a license. . . . So ultimately, if you resist arrest, in a lot of states you have the right to resist arrest to the point of lethal force. . . . My point here is that they're willing to uphold these things all the way to the death. If you don't submit to their arrest, ultimately they're going to bring in more guys and they're going to beat you down or they may shoot you. And that is a standing army. They are holding decrees that are not [constitutional] and they're willing to do it to the death.

Payne also made a lengthy argument comparing specific alleged acts of government overreach against citizens of Harney County to the tyranny of the British against American colonists. Invoking the Declaration of Independence, Payne stated, "Whenever any form of government becomes destructive to these ends [life, liberty and the pursuit of happiness], it is the right of the people to alter or abolish it, and to institute new government." Payne claimed that "abuses" against Harney County's citizens justified revolution:

As soon as the government violates our Constitution, that is not your government anymore. . . . If you want to be free, you have to be willing to give it all up.

The purpose of government is to secure our rights and defend each other. When it gets used for any other purpose, that's when it has to be altered or abolished.

Moreover, Payne stated, the only path to establishing a "constitutional" government would necessarily lie outside the bounds of existing "unconstitutional" laws:

We can talk about trying to do it the legal way. We've been that route. We have fought for years and years and years and we have waved the signs and we have marched around in protest and we have petitioned our state legislators and we've tried to work through elections and we tried to—we thought, "If we can just get this guy in [office] he'll be able to fix the problem." It takes a long time, and if he makes it, he's alone and he can't get it done. It will never happen. If you wait for legal means, you will wait forever.

Picking up on this theme, Ammon Bundy, drawing from examples of the civil rights and women's suffrage movements, argued that civil disobedience is necessary. He argued that taking possession of federal land is necessary, an act he compared to Rosa Parks illegally sitting at the front of the bus:

It took individuals first. And then the courts and the laws followed later. Never has there been in history where the courts and the law took the role [of positive change] first. . . . It does not work that way. It takes individuals standing and then the courts and the laws will follow. Nine-tenths of the law is possession. The people have to take possession and then the law will follow.

Near the end of the meeting, Ammon Bundy finally spelled out his whole plan. In accordance with Bundy's views of natural law, federal land in Harney County would be deeded as the property of ranchers who were currently using the land or had used it in the past under federal grazing contracts. These Harney County citizens would cancel their grazing contracts and declare themselves "free" ranchers. The Bundys and their "patriot" supporters would provide armed "protection" to keep the federal government at bay "as long as necessary." Harney County, under armed "patriot" protection, would become a model of a county "free" of the federal government and inspire others across the United States to follow suit. Bundy stated,

We have teams of people [at the refuge] going through all the records of the allotments. They're finding out all the boundaries and who's using those allotments. . . . What will happen, this is our goal, as people stand and say "Hey, [that land] is mine," those rights will be defined. Natural Law teaches us that the rights belong to those who are using [the land]. . . . We need [local] people who are willing to stand.[62] Our goal is that these rights are going to be deeded in the county. . . . We are here temporarily to defend you. And we have a lot more that are willing to come and defend you. . . . [The government] wants to make you afraid. That's their tool. But when even this group right here, even half this group, if you guys would stand you would be strong enough to do anything you want. Just this ten or twelve people right here [Bundy pointed to a small group], if you were to stand together you would have enough power to stop the federal government. I guarantee it. It's just the way it is. . . . We will stand in defense to make sure your rights aren't violated. We'll do that as long as we have to. That's what we're here for. . . . You'll be an example to other counties around you that are already right on the verge. . . . The opportunity is now, the place is Harney County, and you are the people. . . . You guys will be an example of a federal-free county.

At the end of the meeting Ammon Bundy, with his bodyguard, remained to answer individual questions. The few reporters in attendance—who had by that time heard plenty from Bundy—honed in on several Harney County ranchers who openly expressed doubt about Bundy's plan. An environmental activist and I approached Bundy. I asked Bundy, for sake of clarification, whether he was in fact proposing to replace the existing United States federal government. Bundy nodded and simply said "Yes."[63] It would soon become clear that Bundy accepted the possibility that achieving this goal might require blood sacrifice.

Violence

On January 20, 2016, a reporter and I were exiting the then-occupied headquarters of the Malheur National Wildlife Refuge after touring the site and meeting with occupation leaders when gunfire rang out. Overhead was the imposing hundred-foot watchtower, used by the US Fish and Wildlife Service to house communications antennas, now always occupied by armed guards. We stopped, looked back, looked at each other, in near-unison said "Let's go," and briskly walked back to our cars. As trial evidence and testimony later revealed, shooting practice at the occupied refuge was routine. What no outsiders knew at the time was what role arms played in the occupiers' plans.

The United States government—the most powerful military force in human history—would never simply allow a handful of seditionists to indefinitely seize federal property. Once the occupiers made it clear that they would not leave the refuge, they were in effect forcing a confrontation. As Sheriff Dave Ward later said, "Giving in to an armed criminal takeover, well it's just not going to work. There [would come] a point when people had to be taken into custody."[64] With the large number of guns present at the occupied refuge, there was a heavy sense of foreboding. Ammon Bundy's own statements of his ideology provided reasons for concern. On December 15, 2015—two weeks before he took over the refuge—Bundy stood before Harney County residents to make his case for creating a committee of safety. During that meeting, he made it clear that he perceived that his family's 2014 armed confrontation in Bunkerville, Nevada, was a success—and that it was successful because of armed force:

My family was in the same situation as the Hammonds. However, at this point my family moves about the country freely. In almost two years [since the Bunkerville standoff] we've not seen one federal vehicle on our ranch, or even around our ranch. We've received no certified letters in the mail. They maybe want to threaten us from a distance in Washington, DC, but there's no real imminent threat at all to us. And I'm proposing here, what we're proposing, is that we do similar to what we did at the Bundy Ranch. . . . The Bundy Ranch is the freest place on Earth. I truly, truly believe that. . . . That's because we stood on the correct principles and the people ["patriots"] came around us, they defended us, and we went to ranching and that's what we're doing. I'm pleading with you today to do the same thing. [Bundy in tears:] The people of this country ["patriots"] will come and help protect you if you make the right stand. They will come, they will be glad to come and be your defense. You are not alone here.

You [referring to an audience member] just asked the question, How do we do it? [Bundy reading the Second Amendment of the Constitution:] "A well-regulated militia, being necessary to the security of a free state." [Bundy reads this passage three times for impact, his voice rising to a near shout.] That's how [we do it]. And that's why I'm alive. Because if the militia did not come to our defense I would not be here today. My family would have been murdered. They [federal authorities] told us they were going to murder us. And until the militia came and put a check and balance on them, they were going to murder us. As soon as the militia came, they [federal authorities] shaped up and left the area. This can be done without bloodshed. We don't have to believe that just because the militia comes in we have to have a gunfight. That's not what we're proposing here. We're proposing that the people go about their business according to the Constitution and the militia protects them while they do that. That's what we're proposing here.[65]

Bundy was proposing to build a citizen army that would keep government authority at bay with armed force, as his family did in 2014 at Bunkerville. Bundy's stated optimism that there is no need for "a gunfight" assumed that the federal government would back off indefinitely—an idea that many would dismiss as detached from reality. In the same December 15, 2015, meeting, Bundy's partner Ryan Payne (with a semiautomatic pistol holstered on his hip as he spoke) described pre–American Revolution armed militia groups imprisoning a governor and going from town to town with guns, forcing the resignation of judges considered tyrannical. Payne directly equated conditions of British colonial abuse of American colonists to the contemporary relationship between the United States government and citizens of Harney County,[66] emphasizing the centrality of armed force.

Later, at the meeting with Harney County ranchers at the Crystal Crane Hot Springs resort on January 18, 2016, Ammon Bundy stated that armed force is a natural way to maintain rights, a part of natural law given by God:

> Natural Law teaches us that if we're going to maintain our rights, we have to claim them, we have to use them, and we have to be willing to defend them. . . . You have to decide how far you're going to go to defend your rights. . . . There are certain things that are worth fighting for. . . . If you're not willing to defend it, you will lose it. . . . Since the beginning of time this is how rights are maintained.

Bundy's view that armed force—and the choice of "how far you're going to go"—is part of a natural social order puts him further to the right than even the most extreme libertarians, who contend that the social order should be determined through political processes, not armed revolution. Far-right libertarians staunchly insist that they do not advocate anarchy. Bundy, too, denied advocating anarchy, but the difference between his advocacy for the use of armed force to maintain rights and a primitive might-makes-right, law-of-the-jungle philosophy appears to be a thin line—one that depends on adherence to divinely guided natural law. Bundy did not explain how one knows what is righteous under natural law—only that "we just know." Bundy was confident enough in his knowledge of natural law to be willing to put at risk his own life and the lives of others in defense of these principles.

After taking over the Malheur Refuge, this ideology of righteous change through armed force would become very clear. Guns became emblematic and integral to the Malheur takeover. Immediately after his takeover of the Malheur National Wildlife Refuge, Ammon Bundy asked "patriots" to "bring your arms" to the refuge. They did. Armed guards with long guns were posted at the entrance and in the watchtower, and many occupiers had pistols openly carried on their hips. In office buildings at the refuge headquarters, stockpiles of guns and ammunition were visible. In later court proceedings, video evidence was shown of men practice shooting at the headquarters' boat launch. The video appeared to indicate that the occupiers were preparing for full-scale armed combat.[67] In court, prosecutors showed twenty-two long guns, twelve handguns, 16,636 live rounds of ammunition and 1,695 spent bullet casings that investigators recovered at the refuge following the surrender of the last holdouts on February 11, 2016.[68] Michael Emry, a close associate of Ammon Bundy and Ryan Payne, reportedly told a sheriff's deputy in Burns that he had a fully automatic, belt-fed .50 caliber M2 Browning machine gun on the refuge, which the deputy interpreted as intimidation (Emry was later arrested and convicted for attempting to sell the stolen weapon to an undercover law enforcement officer).[69]

Under what circumstances the occupiers were prepared to use so many guns and ammunition became an obvious and crucial question. To reporters and in later court testimony, the Bundys argued that the guns were necessary for their "peaceful protest" to be taken seriously. In court, Ammon Bundy stated that if the occupiers did not have guns they would have been immediately arrested and would not have been able to communicate their views to the world. Although almost certainly true, that statement left unanswered the question of what the occupiers would have done if confronted by law enforcement. At the Bunkerville standoff in 2014, by all accounts the "patriots" were prepared to engage in a firefight. Guns were pointed toward law enforcement officers. As LaVoy Finicum stated during the Malheur takeover, "You don't point a gun at someone unless you're going to shoot them."[70]

Some Malheur occupiers made these intentions very clear. In one of their first interviews from the occupied refuge on January 2, 2016, Ammon

Bundy and Ryan Bundy told reporters by phone that they would not rule out violence if police tried to remove them. Ryan Bundy stated explicitly that he would be willing to fight and die.[71] At a community meeting in Crane on January 18, 2016, Ammon Bundy's coleader Ryan Payne spoke about the necessity of "sacrifice": "If you want to be free, you have to be willing to give it all up," noting that "thirty-six of the fifty-six signers of the Declaration of Independence died" within several years of signing. Prominent anti-Islamic "patriot" activist Jon Ritzheimer posted a video offering tearful goodbyes to his children: "I am one hundred percent willing to lay down my life." Occupier Travis Cox told reporters in an interview, "If the FBI did come here, nobody would be leaving alive."[72] When reporters asked occupation spokesman LaVoy Finicum what he would do if law enforcement officers attempted to arrest him, Finicum (at the time holding a rifle on his lap and famously sitting under a blue tarp) responded, "I have no intention of spending any of my days in a concrete box. . . . There are things more important than your life, and freedom is one of them. I'm prepared to defend freedom."[73] Finicum had also published a quasi-autobiographical novel with an ominous title: *Only by Blood and Suffering* (2015).

When actually confronted with arrest, some occupiers were not as eloquent as Finicum. One of the last four holdouts at the refuge, David Fry, live-streamed a chilling all-night cellphone call that see-sawed between prayer and profanity-laced tirades about government, patriotism, death, and martyrdom.[74] Blaine Cooper planned to escape in a refuge firetruck and open fire ("lay lead down") if pursued.[75] Sean Anderson called for "patriot" reinforcements, screaming on video, "If they stop you from getting here, kill them!"[76]

Thus, although Ammon Bundy claimed his intentions were peaceful, he and his followers made it clear that the peace would remain only so long as they got what they wanted—to continue to control the federal wildlife refuge unimpeded and indefinitely. Bundy and his followers clearly indicated that if they did not get their way and law enforcement intervened, they would "defend" themselves. Since allowing the occupiers to violate the law indefinitely by occupying a federal facility could never be accepted by the government, a very high probability of a violent confrontation was inherent in the armed takeover from the beginning.

Some of the occupiers appeared to embrace this possibility. Occupier Sean Anderson invoked the specter of the 1993 siege of the Branch Davidian compound in Waco, Texas, that hung over the Bundy occupation—and Anderson almost seemed to welcome such a confrontation.[77] Another "patriot" at the refuge, Gary Hunt, had a history of supporting such confrontations. Hunt describes himself as a former land surveyor in Florida until the 1993 siege of Waco. Hunt left his business "in pursuit of restoring the Constitution," and began a "patriot newspaper" (later a blog) called *Outpost of Freedom*.[78] Hunt became a leader, with Ammon Bundy's top lieutenant, Ryan Payne, of Operation Mutual Defense, a "patriot" network created after the 2014 Bunkerville standoff. Hunt reports that he and Payne cowrote the PowerPoint slide show that Ammon Bundy used in December 2015 to encourage Harney County residents to form a committee of safety.[79] Hunt was among the few "patriots" to openly sympathize with Timothy McVeigh, who bombed an Oklahoma City federal building in 1995 resulting in the deaths of 168 people, including 19 children. (Some "patriot" groups allege that Hunt even assisted McVeigh, helping to load explosives on McVeigh's Ryder truck.[80]) In his blog, Hunt wrote, "I have always said that I am supportive of McVeigh's motivation for bombing the [Alfred P.] Murrah [Federal] Building. After all, for the two years since Waco, as I traveled the country, I heard many patriots say that we should bomb a government building."[81]

Hunt described McVeigh's murders as a "war to restore Constitutional government to the United States," and went on to say, "Timothy McVeigh is dead. And, now, it is time to pass the torch. Will you receive it?" After the main occupation leaders were arrested, Hunt was among the few who remained at the refuge, where he issued a "call to action" on his Outpost of Freedom web page in which he demanded that all "patriots" must report to the refuge immediately in order to protect the "patriots" still there. Hunt withdrew the call when the Federal Bureau of Investigation had clearly sealed the refuge so tightly that no one could enter. Given his open endorsement of extreme violent actions such as bombing federal buildings, Hunt's presence and his "call to action" at a critical juncture greatly heightened concerns about possible violence. Had the FBI not sealed the refuge so quickly and thoroughly (and had "patriots"

responded to Hunt's call as he demanded), the potential for violent escalation was very real.

Although the occupiers expressed their willingness (and in some cases
possibly desire) to use violence to defend the takeover, they maintained that
they would not initiate or condone violence themselves. However, there
were several altercations between competing "patriot" groups, and at least
one instance of a life-threatening situation condoned by Ammon Bundy.
On January 23, 2016, an environmental activist named Taylor McKinnon,
who came to the refuge to counter-protest, found himself accused by
"patriot" journalist Pete Santilli of being an FBI agent. McKinnon recalled,
"The militia crowd, in turn—many brandishing assault rifles, and almost all
with side-arms—began mobbing, getting in my face, and calling me 'fed.'
One told me that snipers were trained on us."[82]

Recalling a pair of Bundy supporters who shot and killed two police officers point-blank after participating in the Bundys' 2014 Bunkerville standoff,[83] McKinnon believed his life was in real jeopardy. When McKinnon's
partner pleaded to Ammon Bundy to stop the mob from what appeared
to be imminent violence against McKinnon, Bundy refused, saying it was
McKinnon's fault for coming to the refuge.[84] Occupier Jason Patrick intervened and escorted McKinnon and his partner to safety. Ammon Bundy,
however, had revealed that he would tolerate violence by his followers
against an unarmed citizen whose views differed from his.

Oregon and the nation were extremely fortunate that no serious violence occurred at the occupied Malheur National Wildlife Refuge. The
claim by Ammon Bundy and his followers that the takeover of the refuge
was a "nonviolent protest" was not consistent with the circumstances they
had created. Ammon Bundy and his supporters knowingly established a
situation in which a violent confrontation between law enforcement and
the armed occupiers was highly likely, and they openly stated that they
were prepared to die. Some stated that they expected to die. Some even
seemed to welcome a violent confrontation, apparently believing that their
martyrdom would serve a noble political end.

Whether via winning through armed threat or (far more likely) losing
through bloody confrontation, violence was a central and conscious part of
Ammon Bundy's takeover of the Malheur National Wildlife Refuge. Even

some far-right media commentators recognized and expressed alarm that the Malheur takeover would "force a showdown with government agents," becoming a spark that could set the "powder keg" of American society "aflame."[85] That possibility was no accident. As Ammon Bundy himself said, the Malheur takeover was "much more than a protest"[86]—forcing a showdown, even at the risk of setting off a "powder keg," was the key to Bundy's goal of establishing government by "federal-free" counties. Those who dismissed Bundy's strategy—including similarly minded "patriots"—failed to understand that in Bundy's mind the Malheur takeover was a win-win. If he had held off the most powerful military force on Earth, his victory would have been obvious and enormous. Had the Malheur takeover ended in violent bloodshed (a possibility Bundy acknowledged and accepted), in Bundy's words, he would also win: "In the worst-case scenario they [law enforcement] come down and kill us all. I don't think they want to do that because they still lose. American people from ocean to ocean will retaliate and their [the government's] power will be taken away from them."[87]

A massacre at the Malheur Refuge could well have sparked exactly the kind of nationwide uprising that Ammon Bundy wanted.

Rejection

The strategic flaws in this plan ultimately lay in Bundy's own hubris, and equally or more importantly in the rejection of his plan by the majority of citizens of Harney County. When Ammon Bundy and other leaders of the takeover were stopped for arrest on Highway 395 on January 26, 2016, they had stepped directly into a carefully planned trap that was patiently set by combined federal, state, and local law enforcement. Highway 395 passes through isolated, narrow canyons surrounded left and right by steep forested terrain. In midwinter the terrain is covered in deep snow. If the road becomes blocked, there is nowhere to go and no one to call—cell phone service ends a few miles outside of Burns. With all the main leaders of the takeover riding in only two vehicles in an area with no human population as potential collateral damage, law enforcement vehicles simply blocked the road from the front and behind. Recognizing the then-obvious tactical blunder, Ryan Bundy observed the hubris: "We got too stinkin' lax, you think things are just all downhill fine, we got too damn lax."[88] Co-occupier Shawna Cox later observed, "It was like a wake-up call—we'd been set up."[89] Cox and Ryan Bundy were correct.

Perhaps an even more important strategic error lay in what had *not* happened at the occupied Malheur National Wildlife Refuge. By various estimates, the number of people occupying the refuge when the main leaders were arrested was fewer than fifty. In military operations, it often assumed that if the leadership is removed, followers left behind and facing likely overwhelming force will dissipate—which all but four of the remaining occupiers at the Malheur refuge did within hours of the arrest of the leaders. The relatively small number of occupiers at the refuge was crucial. From the first hours of the takeover, Ammon Bundy called repeatedly for supporters to come to the refuge, with their guns. The total number increased by several dozen over three weeks—but nowhere near the thousands that Ammon Bundy and Ryan Payne hoped for. None of the full-time occupiers were from Harney County—they were from all over the country, and they suddenly found themselves in an unknown place in cold, hostile terrain without a leadership structure and facing overwhelming force. Had their numbers been greater or had there been more local support, the remaining occupiers might have regrouped.

The relative absence of local support was not accidental: from the first days of the takeover, Harney County sheriff Dave Ward had urgently requested county residents to not go to the refuge and to not provide support, stating, "I think if one person gives them a Snickers bar they're going to go on national media and claim the community supports them."[90] The weakness of local support for the Bundy takeover was, however, even more importantly a spontaneous rejection by the majority of Harney County residents of the methods and, in most cases, the goals of the occupation.

Some local residents did visit the refuge and a few even brought food and supplies, but the numbers were small and none remained at the refuge. Many others were incensed that the Malheur National Wildlife Refuge, which many community members view as an important local asset, was seized by strangers with no consultation with the community. Many not only rejected the takeover, but were also deeply angered. Sheriff Ward recalled that his bigger problem was not keeping local people from supporting the takeover but preventing armed, angry locals from going to the refuge to remove the occupiers by force.[91]

Thus, what did not happen was critical: with no local people physically joining the occupation, and facing considerable hostility from the community, almost none of the occupiers chose to remain in place after the leadership was arrested. Had the community joined the occupation or come to the aid of the takeover in the critical hours after the leaders' arrests, the task for law enforcement would have been vastly more difficult. A Waco-type tragedy could well have taken place. As it was, law enforcement's strategy to decapitate the takeover and allow most of the lower-level players to dissipate succeeded in no small part because appeals by the Bundy group for support were rejected by the majority of Harney County citizens. For the absence of a Waco-type tragedy, the nation largely has Harney County to thank.

What might seem surprising in this outcome, however, is that superficially Harney County fits the profile of the kind of conservative, resource-dependent, economically distressed rural community that might have been expected to embrace the radical politics offered by Ammon Bundy. The community is largely dependent on ranchers and farmers who do often perceive problems of federal overreach. For the most part, however, they do not perceive overreach in the same ways or see the same solutions as Bundy. As many observers noted, Ammon Bundy "didn't do his homework"—he picked the wrong county in which to lead an angry, armed revolution. Bundy's message failed to connect with most Harney County citizens.

3

Disconnect

On January 23, 2016, in front of dozens of reporters and militia activists, a tall red-bearded man with a brown cowboy hat and a black jacket bearing the words "Save Our American Ranchers" stood under a picnic shelter at the headquarters of the Malheur National Wildlife Refuge and fired the United States federal government.

Adrian Sewell had come to Eastern Oregon from Grant County, New Mexico, where, in 2015, he held a grazing permit for fifty cow/calf pairs and six saddle horses on the Walnut Creek Allotment of the Gila National Forest. With dozens of reporters' cameras and microphones jostling to get as close as possible to the main attraction, Sewell read his letter of termination to the federal government:

> Dear Solicitor General of the United States, I am a rancher in Grant County, New Mexico. I am hereby giving notice of termination of all contracts between me and the United States Forest Service. I shall no longer require their help in managing my ranch, nor any range improvements. I shall take full responsibility for these myself.[1]

LaVoy Finicum then presented Sewell with a list of names of individuals who had pledged to Sewell that "if there's any oppression that comes upon you—from Fish and Game, Forest Service, BLM—we shall stop everything and come to your aid."[2] Finicum and the Bundys made a similar pledge when attempting to recruit Harney County ranchers—an apparent reference to armed outside "defense."

For Ammon Bundy and his followers, this moment was intended to be the culmination of extraordinary efforts to bring ranchers into their campaign to break free from all federal control. Before Sewell signed and read his "termination" letter, Ryan Bundy stated, as he had many times before, that grazing contracts are how the federal government establishes control over ranchers, since, in the Bundy view, such authority is not granted under the Constitution. According to the Bundys, by declaring the termination of their grazing contracts and refusing to sign new contracts, ranchers can sever all legal authority of the government over federal land that ranchers claim to own under principles of prior appropriation and beneficial use in natural law. When Sewell dramatically signed his letter, a notary public certified the letter, apparently to lend authority to the occasion.

The contract-breaking ceremony was made awkward, however, by the notable lack of participation by Harney County ranchers. Ammon Bundy, Ryan Bundy, LaVoy Finicum, and other leaders of the occupation repeatedly stated that Harney County would set a national example of a "federal-free" county. Harney County was the place, this was the time, and residents of Harney County were the people who would lead the national revolution against federal control, the Bundys insisted. Yet, not a single Harney County rancher committed to severing their relationship with the federal government. The Bundys kept trying: after Sewell made his pledge, Ryan Bundy called out to the audience, "Do we have any other ranchers who are ready to make that commitment?"[3] Silence followed; no one stepped forward.

As the symbolic climax of the Bundys' campaign to stoke a national rancher revolution against federal control of land, the January 23, 2016, contract-breaking ceremony appeared to be a failure. There was no immediate large-scale wave of rancher rebellions. In a ceremony held almost simultaneously, eight ranchers in Cedar City, Utah, who attended a workshop where LaVoy Finicum had recently spoken, signed letters declaring their "withdrawal of consent" to be governed in their ranching practices by federal agencies.[4] Several months later, these ranchers decided against carrying out their pledges.[5] Federal staffers reported having received no "withdrawal of consent" letters.[6] Meanwhile, several months after his dramatic firing of the federal government, Adrian Sewell (who had multiple violent felony assault convictions and a history of alcohol abuse[7]) signed new Annual Operating Instructions for his Walnut Creek allotment in the Gila National Forest and paid his grazing bill.[8]

Despite the failure of the Bundys' contract-breaking ceremony to spark a nationwide brushfire of rancher rebellion, the moment was still significant. To those old enough to have observed the Sagebrush Rebellion, the wise use movement, and the growing "patriot" militia movements over the decades, the Bundys' signing ceremony could be seen as a watershed moment: what the Bundys put forward was an organized, formal invitation to join a revolution, backed up with armed force. Would rural communities accept the invitation? The fact that few ranchers nationally, and no ranchers in Harney County, did so seemed to reveal limits to anti-federal-government fervor—in practice if not in words.

If, however, Harney County ranchers had taken up the Bundys' call, there could well have been a nationwide ripple effect, as Ammon Bundy expressly hoped. As the nation struggles to understand and cope with radical homegrown antigovernment movements, there is value in examining why Harney County as a whole chose not to join Bundy's revolution. Harney County did not take up the revolutionary call in part because the claims Ammon Bundy made about the Constitution, wealth, poverty, government abuse, and dispossession from land in Harney County did not ring true, and his solutions seemed excessive and impractical. The stories Bundy told were disconnected from the lived realities most Harney County residents experienced.

Poverty

The central story Ammon Bundy and his followers told about Harney County was one of poverty driven by federal government seizures of land and resources. Bundy presented his story in the first hours of the takeover:

> We're out here [at the Malheur National Wildlife Refuge] because the people have been abused long enough. Their lands and their resources have been taken from them to the point where it's putting them literally into poverty. . . . Many federal employees at one time were working for ranchers or as ranchers and loggers. They were forced to leave those industries that many of them had for many generations. They were forced to leave them and go find

a government job. And now [in] Harney County, the US government is the highest employer in the county.[9]

> While we're here what we're going to be doing is we're going to be free-ing these lands up and getting the ranchers back to ranching, getting the miners back to mining, getting the loggers back to logging, where they can do it under the protection of the people and not be afraid of this tyranny that's been upon them. And what will happen is Harney County will begin to thrive again. At one time [Harney County was] the wealthiest county in the state and now they're the poorest county in the state. And we will reverse that in just a few years by freeing up their land and resources.[10]

The story of poverty in Harney County told by Ammon Bundy was deeply flawed: Harney County has struggled, but not more than many other resource-dependent counties across the country, including ones where there is no federal public land. In recent years, Harney County's agricultural economy has taken a significant upward turn. It is difficult to lead people into a revolution when their economy is not collapsing and, in fact, shows a modest upward trajectory. It is even more difficult to make the case for radical change when the causes of economic struggle are incorrectly characterized, and yet more so when the radical path appears likely to make problems worse and not better, as many Harney County residents believed.

Ammon Bundy was not entirely wrong: the existence of poverty in Harney County is not in question. In 2016, the year that Bundy and his fol-lowers took over the Malheur National Wildlife Refuge, the median house-hold income in Harney County was $36,340—the third-poorest county in Oregon.[11] In, 2015 Harney County was at the twenty-first percentile in median household income among all counties nationally.[12] In the same year, the number of people in Harney County living in poverty was 16.3 percent, above the 14.7 percent found nationally.[13] Poverty is not unique to Harney County, however, and in fact its poverty rate is lower than the 17.2 percent poverty rate in nonmetropolitan areas in the nation as a whole[14] (including nonmetropolitan areas in eastern and Midwest states where there is very little federal land). Since the late 1990s, Harney County's poverty rate has spiked up and down without a clear overall upward or downward trajectory.[15] Bundy's claim that Harney County had sunk "literally into poverty" was valid, if overstated. The rest of Bundy's story of federal-government-driven economic hardship in Harney County was at best a stretch of historical and economic facts.

Economic struggle has been a big part of Harney County's history since the arrival of non-Native settlers in Eastern Oregon in the mid-nineteenth century, long before the existence of federal land management agencies. Harney County's high desert was always a tough place to make a living. A handful of cattle barons were able to build their wealth by controlling access to water and forage in the Harney Basin, but for the great majority of homesteaders life always consisted of a struggle to survive the capricious forces of nature (droughts, floods) and brutal competition (including lawlessness and violence) from outside cattle empires (Langston 2003). In the early twentieth century, significant logging and millwork produced periods of substantial wealth that ended by the 1990s when the last old-growth logs were gone and local mills permanently closed. Changing markets, climate, and resource conditions produced a boom-and-bust pattern characteristic of much of the history of the resource-dependent rural American West.

Harney County's economic history was not particularly unique or extreme. Economic struggle is a fact of life in most rural areas in America. Ammon Bundy's telling of Harney County's story was misleading: reliable county-level economic data available since 1969 show that Harney County has never been "the poorest county in the state," and in only one year (1973, when local lumber mills were at peak production) has Harney County ever been "the wealthiest county in the state" in per capita income.[16] Although some industries (especially wood products) have suffered, that has been a pattern in Oregon and the Pacific Northwest generally. Harney County's overall income and employment has been relatively resilient, with per capita income (adjusted for inflation) as well as overall population and jobs declining modestly relative to many resource-dependent rural communities over the last five decades (figures 3.1 and 3.2). Similarly, Bundy's promise to reduce reliance on government paychecks and bring "back" prosperity by getting "the ranchers back to ranching . . . miners back to mining . . . loggers back to logging" had little grounding in reality.

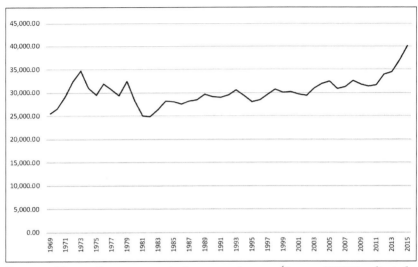

Figure 3.1. Harney County per capita income, 1969–2015. (Source: USBEA, adjusted to April 2017 US dollars)

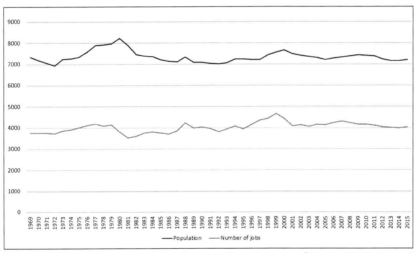

Figure 3.2. Harney County total population and employment. (Source: US Bureau of Economic Analysis)

In the agricultural sector, there is no indication that ranchers or farmers in Harney County have been driven out of business: United States Census of Agriculture data show that from 1969 to 2012, the number of farms in Harney County increased from 276 to 497, and the total amount of land in farms in the county increased from 1.41 million acres to 1.50 million acres (figure 3.3). The value of farm products in the county (adjusted for inflation to 2017 dollars) during the same period increased from $54 million to $95 million (with increases in crops from $7 million to $39 million, and livestock production from $48 million to $55 million) (figure 3.4). Ammon Bundy claimed that Harney County farmers need to "get back" to farming, but the data indicate that Harney County farmers never left farming and, despite ups and downs inherent to the agricultural market, are doing well overall.

As for "getting the miners back to mining," Bundy's statement showed the severe limits of his knowledge of the local geography and economy. Mining, although present at a very small scale, has never been a major part of Harney County's economy, contributing generally fewer than ten jobs per year since 1969,[17] and historically probably not many more.

In contrast, there have been major losses of jobs in Harney County's wood products industry, though these job losses pre-dated environmental restrictions of the late 1980s and 1990s and had almost nothing to do with federal government policies. In 2016, the Oregon Office of Economic Analysis reported that, from 1978 to 2014, Harney County lost 99 percent of its wood products jobs—dropping from 768 jobs in 1978 to just six reported logging jobs in 2014.[18] With the total number of jobs in Harney County standing at 4,074 in 1978, a loss of 768 jobs represented a 19 percent loss of all jobs in the county. The effect of this on the county's economy was felt particularly strongly because in the 1970s wood products jobs were well paid, union-represented, and included generous benefits. Not only were many wood products jobs lost, but these were some of the best jobs the county ever had.

The hardship in the wood products industry that Harney County experienced, particularly in the 1980s and 1990s, was very real, but Ammon Bundy's claim that this was because "lands and resources have been taken" by the federal government was simply wrong. By the early 1980s, a perfect storm of adverse economic factors produced major reductions in timber production and millwork in the county. The most important producer of timber and wood products in Harney County for much of the twentieth century was the Edward Hines Lumber Company, which established a mill

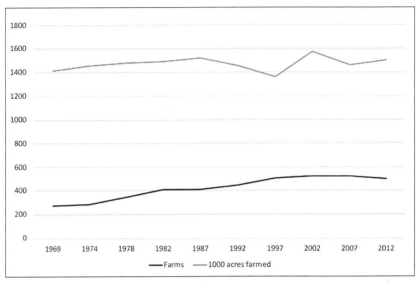

Figure 3.3. Harney County land in farms. (Source: USDA Census of Agriculture)

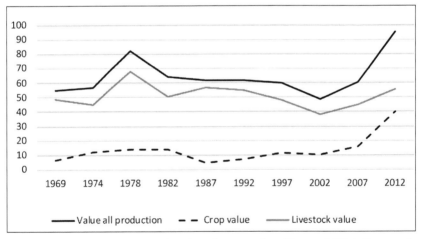

Figure 3.4. Harney County agricultural production value. (Source: USDA Census of Agriculture, adjusted to May 2012 dollars in millions)

in 1928. A Hines post office was established in 1931 to serve the mill and its community, in effect establishing the town that still bears the company's name today.[19] The company and industry thrived during World War II and the postwar era as construction soared. Unionized jobs and strong wages remained steady as the company expanded its product lines, including a new plywood mill in the 1960s and specialized production of window and door frames and molding. As late as the mid-1980s, in the last stages of the wood products boom, unionized mill wages held at about $9 to $11 per hour (adjusted for inflation, $20–$25 of buying power in 2017). In addition, employees received health coverage for themselves and their families, vacation pay, and pensions. Going to work at the mills was what many young people in Harney County aspired to do—for good reason.

By the late 1970s, there were signs that the boom times would not last. In the late 1920s the Edward Hines Lumber Company estimated that there was a fifty-year supply of large-diameter, high-value old-growth Ponderosa pine logs available on nearby US Forest Service lands. The estimate proved accurate. By the late 1970s the available supply of old-growth logs had dwindled. Facing millions of dollars of prospective retooling costs, high wages, and then the global recession of the early 1980s, Edward Hines Lumber Company chose to end its fifty-year run in Eastern Oregon. In 1980, the company closed all four of its divisions, including its stud mill and plywood and veneer plants.[20] The mill was retooled, modernized, and sold off to Snow Mountain Pine Company, which operated with a much smaller workforce from 1983 until the mill closed permanently in 1995.

With increased competition from the southeastern states and other countries (Canada, Brazil, Chile, South Africa, Russia, New Zealand) and, above all, with few large-diameter trees remaining locally, the glory days of the timber industry in Harney County would not return. The Oregon and Northwestern Railroad that serviced local production for both Edward Hines and Snow Mountain Pine shut down, and most of the equipment of the Hines mill was said to have been resold to Russia.

The northern spotted owl was listed under the Endangered Species Act in 1990, further undermining business confidence in access to the few remaining pockets of old-growth trees on federal land.[21] By that year, however, the financial conditions that had led to the end of the timber boom in Southeastern Oregon were already evident. Seeing profits plunge, the Edward Hines mill had closed a decade earlier. The spotted owl may have driven the last nails into the coffin, but it was market forces—scarcity of large-diameter logs, obsolete mill equipment incompatible with smaller trees, high retooling costs, domestic and international competition, and

high wages and transportation costs—that all but killed the timber industry of Southeastern Oregon. Third-generation wood products manager Jim
Bishop, who ran the Frenchglen Millworks in the 1980s and early 1990s,
describes the situation at the time:

> The federal government had essentially nothing to do with the Hines mill
> shutting down. It was all recession-related, it was industry related, and it was
> the quality of the timber [available]. And Hines mill over the years paid really
> good wages—the workers were well paid, middle class. . . . But the world
> changed. So those mills [had to get] incredibly efficient and automated. . . .
> I'd say two-thirds of the workforce would have been laid off anyway if every
> sawmill in Oregon had automated and gotten efficient. So, it was going to
> happen. It had to happen. Coincidentally it happened during the 1980s reces-
> sion. The spotted owl kicked in, when? The late 1980s? People want to con-
> flate those two things. They have virtually nothing to do with one another.
> But it's easy to blame the spotted owl.[22]

Local rancher Keith Baltzor agreed:

> Harney County was one of the wealthiest counties if not the wealthiest
> county in the state when Edward Hines was going full bore, but that wasn't
> even close to sustainable. And the loggers here will tell you that. You couldn't
> [produce timber] at that level for much longer and have anything left. The
> spotted owl might have been part of it, and there might have been other
> issues, but that [timber production] was going to burn itself out anyway.[23]

Although capitalist market forces were the main drivers behind the bust
of Eastern Oregon's timber boom in the 1980s, market forces also provided
a partial remedy. In the period after 1980, sawmills closed or drastically
downsized, and jobs in manufacturing dropped to almost zero, interspersed
with periods when mills briefly reopened or other manufacturing industries (for example, the Monaco Coach company) came and went (figure
3.5).[24] But during the same period that manufacturing jobs were declining,
service jobs outside farming and government were significantly increasing. These included jobs in health care, real estate, finance and insurance,
science and technology, information, hotels and restaurants, and other
services. From 1969 to 2015, service jobs increased from 1,114 to 2,255—a

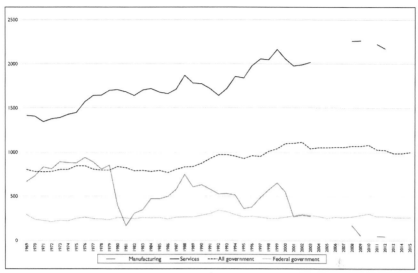

Figure 3.5. Harney County jobs by sector. (Source: US Bureau of Economic Analysis)

gain of 841 jobs, which almost exactly compensated for the near-total job losses in wood products manufacturing, which averaged 835 jobs during the wood products boom of the 1970s.[25] Increased employment in services roughly balanced out losses in manufacturing, but these newer jobs generally had lower salaries and few or no benefits. There is no question Harney County lost ground economically after the 1970s.

Harney County's economy today is very different and in many respects not as favorable for workers as during the wood products boom from the 1940s to the 1970s, but the change had almost nothing to do with the federal government. To the contrary, a fairly small number of federal government jobs provides much of the income that has sustained the local economy through tough times. The total number of federal jobs in the county, however, has never been more than 9 percent of all local employment.[26] Ammon Bundy got the figures wildly wrong, claiming that "the US government is the highest employer in the county." In 2015, farming was the single largest source of employment in the county, outnumbering federal government jobs by almost three to one: in 2015, there were a total of 259 federal civilian and military jobs in Harney County, compared, for example, with 715 farm jobs, 641 state and county government jobs, and a total of 2,311 nonfarm jobs in the private sector (the biggest segment being in retail trade, services, forestry, and construction).[27] Bundy sympathizers and militia claimed that the county would not stand up against federal "tyranny" because as much 70 percent of the voting population are government employees.[28] In fact, since 1969, federal jobs in the county (including military) never exceeded 343 (in 1992), and steadily declined after that time. By 2015, the federal government account for only 6 percent of total employment in the county.

Nevertheless, the relatively small number of federal jobs played a particularly important role in the recovery from the 1980s recession because these jobs tended to be relatively well paid and included benefits, unlike most service jobs that made up much of private sector employment after the end of the wood products boom. Ammon Bundy saw federal jobs in the county as a symptom of government overreach. If so, it is the kind of overreach that many job seekers gladly embrace.

In the view of many local residents, not only was the presence of the federal government in Harney County not a big problem, the removal of the federal government from the county would make things worse. Ammon Bundy's explicitly stated goal was to make Harney County the first "federal-free" county in the nation. Bundy stated that his goal was to hand over federal land to the "rightful owners." When pressed about who, exactly, the "rightful owners" are, Bundy replied only, "We're working on that." Based on his statements to the press, however, it was clear that he wanted to give some land "back" to ranchers; and, based on his interpretation of the Constitution, it appeared that ownership of other federal land would be transferred to the county government. Bundy and his followers seemed to assume that Harney County residents wanted to become "free" of federal government. Had Bundy listened to more local people he might have foreseen the uphill struggle his revolutionary ideal would face in Harney County.

Skeptics included ranchers who opposed Bundy as well as those who were sympathetic to Bundy's message. Ranchers Andy and Vena Dunbar are the closest neighbors to the headquarters of the Malheur National Wildlife Refuge and opposed Bundy from the start. While agreeing with some concerns about government overreach, Andy Dunbar flatly rejected the idea that Ammon Bundy in any way spoke for the interests of ranchers like him:

I think, yeah, the government is in charge of way too much land, and I don't think there'd be a rancher or farmer around who would disagree with that. But it's not really in federal ownership, it's a public trust, it belongs to all of us. The federal government can hardly afford to manage what they have [the land]; how's the state going to do it? One of the things that worries people like us, a lot of us [federal land] permittees here in this county, is that the state can't afford [to manage public lands] and sure as heck the county can't afford it, so it's going to be sold off to the highest bidder and we're going to get big corporations coming in. And that's the last thing we want.

They were making the cry to "burn your [federal] permit," and I was think-ing, oh boy, anybody stupid enough to do that deserves to lose their permit. . . . I've got a private allotment with the BLM, and our refuge (US Fish and Wildlife) permit's private basically. That's close to an ownership, and every-body else can enjoy it. It's a win-win situation as far as I'm concerned. . . . *It's a lot cheaper than owning it outright* [emphasis added]. I don't have to pay taxes on it. We pay for water development and things like that but the BLM [pays] also, it's kind of a cost-share. It just works better all the way around. I wouldn't change it. [Interviewer: Fire protection?] Oh, gosh yeah![29]

Taking a different view of Ammon Bundy and his followers, Buck and Linda Taylor are ranchers who live near Diamond, close to the Malheur National Wildlife Refuge, where they have a grazing allotment (in addition to a BLM allotment). The Taylors visited and spoke with Ammon Bundy at the occupied Malheur Refuge several times, and few other Harney County ranchers were personally closer to Bundy. The Taylors agreed with much of Ammon Bundy's interpretation of the Constitution. Yet, on Saturday, January 23, 2016, when Bundy called for local ranchers to renounce their grazing contracts and declare their public range allotments as private prop-erty, the Taylors were not present. The Taylors explained:[30]

BUCK TAYLOR: I wouldn't want to own that property up there [the Taylor family's BLM allotment]. I couldn't pay taxes on it. . . . We run over 200,000 acres up there. My God, if there was a fire, I would have to call somebody to help. If it's the government's, let them take care of it. That's their land. If we had a fire, which we did in 2012, probably a third of our range was

burned. We were lucky. There were guys on the south end where 100 percent of their range was burned. And the government helped look for other
property. Other places to put you. Because they still want the money from
cattle grazing! If that was my private land? I'd be SOL [shit out of luck]. I'd
be on my own. I don't want to own that property, no way.

LINDA TAYLOR: We couldn't manage it.

BUCK TAYLOR: We couldn't manage it, it's too big.

Leaders of Harney County's government were equally adamant that
from a financial perspective the concept of a "federal-free" county was
simply not realistic or desirable. Bundy never analyzed the budgetary
implications of such a radical shift. Although Bundy did not explain how
such transformation would work, logically a "federal-free" county would
also have to expect to become free of federal payments allocated to the
county government associated with (formerly) federal lands (payment in
lieu of taxes, US Forest Service payments, Bureau of Land management
payments, US Fish and Wildlife Service payments, and others). In 2016,
15 percent of the county's general fund came directly from federal land–
related funding, as did almost 100 percent of the county's non-project-
specific road fund.[31] State or county government would also have to provide essential services, including costly fire protection for 4.7 million acres
of formerly federal land. Harney County then commissioner Dan Nichols,
a rancher from Diamond, near the Malheur Refuge, went to the refuge
during the occupation and asked Ammon Bundy if he had considered this
potential problem:

I listened to Bundy for about three hours. . . . He kept talking about the
resources we have here. And I said, "Have you guys ever done a spread-
sheet on the county taking over all these public lands?" [Bundy] said, "No,
I haven't. Look at all the grass and all the trees." They hadn't [considered the
financial impacts]. They never went beyond their little graphs that they wrote
showing me how I was misinterpreting the Constitution. That got me thinking, and I came up here to the courthouse, and just to run the courthouse
and the schools and the road department we would have to have ten times
the revenue currently generated from property taxes just to run those small

entities and the whole realm of things the county is responsible for. That didn't include the millions of acres of public land and the costs of administering and maintaining that. It's totally out of the question. It doesn't even fall within the realm of possibility.[32]

The visit from Commissioner Nichols was not the last opportunity Bundy had to consider the financial implications of his plans. Jim Bishop, the former manager of the Frenchglen Millworks (and later chief financial officer and chief executive officer of the Harney District Hospital) wrote a letter on January 13, 2016, that was published in the *Burns Times-Herald* outlining exactly what would happen if Harney County became "federal-free." If Bundy read Bishop's letter he might have considered whether his goals were realistic.

Bishop's letter raised the crucial question of how the county would pay to manage so much land in accordance with the law (the Taylor Grazing Act, the Endangered Species Act, the Wild Horse and Burro Act, and many more). Bundy made it clear that he wanted the federal government to have no jurisdiction in Harney County; but unless he could muster an armed force capable of resisting federal law on Harney County's 4.7 million acres of (former) federal land, federal land management laws would still apply. Even if Bundy's militia could somehow eliminate federal laws, some essential management tasks would still have to be done no matter who was in charge, including extremely expensive water management, control of invasive species, and fire protection. Someone would have to pay for those services. Bishop pointed out that if the county took over the role of leasing land to ranchers through permits, the county (which does not have the resources of the federal government and is prohibited by state law from raising property taxes) would likely have to raise grazing fees to levels that would bankrupt most public lands ranchers.

If, on the other hand, Bundy's goal was to simply privatize all public land, Bishop argued that the land would likely become controlled by society's wealthiest individuals, corporations, and organizations (much as it is today in states such as Texas that have enormous areas of land, almost all private). Bishop could have added that if certain federal lands such as the Malheur National Wildlife Refuge and the Steens Mountain Cooperative

Management and Protection Area were privatized (given "back" to "ranchers, loggers, and miners"), the county would likely lose much of its small but important tourism and recreation economy. The annual Harney County Migratory Bird Festival, for example, is an important benefit to local motels, restaurants, and retail businesses.

Such views are shared by former county judge Steve Grasty, who was in charge of the county's budget for eighteen years. When asked what would happen if 4.7 million acres of federal land in Harney County became county property, Grasty replied,

> We might make it a few years. But within ten years, a good share of it we'd have to put up for auction. Our local ranchers wouldn't be able to afford it because by state law we'd be required to sell it at a market rate. The rich guy, whoever that is, would come in and buy it up. They wouldn't allow the existing ranchers to use it in most cases. Maybe [the new wealthy owners] would use it themselves. [That kind of owner] doesn't pay income tax because they write everything off. So those [kinds of owners] aren't particularly beneficial to the economy. . . . We would try to make the money back in property taxes, but in the first big fire we'd go broke. Bankrupt. . . .
>
> We couldn't offset the loss of income from [putting the federal land] into county ownership. Where would it come from? You'd have to raise grazing fees to higher than the state grazing fees. None of our ranchers could have afforded that. The only way I could see to [avoid bankruptcy] is to sell the land. Then what? It goes to the rich guy.[33]

Harney County officials were not alone in their concern about the financial impacts of transferring federal lands to state or county ownership. With some states (most notably Utah in 2012) pursuing legislation to promote transfers of federal lands,[34] by 2015 ten of the eleven western states commissioned studies of hypothetical transfers of federal public lands.[35] The most optimistic study, sponsored by the State of Utah, concluded that if oil and gas prices are high and the state maintains an aggressive stance toward energy development, revenues generated on state-controlled public lands could exceed the costs of managing the lands.[36] Even the Utah study, however, acknowledged unpredictable outcomes including the possible loss of hundreds of millions of dollars in federal jobs payroll. Another study by the State of Wyoming came to a more pessimistic conclusion after carefully examining the many significant costs of managing public lands and losses of federal revenue: "We would not anticipate any substantial gains in revenue production or additional sources of revenue with any transfer of management—certainly not enough to offset the enormous costs such an endeavor would likely entail."[37] Collectively the studies suggest that transfers of federal lands to states or counties are far from a simple path to prosperity "in a few years," as Ammon Bundy promised.

Further indications that privatizing public land is no guaranteed path to prosperity can be seen from the experience of any number of rural farm counties in the Midwestern states, where there is little or no federal land. Evidence of the disappearance of family farms and crises in the agricultural economies of the Midwestern states has been documented in depth for decades (e.g., Conger and Elder 1994, on the crisis of family farms in Iowa).

In 2016, the year Ammon Bundy and his followers seized the Malheur National Wildlife Refuge to protest federal government "overreach," seven of the ten fastest-growing states in the nation were in the West, where federal land ownership is highest (Oregon, with 53 percent of its land in federal management, ranked fourth nationally in job creation).[38] Many of those new jobs are in urban centers, but regional wealth and disposable income benefit resource-dependent rural communities that sell products in urban markets (for example, high-end naturally produced beef raised in Eastern Oregon that sells in upscale Portland and Seattle markets). For every trend there are exceptions, and it is not difficult to find cases of legitimate concern about "overreaching" federal policies. From the scale of county, state, and regional economies, however, there is no evidence to support the general conclusion that the rural West—or Harney County—has been put "literally into poverty" by federal land ownership, as Ammon Bundy claimed. There is better evidence that, if achieved, Bundy's goal of transferring federal lands to states and counties would do far more to put the West into poverty.

Takings

> *Just to make this refuge, it's 180,000 acres—it's fifty miles long and forty miles wide—at one time it all belonged to private ranchers. And now it's all been taken through many deceptions, through improper acquisitions, through condemning of ranches, through flooding that they imposed upon the ranchers. All these adverse ways that the refuge has placed upon the ranchers to put them into duress so they'll either leave the ranch so that [the government] can use it, or they'll put [ranchers] into duress so that they have to sell to the refuge. That's how [the refuge] was built.*
>
> —Ammon Bundy[39]

> *To create this refuge, over one hundred ranching families lost their ranches, homes, their land to the US Fish and Wildlife Service.*
>
> —Ammon Bundy[40]

The Malheur National Wildlife Refuge, operated by the United States Fish and Wildlife Service, consists of 187,166.84 acres, of which 113,828.34 acres (60.82 percent) were acquired from the public domain or from other federal agencies[41]; 73,067.57 acres (39.04 percent) were purchased by USFWS; and 270.93 acres (0.014 percent) were donated.[42] The history of how these acquisitions occurred is complex and, in some aspects, fraught. However, Ammon Bundy's claim that all land in the refuge once belonged to private ranchers and became federal property through "improper acquisitions" is inconsistent with well-documented history. Bundy's claims portrayed a past that did not exist, and obscured the past that did (Robbins 2016).

Bundy said little about the rights of the social group with by far the longest and most indisputable claim to land in the region. Ancestors of today's Burns Paiute Tribe inhabited the land that became the Malheur National Wildlife Refuge for at least 9,800 years,[43] and likely closer to 14,300 years (Jenkins et al. 2013; Jenkins, Davis, and Stafford 2012).[44] Abundant archeological evidence of active, long-term Paiute occupancy of the Harney Valley includes village remains, rock art, weapons and tools, and burials (Aikens and Greenspan 1988). The headquarters of the Malheur National Wildlife

Refuge, which became the base of the 2016 occupation by Ammon Bundy, has been shown to have evidence of particularly concentrated human activity, along with at least another 166 sites of human activity in and around Malheur and Harney Lakes (Newman et al. 1974). By the 1860s and 1870s, however, non-Native people encroached on Paiute territory, forcing Paiute people out of their traditional lands and culminating in a brief Native uprising known as the Bannock War (named after the Bannock people of Idaho who led the revolt) in 1878. For the Paiute people the uprising was a disaster, resulting in their forced relocation (through a deadly three-hundred-mile winter trek) to the Yakama Reservation in Washington State (Couture 1978). By the 1880s the area was emptied of Paiute people who had lived there for thousands of years. In 1972, the US Bureau of Indian Affairs designated a 771-acre area on the outskirts of Burns as the Burns Paiute Reservation. In 2017, the tribe consisted of 410 members.[45]

Decades of warfare against the Paiute made land readily available for rapid non-Native settlement. Federal government programs encouraged migration and land acquisition, including the Swamp Land Act of 1850, the Homestead Act of 1862, and the 1877 Desert Land Act. While intended to support small-scale homesteaders, these same laws also benefited large ranching companies. What would become by far the largest ranching company in the Harney Basin began with the arrival of twenty-three-year-old Pete French in 1872. French, along with six Mexican vaqueros and a cook, arrived with 1,200 cows owned by wealthy California cattle baron Dr. Hugh J. Glenn (Brimlow 1951). Facing new restrictions on grazing in California, Glenn sent French and his men in search of open pastures. French was delighted to find nearly unoccupied, well-watered, productive range in the Catlow Valley and Blitzen Valley in southern Harney County. One of the few occupants was a prospector by the name of Porter, who sold his few cattle and "P" brand to French. The "P" Ranch would become the base of the French-Glenn Livestock Company, one of the largest cattle empires in the nation.

French would not have the land almost to himself for long, however. Heeding the boosterism of the federal government, newspapers, and private, for-profit "land locaters" who advertised land in Harney County from as far away as the eastern states (Jackman and Long 1964), homesteaders arrived in a steady stream in the 1880s and 1890s, creating friction with the "Cattle King." Pete French set about consolidating and expanding his land-holdings by every means, legal or otherwise. French viewed homesteaders as a nuisance and an impediment, and he used every possible tactic including lawsuits, fraud, and physical harassment to drive out homesteaders who got in the way of his expanding empire (Robbins 2016). After French purchased all the land around the property of homesteader Ed Oliver and denied Oliver an easement to access his land (and allegedly beat Oliver), Oliver approached French on the day after Christmas in 1897 and shot him dead. A jury in Burns acquitted Oliver on grounds of self-defense (Gray 1995).

Tensions with homesteaders resulting from French's aggressive land acquisitions persisted after his death, and helped set the stage for the creation of what is today the Malheur National Wildlife Refuge. In 1901, the US Supreme Court, in *Marshall v. French*, determined that Marshall's homestead claim to land below the 1895 Neal Survey meander line around Malheur Lake, Mud Lake, and Harney Lake (the line of the "ordinary or mean high water mark"[46]) was made on United States public domain land, not land belonging to the French-Glenn Company, as French-Glenn had asserted based on riparian law.[47] The court's determination that unclaimed land inside the Neal meander line belonged to the federal public domain provided the legal foundation for the establishment of the Malheur Wildlife Refuge.

In 1908, when ornithologist William L. Finley persuaded his friend Theodore Roosevelt that the decimation of bird populations by plume hunters must be stopped, the 1901 *Marshall v. French* ruling enabled Roosevelt to establish the Lake Malheur Reservation for the protection of migratory birds.[48] Initially, the Lake Malheur Reservation (renamed the Malheur National Wildlife Refuge in 1940) encompassed only Malheur, Harney, and Mud Lakes and the "smallest legal subdivisions" of land surrounding them. The area was not surveyed but was estimated at 81,876 acres.[49] For homesteaders on the lakeshores inside the reservation boundary, life went on as normal so long as they left the birds alone.

As opportunities to acquire adjacent land arose and managers came to understand that managing land as well as water was necessary to maintain bird habitat, managers at Malheur became interested in expansion.

Theodore Roosevelt's 1908 Executive Order 929 prohibited the killing of birds or destruction of birds' eggs and nests, but did nothing to protect the flow of water that just as certainly meant life or death for birds. For decades, ranchers in the Blitzen Valley had channeled water from the Blitzen River to irrigate pasture, reducing the flow into Malheur Lake. In dry years, bird-nesting habitat was reduced to a small fraction of the refuge. William Finley, who persuaded President Theodore Roosevelt to establish the reserve, again played a major role by advocating for the purchase of the Blitzen Valley, which would provide water rights enabling the refuge to assure an adequate flow of water from the Blitzen River into the Malheur Lake to maintain vital bird habitat (US Department of Agriculture 1911).[50]

The severe drought of the 1930s provided exactly such an opportunity. By far the single biggest private land acquisition by the Malheur Refuge was none other than Pete French's old "P" Ranch. The French-Glenn Livestock Company was sold in 1907 to investors from Portland and managed by respected cattleman Bill Hanley, who valued homesteaders and reversed French's confrontational style (Gray 1995). The company was later reorganized as the Eastern Oregon Livestock Company under the ownership of Louis Swift of the Swift Packing Company in Chicago. Facing economic depression and severe drought, profits tumbled. Lacking private buyers,[51] Swift sold 64,717 acres of the Blitzen Valley (including what is today the headquarters of the Malheur National Wildlife Refuge) to the United States government for $675,000 on February 21, 1935.[52] Ownership of the "P" Ranch gave managers crucial water rights over the Blitzen River, greatly increasing their ability to ensure a flow of water into Malheur Lake sufficient to maintain waterfowl habitat.[53] In the words of historian Nancy Langston, an empire of cattle became an "empire of ducks" (Langston 2003, 63).

The second largest opportunity for managers to substantially expand and improve their ability to maintain bird habitat came six years later. Gentleman rancher Bill Hanley, who operated one of the largest ranches in the region, passed away in 1935. Hanley's wife, Clara, continued to operate the two largest Hanley properties, the Bell-A Ranch and the Double-O Ranch. The deep economic depression of the 1930s and the severe drought, however, reduced the number of cattle that the ranches could maintain. Clara Hanley, who lived on the family's celebrated Bell-A Ranch southeast of Burns, found it difficult to manage the Double-O property west of Harney Lake, many miles away on rough, isolated roads.[54] In 1941, the Hanley family sold the 14,517.89-acre Double-O to the Malheur reserve (by then renamed the Malheur National Wildlife Refuge) for $116,143, a choice consistent with Bill Hanley's own strong conservation interests.[55] The Double-O property gave refuge managers access to excellent marshland bird habitat fed by springs and snowmelt waters from the Blue Mountains carried by Silver Creek.[56]

The acquisitions of the "P" Ranch and the Double-O Ranch still make up by far the greatest acreage of private land purchased by the Malheur National Wildlife Refuge, and both sales were conducted on friendly terms—Louis Swift needed to sell the "P" Ranch, and the Hanley family sold the Double-O by their own choice.

Acquisitions of smaller pieces of private land were mostly amicable, but not always. On June 3, 1935, four months after the acquisition of French's "P" Ranch, the United States Supreme Court resolved a key dispute between the federal government and the State of Oregon, concluding that Malheur Lake and adjacent bodies of water were not navigable and therefore constituted United States public domain rather than state property. The decision reaffirmed the 1901 *Marshall v. French* ruling and gave the United States legally settled ownership of the area inside the Neal meander line and the ability to consolidate private inholdings in the reserve.

For homesteaders facing the expanding Pete French empire in the southern Blitzen Valley, the well-watered shores and meadows of Malheur, Harney, and Mud Lakes had been among the places where a homesteading family could stake a claim. When Theodore Roosevelt established the Lake Malheur Reservation in 1908, the goal was to protect the lakes as bird habitat. Roosevelt's order created uncertainty, however, because high desert lakes are not always lakes. Owing to droughts and withdrawals of water from the Blitzen River, lake levels could fall dramatically for years at a time, creating new opportunities for farming and ranching on the exposed lakebeds.

Prior to the establishment of the Lake Malheur Reservation in 1908, settlers homesteaded inside the Neal meander line around Malheur Lake and Harney Lake for the better part of three decades. The new wildlife preserve enclosed more than just birds. After the Supreme Court decision of 1935, the federal government offered to buy out the homesteaders with inhold-ings inside reservation boundaries. Initially not all parties agreed on a "fair" price,[57] but by 1956 the federal government had purchased, exchanged, or condemned all of the 23,947 acres of land that the US district court iden-tified as privately held within the meander lines of Malheur, Harney, and Mud Lakes.[58]

Understanding the history of land condemnations on Lake Malheur requires in-depth knowledge of local history. In 2017, multigeneration Harney County rancher and local journalist and historian Pauline Braymen researched the original deed records and court cases involving these con-demnations, stored at the Harney County Courthouse.[59] Braymen applied a lifetime of knowledge of local families and farm histories, including her own: Braymen's grandfather grew grain on the lakebed, and her father was born near Cane Island, now part of the Malheur Refuge. Braymen once worked in the county records office and has professional-level knowledge of how to read often complex deed records.

Braymen observed that most of the properties condemned along the Malheur lakeshore were very small by Harney County standards, mostly around 160 acres. In the high desert, even on the productive lakeshore, 160 acres is not close to enough land to support a farm family. Braymen noted that most of the properties were extensions of larger family farms and ranches. For example, in a condemnation case that was not settled until 1947 (*United States of America v. Otley et al.*), thirty-six individual owners (or heirs of owners) were named but most belonged to four large local farming families—the Otley family, the Miller family, the Hayes family, and the Ausmus family (Braymen's relatives)—all of whom still farm in the county today.

The lakeshore was generally not their only or main source of livelihood; and Braymen found they were compensated at rates at least equal to mar-ket rates for comparable land at the time. For many, selling flood-prone land inside the meander line meant an opportunity to buy upland ground where they could grow barley and alfalfa hay—something that could not have been done on the ephemeral land they vacated on the lakebed. Other condemned properties, belonging to persons who had long since moved out of the county, were no longer in use. In total, Braymen's deeds research showed that, from 1935 to 1947, 5,027.66 acres of land inside the Neal meander line were condemned, involving twenty to twenty-five families,[60] but almost all in small parcels that did not constitute full farms or ranches. Braymen stated flatly, "The government has not taken anybody's ranch to my knowledge."[61]

When Ammon Bundy occupied the Malheur National Wildlife Refuge in 2016, it was not clear whether he was aware of the condemnations along the shores of Malheur Lake in the 1930s and 1940s. It appears likely that Bundy had instead been told of persistent local myths of alleged condemnations, which, in most instances, were cases in which the Malheur Refuge did not allow a refuge permit to be passed from one generation of a family to the next. It is not US Fish and Wildlife Service policy to extend a permit from one generation to another. These "condemnations" did not occur—despite some younger family members' widely vocalized claims.[62] The only actual condemnations in recent decades at the Malheur Refuge have been so-called friendly condemnations, used to expedite a real estate swap and give private landowners financial advantages.[63]

One well-known case occurred in 1978 involving rancher Walt McEwen.[64] McEwen's 1,518-acre marsh inholding was described as the last large portion of lakebed purchased by the refuge.[65] Private inholdings in protected areas create management problems for agencies and private landowners alike. In its 1978 Annual Narrative Report, the Malheur National Wildlife Refuge described McEwen as a willing seller.[66] After McEwen passed away in 1995, local recollections of his actual willingness to sell differed. However, after a legal settlement was reached in 1981, McEwen received $461.13 per acre for his property ($1,736.44 per acre in 2017 dollars) plus interest since 1978,[67] on par with or above market value for comparable ranchland at the time.[68] Nevertheless, McEwen's case became a celebrated cause among some members of the community who opposed any net loss of private land in the county, including Susie Hammond (wife of Dwight Hammond). Several groups, not including McEwen, sued the federal government, alleging that the transfer was part of a "master plan" by the refuge to acquire another twelve local properties, which would constitute a major federal action requiring an environmental impact statement under the National

Environmental Protection Act.[69] The district court rejected that argument, but to the present day, stories of the McEwen condemnation raise hackles. The word "friendly" disappeared, as did memories of the solid settlement he received. The size of the property increased in some recollections from the documented 1,518 acres to more than 3,600 acres. Ammon Bundy appeared to pick up the McEwen story, and made it one of his key pieces of "evidence" of "improper acquisitions" by the Malheur Refuge.

The most likely source of Ammon Bundy's claim that more than one hundred other ranchers were displaced by the Malheur Refuge was the reduction of refuge grazing permits that occurred during the 1970s, which the Bundy family famously considers a taking of private property.[70] The amount of cattle grazing in the Malheur Refuge had varied over time according to differing management priorities. After John Scharff became refuge manager in 1938, cattle on the Malheur National Wildlife Refuge increased, in some years topping one hundred thousand animal unit months (AUMs).[71] Some in the environmental community were deeply alarmed by such practices (Ferguson and Ferguson 1983), and by the early 1970s, with new environmental regulations from Washington, DC, and a nationwide pro-environmental shift, the accommodating approach that Scharff had established toward local ranchers changed.

When Scharff was replaced by new refuge manager Joe Mazzoni in 1971, Mazzoni's orders were to refocus the refuge on its primary mission: providing habitat for migratory birds. By the late 1970s, AUMs on the refuge had been reduced to approximately forty thousand. The results included reductions in permits, increased fees, and a great deal of consternation among ranchers who had relied on pasture in the refuge for decades.

Although most ranchers in Harney County do not share Bundy's view that a permit on federal land is "private property," over time a sense develops that a permit is part of one's ranch. A withdrawn, reduced, or restricted permit *feels* like a loss of rights. In recent decades, the refuge has worked hard to achieve win-win solutions for ranchers and wildlife, but Bundy was successful in tapping in to and nurturing residual hostility toward the refuge among some in the community.

Another persistent local myth that Ammon Bundy nurtured involves the dramatic floods of the early 1980s. After five or six years in a row of abundant snow pack, in 1984 Malheur and Harney Lakes expanded from a typical 45,000 acres to 160,000 acres. Because the water rose gradually over a number of years, farmers and ranchers were not able to collect on flood insurance and did not qualify for federal disaster relief. Local resentment built because the US Army Corps of Engineers declined to open a silt-filled seventeen-mile channel that would drain to the Malheur River, on the basis that too few people would benefit to justify the large cost.[72] A rumor circulated among a few people locally that the federal government had declined to open the channel in order to force flooded farmers and ranchers to sell to the Malheur Refuge. No evidence was ever presented of a government conspiracy to use the floods of the early 1980s to force condemnations, but Ammon Bundy picked up this rumor decades later to further his political agenda.

No subject was more central to Ammon Bundy's ideology than the history of land, yet in his telling of the history of land in Harney County there was no subject about which he was more demonstrably wrong. Bundy mostly ignored the unresolved historic claims of Native Americans, and it is not true that all refuge land was at one time owned by private ranchers. Of the estimated 81,786 acres inside the original Lake Malheur Reserve boundaries, only 23,947 acres were identified as private property, most of which was purchased from willing sellers after 1935. By far the largest areas of the refuge that were once private ranch land—Pete French's "P" Ranch and Bill Hanley's Double-O Ranch—were purchased from large companies eager to sell, not the downtrodden family rancher that Bundy's words evoked.

Ammon Bundy's claim that more than one hundred ranches were taken by the government was not even close to accurate. Perhaps two dozen owners (or their heirs) did contest condemnations of small pieces of land around the lakeshore in the 1930s and 1940s, but they were compensated at market prices or better. No "ranches" were taken. In total, the condemnations of properties inside the Neal meander line after 1935 make up 2.7 percent of the area of the Malheur Refuge today. The condemnations occurred for a public purpose (to protect migratory birds) and were legal and compensated. Whether or not one considers land condemnation for a public purpose an "improper acquisition," the US Supreme Court has repeatedly ruled that such condemnations are constitutional.[73] In recent decades, there is no record of hostile condemnations. It is true that some ranchers lost access to refuge land in the 1970s, but since then refuge managers, ranchers, and environmentalists have worked to craft win-win rather than zero-sum solutions.

These deliberate efforts in recent decades to achieve collaborative problem-solving buffered the community from potentially the most powerful and compelling story Ammon Bundy told: the story of government "overreach."

Overreach

The twin towns of Burns and Hines are the center of an island of private property in a sea of federal public land. To the north is the Malheur National Forest. To the south is the Malheur National Wildlife Refuge. Surrounding both, and in every direction, is land managed by the US Bureau of Land Management. The Bureau of Land Management office, the US Forest Service office, and the US Department of Agriculture's Eastern Oregon Agricultural Research Center are prominent landmarks. Approaching Burns on the most traveled route from Bend, travelers pass the USDA's Northern Great Basin Experimental Range, and signs that encourage passers-by to "Enjoy Your Public Lands," as well as federally managed wild horse corrals. In remote areas, private property exists in small pockets, and federally managed land is almost always within view. The large presence of the federal government in Harney County—72.5 percent of the total land area[74]—is almost impossible to miss.

It is not difficult to understand a sense that this federal presence may be *too* big, and indeed many in the area feel that way. When Ammon Bundy came to Harney County in late 2015 and early 2016 and spoke tirelessly about federal "overreach," the response was generally one of agreement. Few other words so readily cause heads to nod in the rural American West. In Harney County, as in most of the rural West, there are few individuals who do not at times feel frustration with federal authority. When Ammon Bundy occupied Harney County and then took over the Malheur National Wildlife Refuge, the term "overreach" ricocheted through the community, animating conversations and amplifying long-simmering grievances.

Yet, "overreach" was almost never defined. For Ammon Bundy and his supporters, the definition of overreach was simple, and radical: in their view of the Constitution, as soon as the western territories became states, virtually any continued federal control of land was unconstitutional overreach. Bundy cited the Enclave Clause and insisted that under the Constitution the federal government can control nothing in a state other than "forts, magazines, arsenals, dockyards, and other needful buildings." This interpretation could justify almost any action against federal lands, buildings (other than "needful buildings" specifically named in the Enclave Clause), or employees, since, in Bundy's view, the federal government had no authority to be in those places. To Bundy, the mere presence of federal agencies in the state of Oregon in any way not authorized under the Enclave Clause was overreach. Thus, when he seized the headquarters of the Malheur National Wildlife Refuge, Bundy insisted he was doing nothing unlawful because he was taking the refuge back for "We the People," in whose interest he claimed to be acting.

Observations of public meetings in Harney County during and after the Malheur takeover suggest that few local residents shared such radical views. For most Harney County citizens, the concept of federal "overreach," while important, tended to focus on practical concerns rather than grand ideology. Specifically, Bundy's vision for an anti-federal revolution was centered on ranchers (who he called the "tip of the spear"), but few local ranchers viewed federal ownership of land, in and of itself, as "overreach." By and large, when Harney County ranchers used the word overreach they appeared to see it as specific government actions that, to them, defy common sense or seem excessive, unnecessary, or just dumb—typically resulting from a failure of resource managers to adequately listen to local voices.

Mark Owens is a hay farmer who worked as a ranch manager before buying his own farm in Crane, Oregon (twenty-nine miles southeast of Burns). In May 2016, when the Harney County community was still bruised and reeling from the Bundy occupation, Owens was recruited by community members seeking a unifying candidate to run for a vacant seat on the county commission. Owens won by far the most votes (more than 40 percent) in a nine-candidate primary election, and then won the general election vote by 95.6 percent. Owens reflects the point of view of many local citizens on the question of federal overreach, suggesting that the real question is not whether the federal government is overstepping its constitutional bounds, but whether the government embraces local input:

> I don't like the word overreach. Webster's Dictionary says overreach is try-ing to do something you don't have the ability to do. I think the federal government has the ability to govern. . . . The best verbiage is local input. Local input gets us to what the majority of people in Harney County want. We don't want control of federal lands. I believe the majority of people in Harney County want federal lands to continue to be managed the way they are, with more local input.
>
> I believe if we have local input we can make significant changes in [fed-eral] plans. I think [the government] will listen to us, honestly, if we come to the table with the right position and attitude and understanding that it's a multiple use plan. We live in a new world. There's going to be give and take in how federal lands are managed. There's more people now than ever that want to use that federal land, and they have the exact same right to use that federal land that we do. Even if we're trying to make a living off it, if someone wants to use the land for recreation, they have just as much right to use the land as we do. So hopefully when we put in local input in how to best manage that land, for recreation, for multi-use, they'll listen to us because we're the ones given the responsibility of taking care of that land because we're making a living off it. [75]

Katie and Keith Baltzor are longtime local ranchers near Burns who accept that working on public land may require certain kinds of restric-tions, but agree that the real question is whether government embraces local input. As Keith explains,

> We weren't okay with [the Bundy occupation]. There might be a few ranchers around here who were, but the majority weren't. . . . I think [the question of federal ownership of land] has been so taken care of in the past with court cases and US Supreme Court decisions that it's pretty much a nonissue for me.

Katie elaborated on some complexities of land management and concerns of local ranchers:

We rent and lease a lot of land from private individuals as well [as the federal government]. We don't own that. It's not our right. And if you look at the contracts, they say in there that if the owner decides the grass is used up you may be asked to move to a different pasture. That's just how it works. . . . I don't see it as any different with the BLM. They're the manager of the land. We have a contract, a lease with them, a permit. But in that permit, there's certain guidelines and stipulations that are just part of having that lease. It's no different with private landowners or the government. . . . People just want to have a voice. They want to feel that they're listened to. The truth is it's really hard sometimes when a decision is made away from the location, because we've been here fifty-some years. We've been on this property and this land. We've seen a lot of different things caused by drought and wildfire. You really are tied very closely to the land and have a lot of knowledge.

The Baltzors emphasized that if "overreach" means lack of local input, it is a word that does not fit the Malheur National Wildlife Refuge. Keith said,

The changes that we've seen in the mind-set of the refuge management have been huge in the last twenty years. There have been different managers and some have had different agendas. They've worked through a process there where people have seen managers on the ground and they acknowledge their failures and they say, "Well, that didn't work, so maybe let's try this." . . . Then you start seeing a change in the mind-set of [local] people. We don't have any direct business that we do with [the refuge] but we know people who run cattle at the refuge and their families loathed the refuge thirty years ago. Now they talk about what a great opportunity it is [to work with the refuge], and how well they get along, and how things work now.[76]

Kenny and Debbie Bentz are from a large and prominent Eastern Oregon ranching family that includes Cliff Bentz, a Republican Oregon state senator who took a strong position against the Bundy takeover of the Malheur Wildlife Refuge. Kenny and Debbie Bentz emphasized that the Bundys' view of what is constitutional seemed to favor people like themselves to the exclusion of others from different backgrounds with different points of view, and that public land must allow for multiple uses and multiple users, and multiple use is not "overreach":

Government overreach, it was never defined but it was talked about all winter long [in 2016, during and after the Bundy occupation]. Somebody needed to stand up and define exactly what they were talking about. Especially with regard to the [Malheur National Wildlife] Refuge. To [the Bundy occupiers] it was government overreach because government owned it.

If it was constitutional for [the occupiers] to take the refuge, and they're waving their Constitutions around, and give it to the people, meaning me, I guess, because I own a cow and I live close by. . . . What if [the Oregon Natural Desert Association] showed up with their militia and took the refuge and said they were going to give it back to the Indians? They would have been constitutionally on a lot firmer ground than the Bundys were. So, I asked the [Bundy] supporters, would you have been down there supporting them, with your American flag and your AR-15 [rifle]? The answer is no, they wouldn't have been down there supporting that. That's not consistent. You're either for what is right under the Constitution, or you're not. So, it [government management to protect wildlife] is not overreach.[77]

Stacy Davies manages the 1.2-million-acre Roaring Springs Ranch in the Catlow Valley of southern Harney County, which includes much of what was once Pete French's "P" Ranch. Roaring Springs Ranch, which defines sustainability as its mission and is a member of the Country Natural Beef Cooperative, is owned by Bob Sanders, president of RSG Forest Products, Inc., based in Washington State. From Talmage, Utah, Davies was hired in 1997 and has since become a leading figure in the ranching community in Harney County as well as a major contributor to local collaborative land use management efforts, including his pivotal role in the creation of the Steens Mountain Cooperative Management and Protection Area in 2000. A devout Mormon and political conservative, Davies met with Ammon Bundy at the occupied Malheur National Wildlife Refuge. Davies sympathized with Bundy's frustrations regarding federal regulations and supported his effort to communicate a message calling for change, though Davies does not share all of Bundy's interpretations of the Constitution. With a view that shares some similarities to the frustrations voiced by Ammon Bundy, Davies takes a philosophical view of government "overreach":

Early grazing laws were all brought upon the West mainly driven by the locals, by cattlemen. We had to create some kind of a management system so we weren't overusing the land. Some individuals had a right to use it, others did not. Those early acts created a grazing right. And over time, through policy, that right became a privilege, through a ten-year permit, which is revocable at any time.... To any business, stability is an important factor. When you're in a county that is 70 percent 80 percent, 90 percent federal land, and therefore your economy is going to be dependent on the use of that federal land, you felt like you had a right that was attached to your base property to use that [federal land] with your livestock, and that right gave you some assurance and stability. But as times changed and that right has become a revocable privilege on an annual basis, the stability is gone. The fear overtakes most other emotions and motivations, and people lash out, and they use words such as overreach. And then they will respond in ways as severe as taking over a federal property and making a stand. [78]

In a later public forum in which Davies spoke about collaborative land use problem-solving,[79] he memorably observed that such fear of change and instability is "a close cousin of hate." Times have changed, and ranchers such as Ammon and Ryan Bundy's father Cliven have found the world around them different than the world they once knew; fear is a characteristic human emotion, and it can easily metastasize into hate, and even violence. Davies acknowledged that at times he could have envisioned himself going down that path.[80]

Davies chose a different path, however. While he can understand the fear and anger of working in a more restricted world—a world where the word "overreach" does apply, in his view—he does not see a grand political battle over constitutional rights or property rights as a practical way forward. Davies (like most ranchers in the area) can provide a long list of examples of problems he sees with federal land management. Yet, while Davies connected at a visceral and emotional level with the frustrations voiced by Ammon Bundy and his supporters, he still sees collaboration as a better path forward for resolving these problems:

If you operate in that space where we believe we can [find win-win solutions], and I take your values and interests into consideration and you take mine into consideration, and we find a solution that works for both of us, generally you don't even get into a discussion about rights. When you fall back to [talking about] your rights, you're falling back to the contract, and it's a fight at that point. You're pushing me too far, I have a line and you're not crossing it, because those are my rights. When you're really in a good-quality collaborative process, the word "rights" never comes up. . . . If you're in that space where you're truly concerned about other people's interests and truly interested in finding a solution, then it's not right or wrong, it's what you agree to—it's a win that's good for all.

Every Harney County rancher and farmer is an individual, and views vary widely, but the thoughtfulness and pragmatic, constructive attitude displayed by Harney County farmers and ranchers like Mark Owens, Keith and Katie Baltzor, Kenny and Debbie Bentz, and Stacy Davies is typical. Even those who see federal ownership per se as a form of "overreach" do not see practical value in fighting over rights. Rather, they see greater value in dialogue, wherein all parties genuinely listen to each other's ideas and concerns and seek practical solutions. Prominent Harney County rancher Gary Miller noted succinctly, "When you believe you know the answer, it's tough to wait twenty years for [the government] to figure it out."[81] Miller, like many others, did not want a fight, he simply wanted to be heard. For many Harney County citizens, "overreach" might be better described as *under-listening*. Harney County's citizens—ranchers, government leaders, tribes, and others—worked hard to provide opportunities for listening and finding win-win solutions.

Ammon Bundy seemed wholly unaware of Harney County's remarkable efforts to promote dialogue. In fact, despite all the time he spent inveighing against federal "overreach," Bundy himself did very little listening. Stacy Davies, who interacted extensively with Bundy at the Malheur takeover, observed that, "Ammon doesn't know the issues, and it's hurting him."[82] Fred Otley, a fifth-generation rancher who grazes cows on the Malheur Refuge in the winter, observed,

I don't think the Bundys necessarily have the facts on the history of the refuge. Refuge lands that have forage that you can go in and harvest and you can graze during the winter time when there's too much snow [elsewhere] is a real benefit to the livestock businesses and the community and the economy. . . . I think [a cooperative mode] has been increased in this [2010s] decade. . . . [The Bundy takeover] happens to be here in Harney County, and here at refuge headquarters, and doesn't necessarily represent the recent management and collaborative-type things, and more science-based things, that the refuge has been trying to do.[83]

Ammon Bundy was an outsider who came to Harney County with preconceived ideas about local problems and prepackaged "constitutional" solutions. He did not take time to visit and truly listen to a cross section of the community. If "overreach" is defined, as Bundy defined it, as a violation of the Constitution, revolution may be the answer. If "overreach" is defined as a failure to listen to local ideas and concerns, the answer is more likely to be found in dialogue—as Harney County has done. Starting from a fundamentally different definition of "overreach," it is little surprise that Bundy failed to connect with the hearts and minds of most Harney County citizens. If, as many Harney County citizens believe, "overreach" is really under-listening, Ammon Bundy himself could be said to have severely "overreached."

Deafness

Three days after no Harney County rancher heeded Ammon Bundy's call to join a public ceremony to declare sovereignty from the United States, the internet buzzed with chatter among Bundy's opponents and supporters alike, amazed by his tactical error. Bundy bundled all the leaders of the Malheur takeover into two vehicles (his own driven by a federal informant) and set off on a narrow, isolated canyon road that provided a perfect opportunity for arrest. Bundy's tactical error was an outcome of a profound strategic error he had made months earlier.

Bundy's supporters claimed he was traveling that evening to Grant County to help spread his message about the Constitution. Critics said Bundy was headed to Grant County because he was frustrated that he had gained little traction in Harney County and hoped for better success in Grant County, where the county sheriff, Glenn Palmer, was sympathetic to Bundy's views. If Bundy had gotten Harney County ranchers to join his movement three days earlier, he might not have had the time or need to be on the isolated canyon road that evening traveling to Grant County.

Why, then, did Harney County ranchers not heed Ammon Bundy's call to revolution? In his three months in Harney County, Ammon Bundy lectured almost nonstop about the story of Harney County as he saw it: a story of impoverishment, dispossession, and overreach. He spoke in public forums, he spoke to almost any visitor who came to the occupied Malheur Refuge, and he communicated almost every day with the press and social media. Yet, as the weeks and months of Bundy's presence in Harney County and the takeover of the Malheur National Wildlife Refuge passed, he gained only a small number of active local supporters. As later elections that were widely viewed as referendums on the Bundy occupation indicated, the great majority of the community opposed Bundy's presence, and their hostility and willingness to openly confront the occupiers increased over time.

Ammon Bundy's stories of federal oppression and call for rebellion missed the mark in Harney County, and he knew it. His frustration showed. Bundy may be one of the few persons to ever call a Harney County rancher a coward (and live). On January 18, 2016, at a meeting of ranchers in Crane, Bundy was confronted in a public meeting by a fourth-generation Harney County rancher who told Bundy that his call for revolution was going too far. Bundy replied angrily, "You're afraid." Bundy may not have known that Harney County sheriff Dave Ward had to plead with local people including military veterans to not go to the refuge and "take care of the problem" themselves. Harney County displayed restraint, not fear.

It was an example of Ammon Bundy's core strategic mistake: he did not *listen*. Instead, Bundy lectured county residents on the need to "educate" themselves about the Constitution, property rights, and alleged government tyranny. Much of what he said about Harney County appeared to be his own embellishments on old local myths and half-truths that had circulated among an angry minority for years or decades, but that most knew to be false. What Bundy seemed incapable of grasping was that Harney County as a whole, like the rancher in Crane, was not afraid or uninformed: the majority simply did not accept his story.

Few Harney County citizens would disagree that there are problems with federal land management. However, where Bundy saw black and white, good and bad, and armed solutions, residents of Harney County saw nuance, complexity, and cooperative possibilities. Where Bundy saw poverty induced by government tyranny, most local people recognized that the federal government had made positive contributions to the economy and community. Where Bundy saw the federal government as an illegitimate landlord, most Harney County citizens believed transferring federal public lands to private ownership would cause major financial and social problems. Where Bundy saw "overreach" as requiring the elimination of the federal government from the county, local residents asked only to be listened to so that the federal government could be a better neighbor.

Had Ammon Bundy spent more time listening and less time lecturing, he would have known that most people in Harney County who work the land see the problems not as grand political struggles but as tangible problems—stubble height in sage grouse habitat; overgrazing caused by growing wild horse populations; the diameter of trees that can be harvested; and many others. Had Bundy listened, he would have learned that Harney County has been a leader in finding practical solutions to such problems through the creative, time-consuming, but generally effective craft of collaboration.

4

Collaboration

At 8:30 a.m. on June 28, 2016—a day with a typical Eastern Oregon bright blue summer sky—I joined a diverse group of nineteen ranchers, farmers, environmentalists, tribal members, local organizers, and federal, state, and local employees who bundled into trucks at the Emigrant Creek Ranger Station for an often bumpy one-hour drive to the US Forest Service's Dairy Project northwest of Burns in the Blue Mountains of the Malheur National Forest. The purpose of the trip was to study the results of various experiments in mechanical thinning and prescribed fire, used to thin forests and reduce the danger of catastrophic forest fire and disease.[1] The group trekked all day carrying notebooks, water bottles, and sack lunches through dry, acrid-smelling, partly charred stands of pine, juniper, and aspen to compare different types and combinations of thinning methods. Stopping every few miles to visit different burn sites, facilitator Jack Southworth enforced his rule requiring every participant to voice their thoughts to the whole group.

The field trip was organized by the Harney County Restoration Collaborative, a forest health initiative of Harney County's High Desert Partnership. What was remarkable about this outing was how normal it was: the field trip was a single example of approximately fifty to sixty group events organized in 2016 by the High Desert Partnership[2] alone—one of an expanding number of collaborative problem-solving groups in Harney County.

On the very same day, back in Burns, life was not normal but it was moving that way. The county recorder was tallying votes on a special recall election to remove the county's top elected leader, Judge Steve Grasty. The

The Harney County Restoration Collaborative is one of many local groups that bring together community members to cooperatively resolve resource management questions (June 28, 2016).

recall effort was widely seen as a referendum on the Bundy occupation, which Judge Grasty had vigorously opposed. The recall failed with a 70.3 percent "No" vote. Arguably, the election was about more than Bundy or Grasty: it was about which model of problem-solving Harney County preferred. Ammon Bundy claimed that the county's resource problems could be solved only by armed rebellion against the federal government. At the time of the takeover, many residents specifically rejected that model in favor of a model with a proven local track record—collaboration.

Harney County had invested for decades in some of the nation's most innovative and successful collaborative efforts to address the very same kinds of problems Bundy claimed could be solved only through armed rebellion. The field trip to the Dairy Project in the Malheur National Forest was one of many examples of the successful collaborative approach. In the months following the end of the Malheur takeover, leaders of local collaborative groups reported, if anything, greater community participation than ever. On June 28, 2016, almost six months to the day after the Malheur takeover ended, Harney County citizens made a double statement: at the ballot box, and in their continued daily practice of solving natural resource problems their own way.

Collaboratives

Harney County may be one of the few remote places in the American West where visitors entering the only major populated area by the most traveled route are greeted by not one but two buildings dedicated to natural resource collaboratives—the High Desert Partnership, and the Harney County Watershed Council buildings (both in the town of Hines on Highway 20). Both offices are new since Ammon Bundy and his militia supporters came to Harney County in late 2015, illustrating that the temporary disruption caused by Bundy's takeover of the Malheur National Wildlife Refuge in early 2016 did not stop the momentum of collaborative problem-solving that had been building in Harney County for decades. Bundy appeared unaware that these collaborative approaches were common in Harney County, and that they provided a viable option for giving local people a voice and a degree of influence over the very types of resource problems that Bundy said could be solved only by overthrowing the federal government. Almost immediately after Bundy left Harney County, in custody, the collaboratives resumed operation and continued to thrive.

Almost immediately after the Malheur takeover ended, Harney County residents resumed their collaborative decision-making (High Desert Partnership meeting, March 22, 2016).

In fact, an often-heard complaint about collaboratives in Harney County is that the word "collaboration" applies to such a wide array of groups in the county with substantially differing goals and methods that it is sometimes not clear what the word means. In fact, apart from avoiding "top-down" and "one-size-fits-all" approaches (which almost all "collaborative" groups advocate), collaboration is not easy to define. Collaboration is not a single process or set of goals; rather, by its nature, collaboration is defined in practice by diverse stakeholders, including local people, who make decisions about decision-making processes as well as desired outcomes in ways appropriate to the local ecology, economy, and social and cultural environments. As Charnley, Sheridan, and Nabhan have described it, collaboratives "involve local people in the definition, design, implementation, and evaluation of conservation efforts, both large and small scale, over time; and recognize and build on the long histories of local people in specific places" (2014, 56).

Some aspects of collaboration, such as providing a voice to local people and opportunities to shape their own destinies, are similar to the goals of the Bundy occupiers. Indeed, many local residents agreed with some aspects of the occupiers' goals, but most citizens believed they had better ways to achieve these goals. Where Ammon Bundy and his followers offered armed confrontation against federal agencies, Harney County's many collaborative projects offered opportunities for dialogue, relationship-building, and participation in resource decisions by local people in cooperation with agencies, conservationists, tribes, and local governments. In another respect, however, the goals fundamentally differed: whereas Bundy wanted to make Harney County "federal-free," collaboratives in Harney County seek not to expel federal agencies but simply to "get ahead" of federal policy-making so that local voices are heard and resource decisions reflect local concerns. In this chapter I explore some principles of effective collaboration in Harney based on a few (by no means all) of the county's many successful collaborative efforts.

One of the early and best-known efforts to "get ahead" of federal resource policy in Harney County was the creation of the Steens Mountain Cooperative Management and Protection Area in 2000. Steens Mountain is the largest fault-block mountain in the northern Great Basin, and the 9,733-foot snow-covered peaks of its eastern face plunge a vertical mile to the usually bone-dry Alvord Desert. On the mountain's more gradual western and northern slopes, ice age glaciers carved half-mile-deep U-shaped valleys into stream channels. Steens offers extraordinary scenic value and ecological diversity. Steens was anything but an untrammeled wilderness, however. In the arid desert environment, the graduated elevations of Steens Mountain provided precious summer grazing. With the arrival of substantial numbers of Euro-American cattle and sheepherders from the 1870s onward, at times the mountain was grazed by tens of thousands of cattle and hundreds of thousands of sheep. In 1902, David Griffiths of the US Department of Agriculture estimated 182,500 sheep on the mountain at an average density of 450 animals per square mile, and possibly as many as 1,000 per square mile. Griffiths described the "evil effect" of overgrazing, with parts of the mountain having "no more feed than the floor of a corral" (Griffiths 1902, 29–30). By the late twentieth century, sheep numbers had been drastically reduced, but cattle still grazed the mountain on a mix of private and federal public land.

Recognizing the exceptional scenic and ecological values of the mountain, as well as its history of overuse, in summer 1999 Secretary of the Interior Bruce Babbitt tagged Steens Mountain for designation as a national monument under the 1906 Antiquities Act. Babbitt also pledged, however, to preserve ranching on Steens—a promise that was "met with skepticism from the thirty-five ranchers (with their eighteen thousand head of cattle) who used the mountain" (Langston 2003, 148). Local ranchers asked Secretary Babbitt if options other than a national monument would be considered.[3] Babbitt said he would consider a legislative alternative, but the clock was ticking, and he insisted that if a legislative solution could not be found, President Bill Clinton would designate Steens as a national monument before the presidential election of November 2000.

Environmentalists, led by the Oregon Natural Desert Association's (ONDA) executive director Bill Marlett, at first strongly supported the designation of a monument. Ranchers, however, argued that, with the large amount of private land on the mountain, a monument designation would create different kinds of land management, fragmenting the open, seamless landscape that local people had enjoyed on the mountain for everything from water to wildlife to recreation. Ranchers also expressed concern that a monument would devastate Steens Mountain ecologically by attracting thousands of new visitors.

In response, Secretary Babbitt asked the Southeast Oregon Resource Advisory Council (RAC) to try to come up with alternative commendations, but when the RAC was unable to create a plan that could be supported by all the key constituencies, Congressman Greg Walden created a small working group that included a member of the Burns Paiute Tribe, a private rancher, a hunter, a county commissioner, environmentalists, and the chair of the RAC. By early summer 2000, with the clock ticking, ranchers made an offer environmentalists could not refuse: they proposed to designate a cow-free, "no livestock grazing" wilderness area on the mountain. Because the wilderness designation would be written into law, it could not be revoked except by an act of Congress. Unlike a national monument, the cow-free wilderness would completely ban grazing in sensitive areas of the mountain. The offer of a cow-free wilderness brought ONDA's Bill Marlett to the table.[4] The group hunkered down at the home of the manager of Roaring Springs Ranch (the largest ranch on the mountain) for three days, penciling lines on maps and wordsmithing the agreement, which Congressman Greg Walden brought as a bill to the House floor; it was signed into law by President Bill Clinton on October 30, 2000.

The Steens Mountain Cooperative Management and Protection Act of 2000 established the Steens Mountain Cooperative Management and Protection Area (CMPA), consisting of 428,156 acres of public land, including the 172,000-acre Steens Mountain Wilderness Area, with 105,000 acres of cow-free wilderness ("no livestock grazing areas"). The Steens Act consolidated public lands on the mountain through land exchanges with private owners, trading high-ecological and scenic value private lands on the mountain for suitable public grazing lands in other areas.

The act established Wild and Scenic Rivers and Trout Reserve areas, prohibited off-road travel in federal lands in the CMPA, and banned commercial timber and mining activities. The act allowed fishing, hunting, and trapping in some areas as authorized by the CMPA, and permitted grazing outside the Wilderness Area. Environmental groups including the Oregon Natural Desert Association (ONDA) and the Wilderness Society praised the act, calling it precedent-setting in the West.[5]

Local ranchers, however, also got some things that were very important to them: above all, they eliminated the possibility of a national monument designation, which they viewed as a guarantee that ranching would ultimately be eliminated on Steens Mountain. In addition, the act provided attractive land trades for owners of private land on the mountain. Critically, the Steens Act also provided an ongoing voice for landowners, permittees, the Burns Paiute Tribe, and other stakeholders through the twelve-member Steens Mountain Advisory Council (SMAC), which serves to "enhance cooperative and innovative management practices between the public and private land managers."[6] The role of the SMAC is to develop "new and unique approaches to the management of lands" on Steens Mountain, and the secretary of the interior and Bureau of Land Management "shall consult with the advisory committee as part of the preparation and implementation of the management plan."[7] Local ranchers had already been cooperating on their own for years on habitat restoration projects such as juniper control, and the prospect of serving only as advisers to the BLM rankled some. Yet, the provisions in the Steens Act formally requiring BLM to consider the advice of stakeholders made the deal doable, albeit at a price many considered quite high. Even so, ranchers got what was most important to them: keeping a seat at the table and a local voice in the process.

Although the Steens Mountain cooperative agreement represented a landmark achievement in managing and protecting an enormously important landscape feature in Harney County with a significant level of local input, some would argue that it remained largely rooted in a model that seeks compromises among stakeholders with specific, often conflicting, outcomes that they want to achieve. Another important group in Harney County, the High Desert Partnership (HDP), chose to focus instead on building relationships among members of the community who represent different perspectives but are not necessarily invested in specific outcomes. By building these relationships, the HDP strives to find innovative, win-win solutions to social-ecological problems in a manner that avoids adversarial approaches. As a private nonprofit, the HDP is relatively free to pursue paths not directly mandated or constrained by government rules.

The HDP was founded by Harney County ranchers Gary Marshall, Dick Jenkins, and Mike Bentz, along with Malheur National Wildlife Refuge then deputy project manager Chad Karges, in 2005. The impulse to create the HDP was generated by a desire to improve relationships between the Malheur Refuge and the local community, building capacity to avoid the conflict-ridden, failed interactions of the past. Marshall and Karges knew that the Malheur National Wildlife Refuge would be required to begin developing a Comprehensive Conservation Plan (CCP) by 2010, and they set out to study collaborative methods and relationship-building to be ready for the CCP process. They invited participation from outside stakeholders including conservation groups. Marshall and Karges set out on a road tour of the state, trying to enlist support from key players including government officials, whose support they would need to pursue their alternative approach at the Malheur Refuge. They spoke with "anyone who would listen to their pitch."[8] They initially found skepticism among agency officials, but support from the Portland-based collaborative facilitation group Oregon Consensus. In the meantime, Marshall and Karges knocked on doors and shook hands throughout the local community to build the relationships and trust needed to persuade a community more accustomed to conflict with the Malheur Refuge to give the new non-adversarial, collaborative approach a try.

The High Desert Partnership does not do projects; it builds relationships and facilitates conversations with the intent to find collaborative win-win solutions to problems that might otherwise result in conflicts and litigation. The group does not advocate particular outcomes; it supports dialogue with positive outcomes for the ecology, economy, and community.

The signature accomplishment of the HDP's approach was its establishment of a diverse working group of about thirty stakeholders to craft the 2013 Malheur Comprehensive Conservation Plan, which detailed the goals and methods for managing the refuge for the following fifteen years. After three years of dialogue, the working group produced a 779-page document that became what the HDP describes as the nation's first collaboratively created comprehensive conservation plan.[9] Given the contentious relations between the Malheur Refuge and the local community in the past, the fact that local ranchers and farmers, the Burns Paiute Tribe, and county government, as well as conservationists and agency officials, all endorsed the plan was an astonishing achievement. Possibly the most powerful evidence of success is the fact that the Malheur CCP was the first plan of its scale in Harney County for many years that was not sued. Current refuge manager Chad Karges observed, "No one thought it could be done."[10] After the plan was approved, the CCP working group continued meeting to collaboratively decide on necessary adaptions in the plan's implementation.

With only five full and part-time staff, the HDP prioritizes initiatives in the early stages of problem-solving with enough time to build necessary relationships (before what Marshall calls the "train wreck" stage, when it's "almost too late"[11]). At the end of 2017, the HDP was facilitating four other initiatives in addition to Malheur CCP working group. The HDP's first initiative, formed in 2006, was the Harney County Restoration Collaborative (HCRC). Facilitator Jack Southworth described the initiative's mission: "We believe a diverse group of people with a desire for a biologically sustainable forest can, through consensus decision making, give the Forest Service valuable input on proposed projects that will decrease contention, reduce litigation, improve the quality of the projects and help result in biologically sustainable forest and rangelands for generations to come."[12] The Harney Basin Wetlands Initiative (HBWI) coordinates activities between the Malheur Refuge and private landowners to control common carp and to maintain and enhance riparian and wet meadow bird habitats through conservation agreements and appropriate management of flood irrigation.[13] The Youth Changing the Community Initiative looks to the community's future, providing career information and training opportunities to help retain youth in Harney County. The Harney County Wildfire Collaborative seeks to identify consensus-based steps to cope with a problem facing every member of the community with increasing urgency: the threat of mega-fires.

Along with fire risk, no issue affects every citizen of Harney County more than water scarcity. By 2017, there were good reasons to be concerned about the future adequacy of water supplies in the Harney Basin. In the early 2010s, beef and alfalfa prices hit new highs, creating opportunities for Harney County agriculture. With an average of less than eight inches a year of rainfall and periodic droughts, however, agriculture in the Harney Valley depends heavily on groundwater to grow hay for local livestock or export. For years, the Oregon Department of Water Resources (ODWR) granted permits to drill wells for irrigation despite having little current knowledge of the groundwater supply.[14] Lacking current data but faced with drought and increasing concerns that the Harney Basin's groundwater was over-allocated, in 2015, ODWR abruptly stopped taking applications for new wells, creating alarm among agricultural and domestic groundwater users throughout the basin.[15]

Facing nothing less than a potential crisis in agriculture—the economic mainstay of the county—as well as a possible crisis for domestic water supplies, Harney County turned again to the tested model of problem-solving through collaboration. The State of Oregon has one of the nation's oldest and most developed systems of support for voluntary, community-based watershed planning. The Oregon Watershed Enhancement Board (Benson 1996),[16] a state agency, facilitates the establishment of voluntary, locally supported watershed councils. The Harney County Watershed Council was established in 1998. The state's 2012 Integrated Water Resources Strategy recommended that the Oregon Department of Water Resources help establish "place-based planning" to coordinate efforts to address future water issues. In 2015, ODWR funded the Harney County Watershed Council as one of four "pilot" projects selected statewide, noting specifically that "the citizens of Harney County have a history of successful collaborative planning."[17]

The overall purpose of the place-based water planning model (referred to in Harney County as "community-based") is to "engage a broad, representative group of stakeholders and other interested members of the public to begin the process of developing a long-term integrated water resources strategy that will meet the needs of Harney County."[18] Participants recognized the urgent need to plan for what many assumed to be the likely conclusions of a new ODWR/US Geological Survey study that was in progress at the time: that the amount of water withdrawals exceeded the rate of recharge of the aquifer. One participant observed that the "bottom line" is the question of "are we going to be able to continue to live here?" Another participant noted that the community-based process provided an opportunity for local people to "get ahead" of otherwise seemingly inevitable and possibly drastic state-level regulation. Yet another participant noted the mantra of the American West, "Water's for fightin'"—and expressed hope that the collaborative process could help prevent a community-wide water brawl.[19]

With the Bundy occupation, Harney County faced a different kind of crisis—one that was brought to them by outsiders, and one that many considered to be built on imagined problems and unrealistic goals. In 2017, the community began to grapple with a problem that seemed all too real, and one that most would acknowledge as at least partly homegrown. Outside claims about alleged constitutional abuses seemed far-fetched to many in the community. Water problems, in contrast, are a problem self-evident and very real to almost everyone in Harney County.

Harney County would not enter into a likely water-scarce future without some useful tools. Whether grappling with water scarcity, grazing on Steens Mountain, providing bird habitat on and off the Malheur Refuge, or building the capacities of the community's youth, through its many years of collaborative experience,[20] Harney County had learned some principles for working together effectively.

Relationships

During the Bundy occupation of Harney County in late 2015 and early 2016, one of the often-expressed worries was whether Harney County would still "be Harney County" after all the disruption, division, and anger that the occupiers and the media and law enforcement that followed had generated in the community. A small population, geographic isolation, and sometimes harsh environment made the ability—the necessity—to work together cooperatively highly prized in Harney County. After the occupation, in some ways Harney County was indeed no longer quite the same place it had been; but the cooperative spirit mostly survived and, in some respects, seemed even stronger, having endured shared hardship.

Harney County's many collaborative groups both built on and contributed to Harney County's close-knit culture and commitment to working together. This close-knit culture provided an opportunity for innovative federal managers to explore management approaches that broke away from the old confrontational, top-down models that had often produced poor relationships with the local community as well as often-failed conservation methods. After coming to the Malheur National Wildlife Refuge in 1999, Chad Karges[21] saw that the old management approaches were not working. When asked why he took a gamble by pursuing a collaborative approach to the Malheur Comprehensive Conservation Plan (CCP), Karges responded,

> Failure. Failure is a good learning tool. Why should you keep repeating processes that cause failure? Try something different. Did I know this was going to work? No. But it was different from the processes that we were using that were failing. And we tried to increase our odds of success by borrowing from some other success stories, and also looking at their failures, too.
>
> When you looked at issues at the refuge, even if it was something simple like moving a fence, many times it became very complicated. That was all due to failed relationships between the refuge and the local community. The refuge wasn't interacting with the external conservation community, and definitely the conservation community wasn't interacting with the local community—except in negative ways. . . . At that point in time, the Forest Service had been going through years of litigation on all their projects, BLM was constantly being litigated or appealed. The only reason the refuge wasn't was because we hadn't done anything new that would generate an opportunity for an appeal or litigation. I thought, you know, there's got to be a better way of doing business.[22]

The first step for Karges, along with his strong supporter Gary Marshall (a fifth-generation local rancher and permittee on the refuge) was to begin drawing on existing relationships and building new bonds of trust and friendship. Bruce Taylor, a bird conservationist who became a core member of both the High Desert Partnership and the later Malheur CCP, describes the time in the mid-2000s leading up to the establishment of the CCP process:

> The outcome that Chad wanted was something that's good for wildlife and the refuge and would bridge the divides and heal the wounds of a couple of decades of acrimony around the refuge here.
>
> Chad did most of the outreach, the one-on-one. He called people up, probably cold-calling people, saying "We really need you to be part of this."

Chad, as a Fish and Wildlife Service manager, he can certainly make those kinds of calls to certain people. Having someone like Gary Marshall, with his standing in the community, there to help make the calls or introduce Chad to people, I think that was critical.

Chad wouldn't tell you this, but he was the guy behind the scenes always touching base with every discrete interest that needs to be at the table, gauging the comfort levels and trying to get things worked out before you go into the meeting together.[23]

Karges explained his approach:

The whole process is relationship-based. There were intentional efforts as the refuge developed relationships locally and externally with conservation groups, in which we intentionally tried to make sure they built relationships amongst themselves. That created a whole new dynamic that never existed here before. For example, we have Dan Nichols, a rancher, talking with Bruce Taylor [an environmentalist]. They never would have talked with each other before.[24]

Karges recalls that through working closely together in the same room over a number of years and learning to understand each other and see the humanity in each other despite certain differences, these relationships became more than simply the ability to transact business—they became true friendships: "When some of our local ranchers go to do business in Portland, they'll stay at the homes of conservationists they've gotten to know in the CCP. Those are the kinds of relationships we've built in the High Desert Partnership."[25]

Despite initial concerns that the Bundy occupation might damage relationships among federal agencies and the local community, the actual outcome seemed to be the opposite. Federal managers were reminded of the value of building good community relations, and encouraged staff to redouble their community outreach. Hay farmer and Harney County commissioner Mark Owens observed,

I go to a lot of meetings, and for a while now they've had a BLM rep at different meetings asking for input on things. Tara Wilson [Thissell], the BLM public affairs specialist, has showed up at every meeting since [the occupation], trying to be more open about how they're doing things. I'm just talking about what I've seen in Burns. [BLM district manager] Jeff Rose has been doing an excellent job trying to engage the community so we feel part of a team, so we're more willing to work together. I think it's genuine.[26]

Also, after the Malheur takeover, the BLM began posting weekly newspaper columns responding to topics that came up during the Bundy occupation, with the goal of ensuring that "these topics haven't been lost" or ignored by the BLM.[27] BLM district manager Jeff Rose observed, "We made a concerted effort to make sure people understand what the BLM is, who the employees are, and how proud we are to be not only managing our public lands but also how proud we are to be part of the community."[28]

The positive relations among the federal agencies and the local community went both ways. For most people in Harney County, the attitude about federal employees could hardly have been more different from the views of the Bundy family and their supporters, who used language to describe federal workers that appeared intentionally dehumanizing—for example, calling Bureau of Land Management employees "jack-booted thugs."[29] Harney County's community is too small and tight-knit for most who actually work with federal employees to fail to see federal workers as people—and even as friends. Harney County rancher Keith Baltzor observed, "At the local level we can work very well with [federal agencies], as long as long as you're honest and do the right things on your range, they're very good to deal with. The people at these agencies, they're our neighbors and our friends, and in some cases our family."[30]

In reflecting on the appreciation dinner that refuge permittees held for refuge employees after the end of the Malheur takeover, Baltzor also observed, "Why are they going to do anything to support and help us if we don't help and support them? It has to work both ways. Our idea [with the appreciation dinner] was to show them support, to say 'We've got your back.'"[31]

The experience of collaborative problem-solving in Harney County suggests that if a core objective of collaboration is to find win-win solutions that benefit all parties, there is no principle more essential than building positive relationships that break out of an old adversarial mind-set. When crouched into defensive posture, the human mind sees only two directions, attack and retreat. Alternatively, creative win-win possibilities become real possibilities if all parties agree that the outcomes have to be right for everyone. Such possibilities begin from the mind-set that all participants truly have each other's backs.

Mind-Set

To collaborate effectively it is necessary to be able to conceive of relationships among parties that are cooperative rather than adversarial. In the Bundy mind-set, the relationship among federal agencies and local communities is presumed "unconstitutional" and illegitimate. In the Bundy view, the only goal of federal agencies is to control local people and resources to serve distant political interests.

Had the Bundys come to Harney County a few decades earlier, they would have found more people who shared their way of thinking. In the 1970s and 1980s, new land use laws and changes in management personnel contributed to hostility between managers and local people. By the early 2000s, however, managers of federal agencies working with local people in Harney County intentionally set out to improve these relationships. They had to overcome a great deal of long-standing distrust between federal managers and local people. Mind-sets did not transform overnight. Harney County rancher Gary Miller described his changing views:

There was an acting refuge manager for a while. I was mad at him. Actually, I hated him. I said bad things about him. But I think actually, looking back, he did one of the biggest favors for me in life. We don't like change. He said to get our cattle out of the canal because we didn't have water rights. [The refuge] fenced off the rivers because they wanted to save the riverbanks. . . . So, we were upset that we couldn't use the free water, that it was going to cost us, because they made us drill wells and made us pipe the water up to a trough. . . . I drove down into the field and they're setting this water trough up, which we're piping water to from the well that we just drilled. That was in the very lowest place in the field. My son says, "Dad, once that water trough fills, do we leave it running? What happens to all the water? It's going to flood around there and in the winter it's going to be ice and cows aren't going to be able to get to the trough." He was six years old. And I saw it too—it wasn't going to work. So, I called the refuge . . . and [after Miller launched an angry tirade] they hauled in gravel, they built that area up, and they drained it, and it turned out that our cattle do better, there's more water, it's fresh water. I found that positive. If I had wanted to find the negatives, I could *still* be fighting. I could still hate that water trough just because they made us do it.[32]

Even after local agencies shifted to more cooperative approaches, not all Harney County resource users chose to accept or extend an olive branch. In Harney County, certainly the most high-profile holdouts were members of the Hammond family. At least since the mid-1980s the Hammonds had engaged in a campaign of confrontation with the Malheur Refuge. Dwight Hammond let his cows trespass, he cut fences, and refused to tell refuge managers when he would trail his cattle through the refuge. Longtime local ranchers recalled that Hammond demanded that the refuge should act like a "good neighbor," a position some local ranchers considered an unreasonable expectation, even if it *should* be reasonable. In the 1970s and 1980s, refuge managers were required by law to carry out their conservation role by conventional methods that included restrictions that many local people considered unreasonable. In 2010, however, when the Malheur Refuge began the collaborative process leading to the 2013 Malheur Comprehensive Conservation Plan, the refuge as well as the Oregon Consensus facilitation group specifically invited the Hammonds to participate. The Hammonds declined and never engaged.[33] It could have been a working relationship. The Hammonds chose instead to continue fighting.

When Ammon Bundy, who held a similar confrontational mind-set regarding federal agencies, came to Harney County, he conversed primarily with the Hammond family and appeared to assume that the Hammonds represented the broader mind-set of the community. As Bundy found when Harney County ranchers declined his invitation to repudiate their federal land contracts, by 2016 the old adversarial mind-set had become the exception rather than the rule in Harney County.

Mind-sets can change slowly in federal agencies as well. Former USFWS biologist Rick Roy recalled that when he and other Malheur Refuge staff asked regional managers to allow a more community-based approach, one manager resisted, insisting that "it's *our* (USFWS) refuge."[34] Earlier, when the Steens Act passed, the BLM was required by law to consult with the Steens Mountain Advisory Committee in the preparation and implementation of management plans.[35] Rancher Fred Otley, a key member of the group that created the Steens Act, recalled that at first the agency did not seem to know how to cooperate with the advisory group:

> One of the problems from my standpoint is how the agency handled the requirements of the Steens Act.... After the Steens Act passed, they basically wrote interim plans that were based on the preservation aspects of the act instead of using the whole body of the Steens Act. . . . They wrote all these interim plans that had no language or actions or anything from the Steens Act. They pulled us clear over here [in one direction], and it took us over five years before we could start saying, "You've got to put this language forward on special recreation permits, and programs and stuff." . . . They didn't know how to deal with the very creative, unique language in the Steens Act. They lost an opportunity to do things in a new, creative way of doing business. It was like they went back to their old handbooks and dug in deeper than they were before the Steens Act.[36]

Even members of groups that consciously aspire to be collaborative can struggle to adjust mind-sets. Gretchen Bates, project manager for the Harney County Community-Based Water Planning Group, observed that sitting down with someone you are accustomed to thinking of as an opponent takes courage and practice: "It was hard thinking, 'You mean Waterwatch [an environmental group] is going to be here? And they have a voice in what happens in Harney County?' At first that's really hard."[37]

Change of mind-set may require not only thinking differently about other people, but also thinking differently about the landscape. When asked why he cofounded the High Desert Partnership, rancher Gary Marshall explained that seeing the world from the perspective of a single landowner or manager fits poorly with a landscape where all things—water, vegetation, wildlife—are interconnected:

For me personally it never made a whole lot of sense that we look at these landscapes as fragmented. That ranch that I was on, I was looking at it from that regard. It was just across the fence from the refuge or just across the fence from neighbors that had a lot of the same soil, a lot of the same birds, the deer travel through—mine as well as theirs. We share the water that comes down. To just silo yourself and say, "I'm going to manage this for me and for this [purpose] right here," seemed like a pretty narrow way of looking at it. So, I was thinking along the lines that what affects a neighbor upstream affects me, and affects the refuge.

Really, in order to make this whole system work, we needed to get together and talk about the important things up and down this system. . . . I proposed to the refuge a long time ago that they had a certain set of resources and I had some resources: "Frankly the birds like my place better than they like yours." So, let's do what we can to [work with] that. If it means a different approach to water, then maybe more water needs to be put in this pond up here to allow these birds, these ducks, to fledge rather than sending the water over there just because the water right is over there on that dry forty acres where it's just going to evaporate. Then maybe we can enhance the whole wildlife [condition] up and down the system.[38]

Conservationist Bruce Taylor, one of Marshall's partners in the High Desert Partnership, observed a parallel change of mind-set among refuge staff:

If you're worried about carp, carp run up the Silvies River, they run up the Blitzen River, they run up Silver Creek. You need to address carp off the refuge as well. But also, just for the refuge's mission as a bird habitat, the private lands are really important. The birds don't know where the property boundaries are, sometimes those lands are even more important [for birds] than the refuge. The refuge staff understood, as most everybody else did, that we need to think about conservation on that system-wide level, not this side of the fence or that side of the fence.[39]

Refuge manager Chad Karges recalled how improved relationships with the community enabled managers to focus on this challenge of confronting the ecological destruction wrought by carp:

Everyone agreed that the number one issue was addressing aquatic health on the refuge, and one of the primary issues on that was common carp. In the past, as a refuge we did not even talk about carp because it's such a complex and large issue. It was way beyond the boundaries of the refuge. Because of failed [human] relationships in the past we couldn't work beyond the boundaries of the refuge. So, there was no way we were going to be able to deal with carp. All of our energy was focused on talking about grazing in the Blitzen Valley when really your number one issue is carp in Malheur Lake. But through the CCP process, those relationships improved so that we could talk about things outside the boundaries of the lake. So then aquatic health and carp in the lake became the number one issue in the CCP. So, we were finally able to focus on what should have been focused on for a long time.[40]

Karges and the Malheur Refuge were able to build those relationships in no small part because of the presence of local ranchers and refuge permittees like Gary Marshall and Dan Nichols and many others like them who recognized the interdependent and reciprocal benefits of collaborating with rather than battling the refuge. Collaboration—sitting at the table and finding commonsense, mutually beneficial solutions—was, in their view, simply a better way. Not all agreed—the Hammonds were known locally to oppose what they described as "collaborating with the enemy."[41] Most local land users, however, came to see that a mind-set of collaboration produced better outcomes—economic, social, ecological—than a mind-set of confrontation. Out of "failure" and some courageous, outside-the-box thinking, federal agencies in Harney County learned to be better neighbors. Most Harney County citizens will never turn away a neighbor.

Time

When asked what makes collaboration work, Karen Moon, a rancher and Coordinator of the Harney County Watershed Council, had a simple and emphatic answer: "Collaboration takes time. In short, that's it."[42] Similar views were expressed by almost everyone involved in collaborative groups in Harney County. The role of time in collaborative processes takes two forms: the years it takes to develop positive relationships between stakeholders, and the many hours out of people's busy days spent sitting at tables discussing in detail the necessary but sometimes tedious nuts-and-bolts of solving resource management problems.

Gary Marshall, the cofounder of the High Desert Partnership, described the importance of allowing enough time to develop relationships in advance of beginning the actual collaborative decision-making:

> When we started the High Desert Partnership [in 2005], we knew [the Malheur Comprehensive Conservation Plan process] was coming up. . . . The timing was perfect because we had enough years ahead of time to work our way through a lot of stuff and make a lot of different connections, build the relationships before we got into actually working on that plan. It allowed just the perfect amount of time [about five years before the actual planning process].
>
> The High Desert Partnership is unique. So many of these [collaborative] projects get started because there's some kind of emergency coming up. That doesn't allow the time to build relationships and create some trust. All of a sudden you're into solving the problem before you know one another or before you're able to work together and think about what you want the outcome to be. . . . That's what was so completely different about the High Desert Partnership. We didn't have that hanging over our heads, an urgent thing right at that time. . . . We were able to get a lot of feedback from other people who were going to be stakeholders in it, and heard their concerns about what outcome was important to them. . . .
>
> Once it gets to a certain point, it's really too late to do collaboration right because everybody already has their opinions made. "They're on the other side; I'm on this side." Then we're going to have a clash, I'm sure of it. Then it's too late.[43]

Chad Karges added that the time required for successful collaboration may not end with the completion of a management plan—those involved in creating plans need to remain involved to address the inevitable unexpected issues that arise in the implementation phase:

> At the end [of the CCP], everyone was in agreement that they wanted to continue to work together on it. . . . We recognized that if you do the plan and

then all your stakeholders disperse, no matter how good your plan is, you've got to make adjustments to it as you go through time, and the stakeholders aren't part of that adjustment so they come back and say, "Hey, this isn't what we agreed to." And then you're right back in the same cycle of appeals and litigation while you're trying to implement the plan. . . . That group is still in place. I can't even remember how many years we've been together now, quite a while. We still don't have all the answers we would like, but we're still all working, moving forward together.[44]

Beyond even the creation and implementation of collaborative management plans, some participants in collaborative processes in Harney County think in even longer time frames—spans of decades and even generations needed to develop and sustain a "culture" of collaborative conservation. Bob Sallinger, conservation director of the Audubon Society of Portland, described his group's long-term commitment to collaborative conservation in the community that is the custodian of his group's signature conservation effort, the Malheur National Wildlife Refuge:

We have always had a focus on the culture of conservation. . . . Ultimately, we want to be sustainable. We want to change people's hearts and minds about [conservation] and invest them in it, because that's what's going to make it sustainable. We know that the policy work is ephemeral. It comes and it goes, and changes in administration can wipe out a whole lot, and so how do you build something that's truly sustainable? Malheur [Refuge] is not a two-year or five-year project. To get where we need to go takes decades of work. It's got to be able to withstand all kinds of stuff.[45]

This view of a long-term culture of collaborative conservation is not merely wishful thinking: newer collaborative processes are already benefiting from the decades of investment in collaborative projects in Harney County. Gretchen Bates, the project manager of the Community-Based Water Planning Group that began in 2016, observes that her project probably could not work without a local history of collaboration:

If we hadn't done it for so long, you couldn't come here and do this if there hadn't been a bunch of collaborative work already. I think that's really the takeaway. It takes time. The [new water planning collaborative] is a huge,

huge thing. . . . Everybody needs water. . . . It's rather ambitious, but if anybody can do it, Harney County can.[46]

As the BLM district manager Jeff Rose observes, while the long-term investments of time in collaborative processes may appear daunting, the status quo is not only likely to produce less-satisfactory outcomes, it is also possible that status quo approaches will absorb *more* time than collaborative process in the long run, since the status quo is more likely to produce time-consuming (and costly) litigation:

> Collaboration started happening here thirty years ago. I started working in Harney County in 1988, almost thirty years ago. . . . That's when you start collaboration. That's what got me to this point, to be able to do things and have those relationships and bring that into the [collaborative] group. [Collaboration] is hard. It's extremely hard. It takes a lot of time. It takes a commitment. But it pays off in the end. You invest the time in the front end, and on the back end when you're making decisions, you're not being challenged by anybody about your decision.[47]

To someone who observed meetings in which the Bundy occupiers spoke of solving Harney County's problems in a few months or years but almost never dug into the specifics of land use management, the contrast was striking. Bundy's revolutionary approach promised quick solutions, rousing speeches, and nonstop drama. The collaborative approach offered no quick fixes, just people meeting and talking, often at length over minutiae, for long hours. Only one of these approaches, however, had a proven track record of tangible positive results for Harney County.

Listening

The long hours involved in collaboration consist, however, not only of talking, but also of listening in equal measure. Listening is at the core of collaboratives in Harney County. It is not a simple or passive kind of listening. Many conventional forms of land use management also involve some form of public input—for example, the US Forest Service or Bureau of Land Management may take public comments at the end of a review process under the National Environmental Protection Act. Unlike these conventional exercises in public input, the basis of success in Harney County's homegrown collaborations is to actively engage the voices of all interested parties from the beginning, and in a way that every single person involved knows that their views are genuinely taken into account. Whether or not their views prevail, participants leave with the knowledge that their views have not merely been put in a file but have actually been listened to and considered.

This kind of deep listening has become the standard in Harney County collaboratives, but it is a relatively new practice in land use management—born perhaps of deep frustration from an earlier time when listening often barely occurred at all. Rancher Pauline Braymen recalls,

> This [collaboration] is what ranchers wanted to do in the first place. The frustration of the local community and the ranching community was that we know things that will work, but you won't let us share in implementing the things that will work. The ranchers were shut out, they really were. Some of the older people that are gone now, like Marcus Haines, had lived here all his life and he was an educated man, interested in history, and lived right by the refuge where the Dunbars live now. He so much wanted to share what he knew, but he was shut out. He was made fun of, he was invited to meetings and literally put on the hot seat and insulted. It was bad. How we went full cycle to what's happening now, it's just tremendous.[48]

Rancher Gary Marshall observed that Harney County's collaboratives addressed the very real desire among local citizens to have their voices heard, making Ammon Bundy's claim that only revolution would give "the people" a voice ring hollow:

> [Collaboration] allows people to feel like they have a voice in what's going on. How much did we hear that during the Bundy thing? "My voice, your voice." People said they were frustrated with the government because they never were listened to. They didn't feel like they had any kind of voice. That's one thing that the High Desert Partnership does. That process allows and encourages people's voices to be heard. It almost enforces it.[49]

Jack Southworth is a rancher in Seneca, Oregon (Grant County), and since 2008 has been a facilitator for one of the main initiatives sponsored by the High Desert Partnership—the Harney County Restoration Collaborative (HCRC), which addresses forest health in the Malheur National Forest. Southworth offered important insights about how the process of truly listening to all points of view psychologically enables individuals to, in turn, truly listen to and even empathize with the views of others, which opens new ways of thinking and problem-solving:

> The HCRC gives them a chance to have input on how the forests are managed. We have pretty good examples that the Forest Service has been listening. . . . We're evolving [our management practices] and that comes from learning and that comes from working together as a group and respecting each other's opinions. And since we respect each other's opinions, we don't feel threatened by them and our own opinions can evolve. That's been the critical thing that has occurred in HCRC is this gradual evolution of opinions. . . .
>
> Once they're part of the group and listened to, they say, "Okay, I get it now." Whether it's a road closure, or not cutting a twenty-one-inch tree, "Okay, I can see it in this situation." And when they can see it in that situation, that gives an opportunity for people on the opposite side to give a little, too. I think it's been a very successful process. . . .
>
> We are very definitely giving direction, or suggesting things, to the Forest Service—we can't give directions, we can only suggest—that are being listened to and followed. So, what is more local than that? Perhaps with collaboration we already have that local control [that Bundy supporters wanted]. Maybe it's the non-radical takeover that we've been looking for. Being allowed to speak and feeling that your opinion is as important as anyone else's in the room, that's got to be good for your emotional reserves. "If I go to this meeting, they're going to listen to me."
>
> And that enables us to listen and not feel threatened. "Okay, that person I disagree with, but I'll try to see their perspective." Those emotional reserves, that trust, that's a big thing. I think that's what the Bundys didn't realize was in Harney County. These people have trust in the federal employees, the federal agencies, and [the Bundys] coming in and saying things ought to be different—people weren't ready to abandon all that trust that they had built up over the last decade.[50]

These observations may provide insight into the seemingly perplexing motivations of those from outside Harney County who joined the Bundy occupation as well as some local people who sympathized. Most did not have livelihoods that were directly affected by federal resource agency decisions. Only one of the Bundy occupiers—LaVoy Finicum—was (arguably) a rancher.[51] Ammon Bundy spoke in vague terms about "BLM tyranny," but apart from his father's choice to confront the BLM in Nevada, he provided almost no specific examples. He did not need to: the occupiers at the refuge were plumbers and welders and fast-food restaurant workers—almost everything except ranchers. The Malheur takeover was not about ranching. Journalist Hal Herring, a leading writer on rural militancy in the American West who spent time at the refuge during the occupation, observed, "I could not find anyone who actually knew what it was they were opposing." The Malheur occupiers were mostly marginalized people looking for a larger meaning to their lives, they "weren't looking for answers." Rather, the occupation provided a huge megaphone, and "it was empowering for people who felt they were finally being listened to."[52]

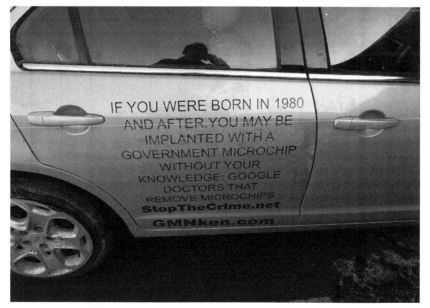

A vehicle with Michigan license plates that often appeared at the occupied Malheur Refuge illustrated the fringe mind-set of some of the people attracted by the occupation.

Ammon Bundy was able to evoke real emotions with what often appeared to be little more than fuzzy buzzwords, such as "government overreach." The words Bundy chose—freedom, tyranny, overreach—evoked real emotions because they described a government his followers believed no longer cared about or listened to people like them. To the extent that Bundy and Harney County ranchers had any shared understanding of the meaning of a word like "overreach," it mainly appeared to mean under-listening. Bundy seemed unaware that Harney County collaboratives were decades ahead of him in providing real platforms for local voices.

Flexibility

When Jack Southworth speaks of collaboratives boosting the "emotional reserves" of participants, the outcome can be not only to reduce the frustration of feeling unheard, but also to enable more flexible thinking and innovative solutions. HDP board member and CCP participant Bruce Taylor described this dynamic:

> Collaborative processes work best when it's not obvious to anyone what the best outcome is. For problems like, "Boy, this is a big problem, I don't know what we're supposed to do about it," that's when it really works. . . .
>
> [For example, US] Fish and Wildlife had made a decision that they weren't going to address [common] carp in Malheur Lake because it wasn't fixable. Why would you waste a lot of time working on something you can't fix? Then you fail and look bad and all that. But [carp] really is the big issue for the refuge. So, it was really useful having all the stakeholders there, and the biologists from other places and agencies saying, "You can't ignore this [carp]— that is the issue." So, we have common ground, and that's probably why this process [CCP] worked well, because it became clear to most everybody early on that the issue that people wanted to fight about—cows—wasn't the issue.

In addition, Taylor suggested that people involved in a collaborative project—where all parties share both successes and failures—are more likely to explore new approaches that involve some risk of failing but may also lead to far better outcomes:

Nobody gets promoted in a federal agency for failing, or admitting failure. It's not a recipe for success normally.... You need to be able to admit failure, say "Yep, it seemed like a good idea at the time, and now we know better." That's a really unique feature of the way the [Malheur CCP] plan came out. ... Chad [Karges] fought to have this collaborative process at great cost to his standing professionally within the [US] Fish and Wildlife Service. It's a little less so now, but back then the approach was all command-and-control, top-down.[53]

Steering a different course, however, also requires leaders—in government and the community—willing to go off the beaten path. Rancher Gary Marshall, who blazed new trails himself, observes,

This Harney County style of collaboration takes an issue, and it helps a little if there's some urgency, . . . and it takes a leader. Someone who's going to really be at the point of a spear, but gets the whole concept in the first place. Someone who understands how important it is to [solve the problem] collaboratively. And it takes the right core group in that community that have mutual trust and respect, and it can work. You can't just pick up this model and move it somewhere else. If you're missing that person who's really passionate about making it work, you can't do it with a committee or people who are fairly lukewarm about it, or if you're missing those other core stakeholders who really want to stay with it.[54]

Although federal agencies may be slow to adapt, proven positive outcomes such as the Malheur CCP may create a virtuous cycle, making institutions and individuals more willing to go off the beaten path to pursue collaborative approaches. Rick Roy, refuge biologist at the time, recalls that when refuge manager Chad Karges made the choice to pursue a collaborative approach to the upcoming CCP, he did so at extreme risk to his career in the US Fish and Wildlife Service.[55] In 2016, however, Karges was awarded the Theodore Roosevelt Lifetime Achievement Award by the National Wildlife Refuge Association and was honored by the US Secretary of the Interior and the director of US Fish and Wildlife. The Bundy occupation helped bring recognition to the success of the collaborative approach that Karges helped lead:

When the community showed their support for the refuge during the occupation, it was evident that Mr. Karges and his staff have been tireless in their pursuit and development of community partnerships and engagement in refuge activities for many years—when militants took out a fence between ranch land and refuge land during the illegal occupation, the rancher put the fence back up.[56]

Flexibility is not only a key principle in seeking solutions, it can also be an indispensable tool in collaborative processes themselves. Robin Harkless, a professional facilitator from Portland State University's Oregon Consensus program who facilitates both the High Desert Partnership's Youth Changing the Community initiative and the Harney County Watershed Council's Community-Based Water Planning Group, observed that the methods of each collaboration are tailored for the individual group, the topic, and the region.[57] In collaborative resource planning, an important conceptual tool is the idea of adaptive management—learning by doing, and making necessary course corrections. Collaborative processes succeed when they, too, constantly monitor the outcomes (the mood, the concerns, the level of trust) among their participants and make necessary adjustments.

During the Malheur takeover, there was a poster at the main entrance to the occupied refuge headquarters that read, "Tyranny is cruel, unreasonable, arbitrary use of power or control." The occupiers appeared to have no awareness that the refuge headquarters they forcibly seized had hosted countless stakeholder meetings over many years to achieve one of Harney County's landmark collaboratives—the Malheur Comprehensive Conservation Plan—which had invited all stakeholders to work together to build relationships, to remain flexible and open-minded, and, above all, to listen. After the change of management approach that the refuge adopted in the mid-2000s, it would be difficult to defend the argument that the refuge symbolized "cruel, unreasonable, arbitrary" government. A more fitting poster might have read, "Democracy: at its best."

Hammer

Change is not easy and typically it does not happen without a push. In most of Harney County's many successful collaboratives, there was a degree of urgency, a deadline, or a specific event that motivated agencies, conservationists, and citizens to act. Harney County rancher Stacy Davies recalled a dramatic event in 1999 that spurred him and other Steens Mountain landowners to create the Steens Act:

> When the [Oregon] governor and [Interior] secretary were here we went up to Big Indian Gorge [Steens Mountain] to take photos. What always happens in these situations is the secretary gets a picture of the local and then it comes out in the press and it says there's a local supporting what the secretary wants. So, we got up there for the photo op, and the governor and secretary were standing with their backs to a cliff that's a couple thousand feet straight down. It's a neat place to take photos, a little dangerous actually. I stayed way back because I knew I was going to get set up if I got in front of a camera. . . . So the secretary said, "Davies, get up here!" I said, "I don't want to ruin my reputation—I don't want a picture taken with you." Everybody just cracked up. . . . [After insisting that the reporters not report that Davies supported a national monument] I walked up and the secretary said, "Don't you push me." I said, "You don't know how bad I want to." We smiled and shook hands and got our picture taken. . . . [The reporters] got it right. That was the beginning of the process. It was kind of a love-hate relationship. . . . [The Clinton administration] had the hammer, and they knew it.[58]

Knowing that Secretary of the Interior Bruce Babbitt would recommend to President Bill Clinton the Steens Mountain should be declared a national monument unless there was a viable alternative, ranchers chose to work with their erstwhile nemesis, the Oregon Natural Desert Association, to create a legislative alternative that would leave all parties— not least the ecology of the mountain—better off. Through extraordinary local efforts by all parties, a cooperative solution was found and written into law. Almost two decades later, Gretchen Bates, the project manager of the Harney County Watershed Council's Community-Based Water Planning Group, observed a similar dynamic: "With the water issue, we're trying to avoid the state coming in and further regulating without taking into consideration what people here want. If we come up with a plan and some scenarios, we believe that will have some impact on what the state does."[59]

As rancher Gary Marshall noted, there are cases when it is "too late," and there is simply not enough time to establish necessary relationships of trust and cooperation. Although difficult to measure, there may often be a "Goldilocks" window of opportunity when there is a "hammer" over the heads of participants, but still enough time to establish an effective collaborative process.

Resistance

After decades of investing in building collaborative problem-solving methods, Harney County—a poster child of collaboration—was arguably one of the worst possible locations for Ammon Bundy to launch an anti-federal-government revolution. In Harney County, bringing different stakeholders to the table and looking for win-win solutions (or at least mutually acceptable ones) had become the default model of problem-solving, one with proven results. This history of collaborative efforts in Harney County provided a model of problem-solving that works, if not always perfectly. It proved to be a path most local people chose over the Bundy revolution, with its unknowable outcomes. The Bundys were unable to persuade even their strongest sympathizers to abandon the existing social order, which in Harney County is largely defined by collaboration.

In some cases, members of the community actively advocated for resistance against the changes that Ammon Bundy advocated—for example, in locally made posters that encouraged Harney County citizens to use their voice: "No to the Bundy Caliphate in Harney County—Take Your Hate Somewhere Else!" In the one and only time that a cross section of the community met Ammon Bundy face-to-face (at the Burns High School gym on January 19, 2016), the majority stood and chanted directly at him, "Go home! Go home!" Perhaps an even more powerful form of resistance, however, could be seen simply in the quiet refusal of the great majority of the community to give up the way of doing things that they had intentionally cultivated for decades.

In science, resistance to change is considered part of the broader concept of resilience, defined as the capacity to absorb a disturbance and return to a condition that maintains the fundamental qualities of the system before the disturbance occurred. In Harney County during the Bundy occupation, that exact word was used by members of the community— for example, on a homemade placard nailed to a telephone pole declaring, "Harney County is resilient"—a defiant declaration that, after the Bundys left, Harney County would still be Harney County. Some of the leaders in Harney County's collaborative problem-solving model would argue that it was collaboration that, in no small part, helped give Harney County its resilience.

5

Resilience

On the night of January 26, 2016, the moon was just past full and its light reflected pale blue on the snow along Highway 26 entering the town of John Day (population 1,707), in Grant County, Oregon. Owls flew like silent-winged ghosts in the frozen air. From above, one would see beams of foggy yellow light as cars and pickups converged at the John Day Senior Center. Ammon Bundy and his followers were coming up from the occupied Malheur Refuge and scheduled to speak. Inside, the warm and brightly lit meeting hall was filled to capacity with about two hundred Bundy supporters, as well as several dozen Bundy opponents holding protest signs. As the starting time of 6:00 p.m. came and went without the arrival of the celebrity militia guests, anxiety, murmurs, and gossip swirled around the room. Then, the event's organizer, Tad Houpt of nearby Canyon City, held a microphone and announced, "I have really bad news, our guest speakers aren't going to be here tonight. It seems that there was an altercation between here and Burns." Odalis Sharp, the mother of the Sharp Family Singers who supported Cliven Bundy at the Bunkerville, Nevada, standoff in 2014 and Ammon Bundy at Malheur in 2016, took the microphone and six of her ten children, some crying, sang Christian songs. An alarmed cacophony of voices nearly drowned out the crying, gospel-singing children. Nearly everyone tapped furiously at smartphones trying to get information about the "altercation."

Highway 395, the seventy-mile stretch of winding mountain road between John Day and Burns, was icy and nearly pitch black in the tall pines of the Malheur National Forest that night. At the normally sleepy mountain town of Seneca, however, the highway abruptly came ablaze in red and blue lights of law enforcement and emergency vehicles. Men with tactical vests, military-style rifles, and powerful flashlights that cut through the freezing fog stopped all approaching vehicles and ordered them back to John Day. Forty-five miles south, where Highway 395 joins Highway 20 near Burns, another set of lights, barricades, and armed men blocked vehicles going north. The tiny Burns Municipal Airport that served as the base of FBI operations during the Bundy occupation was illuminated with giant, blinding floodlights, like a brightly lit spaceship in the black, frozen desert. In John Day, as word spread that Ammon Bundy's group had been arrested and one person was shot and killed, speculation grew that law enforcement would attempt to block angry militia groups from moving out of Grant County into Burns.

Speculation about spreading militia activity was not misplaced. At the John Day Senior Center that night, angry Bundy supporters declared the arrests and shooting would be not the end but the beginning of a revolution. On social media, Gary Hunt (a Bundy supporter who openly supported the bombing of the Murrah Federal Building and killing of 168 people—including 19 children—by Timothy McVeigh in 1995[1]) activated "Operation Mutual Defense," declaring that "patriots" have "an obligation to proceed to the Harney County Resource Center [the Malheur Refuge] immediately, in order to protect the patriots still there."[2] In Burns that night, however, reports emerged on social media that the remaining occupiers at the Malheur National Wildlife Refuge were scattering into the night, and it was anyone's guess where they might go or what they might do. At the Silver Spur Motel in Burns, where I stayed that night (after driving 228 extra miles to circumvent FBI roadblocks) and where many militia stayed, there was no visible activity. The town appeared frigid, motionless, silent. Burns residents later reported waiting that night with doors locked and guns ready. On one matter, there was little disagreement: although all but four occupiers left the refuge within hours, everyone knew this was not the end—for Harney County, or the nation.

Lingering

To the outside world, the Bundy occupation began with an armed takeover on January 2, 2016, and ended with the arrests of Ammon Bundy and other occupation leaders twenty-four days later (and the arrests of four "hold-outs" at the refuge sixteen days after that). For residents of Harney County, the beginning was November 2015—and there was never a clear end. Whereas most in the Harney County community wished deeply to put the occupation behind them, outside militia as well as some locals who felt empowered by the Bundy occupation were not willing to let their movement simply stop. Taking new forms, militia activities in Harney County remained an ongoing reminder of the Bundy occupation, and a source of continuing aggravation and tension in the community.

A new phase of militia activity began almost immediately after the arrests of Ammon Bundy and the main occupation leaders. Antigovernment internet personalities such as Gavin Seim posted online videos declaring that, with the arrests of the Bundy brothers in Harney County, the nation stood "at the brink of revolution."[3] Militia leaders called on "patriots" to protest the shooting death of LaVoy Finicum. In response, on the evening of January 30, 2016, dozens of vehicles, including elevated pickup trucks bearing American flags and "Don't Tread on Me" flags, slow-rolled through downtown Burns, honking horns and shouting.[4] For several hours Burns resembled small towns in Syria or Iraq overtaken by antigovernment militia in similar vehicles.

For three months, the community endured an invasion of their community and their daily lives by militia groups, followed by media and outside law enforcement. After the arrests of the main occupation leaders and the scattering of the lower-level occupiers, finally there was hope life might return to normal. To many in the community, the choice by militia groups to command the streets of Burns yet again—even more aggressively— felt like a painful final straw. Several residents stood at the roadside in the dark and freezing weather shouting at the militia to go home. One made obscene gestures at the passing militia vehicles.[5] The defiance was notable because residents knew the militia were armed and angry, and no one knew their intentions. Local defiance intensified two days later when hundreds of local people stood on the steps of the Harney County Courthouse to block a militia protest (chapter 1)—clearly surprising the outside militia.

What no one knew at the time was that the end of the Malheur take-over would become the beginning of years of efforts by outside militia, with support from a small minority of locals, to keep their anti-federal-government agenda alive in Harney County, which became symbolic of their movement and a rallying cry for anti-federal-government militia. National and local militia used every opportunity to leverage Harney County's new-found fame into further political gains.

In this next stage of occupation, LaVoy Finicum became an even more important figure in death than in life. In the "patriot" community, Finicum was elevated to the status of a hero and martyr. Much of the militia activity in Harney County after the Bundy occupation centered around Finicum's death. The location where Finicum was shot by Oregon State troopers on Highway 395 became a makeshift shrine. The site was decorated with American flags, flowers, a cross, an engraved rock with Finicum's ranch

Militia supporters created a makeshift memorial to LaVoy Finicum where he died on Highway 395 north of Burns (February 6, 2016).

As late as summer 2016, supporters camped near the site where LaVoy Finicum was shot, guarding a makeshift shrine.

brand, a blue tarp,[6] and red paint to emulate Finicum's blood. The site was repeatedly vandalized, purportedly by angry locals. The US Forest Service and the Harney County sheriff attempted to minimize traffic congestion and accumulations of objects at the roadside, creating ongoing tension for much of 2016. Several individuals camped in a US Forest Service campsite nearby, vowing to guard the site and hinting that any federal worker who disrupted the memorial might be killed to avenge Finicum's death.[7] Nineteen miles from Burns, the site became a focus of militia activity and an ongoing source of stress for the nearby community through much of 2016, and even at certain times much later.

The celebrity Harney County gained as the site of one of the most dramatic anti-federal-government protests in American history also attracted an array of anti-federal speakers from across the nation. Only one day after the arrests of the final four "holdouts" at the Malheur National Wildlife Refuge, "constitutional" sheriff Richard Mack spoke at the Harney County Fairgrounds Memorial Building, where Ammon Bundy had made his first public appearance in the community two months earlier. At the meeting, Mack stated that he told Ammon Bundy he opposed the Bundy

The day after the final four militia members surrendered at the Malheur Refuge, "constitutional" sheriff Richard Mack spoke in Burns on his views of the Constitution (February 12, 2016).

occupation, but he strongly endorsed Bundy's view that county sheriffs have a right and duty to intervene against allegedly unconstitutional federal actions. The homepage of Mack's Constitutional Sheriffs and Peace Officers Association featured images of Harney County ranchers Dwight and Steven Hammond as symbols of alleged federal abuse.[8] Other speakers who visited Harney County included anti-federal-government legal activist KrisAnne Hall[9] and her associates, and property rights advocate Angus McIntosh.[10]

The internet war, including overt threats of violence, that began during the Bundy occupation also dragged on. Entire web pages were devoted to either supporting or mocking the Bundys and their militia supporters. Some internet activity took an even darker tone. A year after the takeover of the Malheur National Wildlife Refuge, for example, Sheriff Dave Ward observed that he still received hateful and threatening emails.[11] Ward described one email sent to him on October 29, 2016, apparently celebrating the acquittals of Ammon Bundy, Ryan Bundy, and other occupation leaders by an Oregon jury in Portland two days earlier:

> You piece of trash. You put peoples' lives at stake. One man dead. Others in jail for crimes they didn't commit. Take this you son of a bitch: not guilty. In your face. Swallow that you cock sucker. I hope somebody comes and does the same thing they did to LaVoy Finicum. You piece of trash. You're not a man. You should be tried and hung for treason.[12]

Ward observed, "I still get this stuff rolling in, though not on the same level.... There was a point when I was getting hundreds of emails in a day. Most of them would be rhetoric like this." Not all internet threats remain confined to the internet, and when asked a year after the takeover of the Malheur National Wildlife Refuge if he still feared for his life, Ward said he did:

> I think about it quite a bit. In the case of the Bundys, that's actually already happened once. [Jerad and Amanda Miller] walked into a pizza restaurant and shot two police officers having lunch.[13] [The Millers] had been at the Bundy Ranch [standoff].... It's the same type of people who get drawn into these [events]. When I met with Ammon Bundy on January 7 last year, ... I told him that to his face. I said, "I'm not saying you're going to do these things, but it only takes one unstable person and you know that." He acknowledged

At the occupied Malheur Refuge, sovereign-citizen "judge" Joaquin Mariano DeMoreta-Folch promised "common-law grand jury" trials for opponents.

it, it only takes one unstable person, . . . someone who thinks they're doing God's work by taking a cop's kid or shooting up our community. These people put out this distorted message and we still get, well, wacko phone calls from these people.[14]

Other lingering militia tactics took the form of "paper" harassment. As late as summer 2017, outside Bundy supporters continued to use legal tactics to keep the anti-federal-government flame alive in Harney County. In June 2017, self-described "God Grace Administrator" Joaquin Mariano

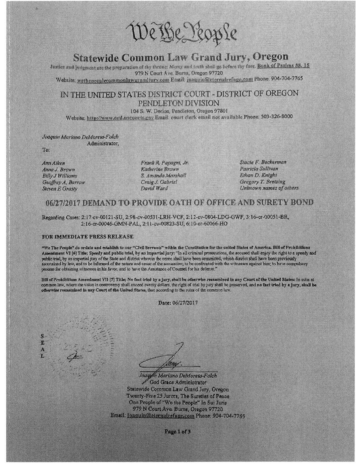

A year and a half after the end of the Malheur takeover, sovereign-citizen "judge" Joaquin Mariano DeMoreta-Folch demanded proof of "oath of office and surety bond" from the Harney County government.

DeMoreta-Folch (a Tea Party activist and self-appointed "judge" from Florida[15]) representing the "Statewide Common Law Grand Jury, Oregon,"[16] submitted papers to the Harney County Court (using an address matching the Hammonds' home in Burns) demanding proof of oath of office and surety bond for county, state, and federal officials who had opposed Bundy.

On September 26, 2016, acquitted Malheur Refuge occupier Shawna Cox filed suit in the Harney County circuit court "to show the people of Harney County how Federal Government is involved in taking their lands and opportunities from them," and to "assist the people of Harney County to recover lands involved in the Malheur that has wrongfully been taken from them."[17] The Harney County circuit court remanded the case to the US district court. On July 24, 2017, the US district court dismissed the case on the basis that Cox failed to meet legal standards including proving a personal interest in the case and filing the complaint in a timely manner from the time that the alleged "takings" occurred, and on the basis that Cox had not presented any "cognizable legal theory or argument."[18] In both the Harney County case and the federal case, Cox listed as her address the Burns residence of Harney County Committee of Safety member Chris Briels. While these cases were exasperating for the courts, to the local community they served as disquieting reminders that some of the acquitted Malheur occupiers would not let go of their seeming fixation on Harney County.

By mid-2016, however, the overall number of groups and individuals interested in associating with the occupation of Harney County had dwindled, although activity continued in neighboring counties: a major event honoring LaVoy Finicum took place in neighboring Grant County on January 28, 2017, and acquitted Malheur occupier Shawna Cox spoke in nearby Baker County on September 23, 2017. Cox, a resident of Utah, called her talk "What Really Happened in Harney County." For the majority in Harney County who had opposed the Bundy occupation, each such event was at a minimum aggravating, and for some it kept alive old anxieties about militia activity in the area.

While fully acknowledging the right in a democratic society for people of all views to participate in the electoral process, many came to see the elections of 2016 as referendums on the Bundy ideology, and for many the presence of candidates associated with Bundy and the Committee of Safety

A year after the end of the Malheur takeover, approximately five hundred supporters attended a rally and memorial for LaVoy Finicum in neighboring Grant County (January 28, 2017).

(almost all of whom lost[19]), prolonged a sense of community tension. At the 2016 Harney County Fair, Committee of Safety members operated a "constitutional" booth that sold anti-federal books and gave away copies of the very same "pocket Constitutions" that the Bundy occupiers carried—injecting an unfamiliar level of politics into the fair. The Committee of Safety also sponsored a float in the 2016 fair parade, as well as a pro-Hammonds vehicle in 2017. When the 2016 Committee of Safety float passed by, applause softened and some residents turned their backs. Privately, some exasperated citizens bitterly spoke of the Committee of Safety as the "Committee of Sedition and Treason." It was not the Harney County most people knew.

The sense that the community was not what it was before the Bundy occupation persisted through much of 2016 and 2017, and there was worry about whether the community could ever be brought fully back together. Gretchen Bates, chair of the Harney County Republican Party, is both

In fall 2016, a challenger for Harney County sheriff campaigned with a rider-less horse representing LaVoy Finicum.

a facilitator for a local water collaborative and a friend of some of the Committee of Safety members, and attended some of their meetings. Bates described the sense of division that built up, and blamed much of it on social media:

> Being reasonable takes too much thinking. It takes a lot more energy to think, "Hmm, do I see any value in what you say?" Or am I going to sit here and spout all these things that I've always been spouting. . . . It's an echo chamber. You're listening to the same opinions, and your opinions are being reinforced. That's comfortable, that's nice. . . . People say horrible things to each other on some Facebook groups, but that's because those ideas are reinforced in some other Facebook group. I don't do social media at all, so I was really shocked when I saw printouts from somebody about what someone's neighbor was saying. That's not Harney County. . . . People here are nice. Until this happened. . . . People got pushed to extremes.[20]

Bates, like many others in the community, suggested that the hardening of opinions occurred in part because support for the Bundys became a kind of proxy for general frustrations with the federal government, and also with commitment to "stand" with the Hammond family (who still had widespread local support)—even though in hindsight it seemed clear the Bundys were more interested in their own political agenda than in Harney County's land use issues or the well-being of the Hammonds:

> All these things became intertwined. Some people couldn't separate what [the Bundys] were doing from the underlying issues of land use and what they saw as federal overreach. In retrospect, people now should be able to say, "It's separate." You can see that [the Bundys] came here with an agenda. They knew all along that this [some kind of dramatic face-off with the government] was something they wanted to do, and they were using the Hammonds as a pretext.[21]

Brenda Smith, executive director of the High Desert Partnership collaborative, agreed:

> I think what has tangled this up is the Bundys using the Hammonds as a platform. It's the personal piece with the Hammonds. People would have been much more united if the Hammond piece wasn't tangled up in that. I mean, they [the Bundys] knew strategically that's how they had to go about it.[22]

By late 2017, however, local support for the Bundy ideology, as embodied in the Committee of Safety, had faded, with the committee's public profile and activities significantly lowered. To the extent that the Committee of Safety remained active, it appeared the Hammonds—rather than bigger land use or constitutional issues—remained the primary motivating force.[23] Some in the community believed the lingering tension would not be resolved until Dwight and Steven Hammond came home from prison, though some also worried about possible renewed militia activity when the Hammonds returned.

Reweaving

Despite lingering tension and uncertainty, Harney County displayed determination to reweave its torn social fabric. This capacity was displayed through special efforts in direct response to the disturbances that had occurred, and also through the numerous ordinary social activities that characterize Harney County's community.

No other social event is more important in Harney County than the annual Harney County Fair. One of the most anticipated events each year is the Harney County Ranch Rodeo. Although the fair attracts performers from far and wide, the Ranch Rodeo is limited to locals. Contestants compete in bronc riding, cow milking, steer riding, and junior, intermediate, and senior barrel races. Winners are awarded western belt buckles, but all participants win cheers and applause for their successes or their efforts because they are members of the community. So it was on September 8, 2017—much as it had been since the fair began in 1900.[24] The grandstands were filled almost entirely with local families. Echoes of the events of late 2015 and early 2016 were not absent (a few wore "Free the Hammonds" t-shirts organized in a social media campaign to "Flood the Fair" with support for the Hammond family[25]); but any divisions seemed eclipsed by the community spirit of the event. Members of the Committee of Safety sat with others who stood against the Bundys. *Everyone* cheered for all of the local cowboys and cowgirls.

At the fair that same day, the Harney County Fairgrounds Memorial Building, where so many of the seminal events of the Bundy occupation had occurred (including Ammon Bundy's meeting on December 15, 2015, to create the Harney County Committee of Safety as well as Sheriff Ward's community meeting in which a straw vote on January 6, 2016, first showed overwhelming local opposition to the refuge takeover) was entirely occupied by the works of local artists: paintings, photographs, and truly extraordinary, individually handcrafted quilts. Some artworks were adorned with ribbons and awards, and each one bore the name of the artist: some who opposed the Bundy occupation, and others who supported it. However, those differences would have been completely invisible to anyone who had not intimately studied the local social dynamics of that time. To anyone else, the room was simply full of art for the love of art—much of which would impress any art lover anywhere, urban or rural.

In these and many other ways, the 2017 Harney County Fair was more like fairs of previous times than the 2016 Harney County Fair had been. In 2016, the Committee of Safety sponsored a "constitutional" booth that became a magnet for reporters from across the nation; there were campaign booths for the reelection of Harney County sheriff Dave Ward, and for his opponent, who some considered to be allied with the local "militia"; and the booth for the Harney County Democrats (who surprise outsiders by their existence) was vandalized, with suspicions aimed at local Bundy supporters. Such events were unique in the history of the fair. The year 2017 was perhaps more auspicious if for no other reason than that there were no major local or national elections to split the community. The mood of the fair was more relaxed. At the 2017 fair, the new Harney County judge, Pete Runnels, volunteered as a cook at the Lions Club food concession. In the fair parade the next day, the county commissioners walked behind horses carrying scoopers and brooms to clean up what many believe both horses and politicians produce in abundance—intentional self-mocking that produced good-natured laughter. The feel of a more unified community, if not entirely what it had once been, was palpable.

The laughter and opportunity for all members of the community to support each other with politics at a distance was needed. Almost two years after the events of late 2015 and early 2016, many spoke of being sick of talking about it and wanting only to move on. One exasperated resident was overheard expressing a widely felt emotion: "I just want to pretend it never happened."[26] Some spoke half-jokingly of refusing to use the "B word."

The often-stated and genuine desire to put the Bundy events behind, however, indirectly revealed the considerable extent to which memories of that difficult time remained fresh, and raw. In private settings, the Bundy occupation remained a topic of often intense discussion, combined with feelings of disgust and exhaustion—especially as news from the multiple criminal trials of the Bundys and their supporters in Nevada as well as Oregon dragged on more than two years, constantly refreshing difficult memories.

In a community that prides itself for cohesiveness, there was a diminished sense of trust, and a sense of wariness. Relations between neighbors, coworkers, longtime friends, church congregations, and even family members were strained by memories of individuals who had taken the opposite side during the occupation. These feelings of wariness and strained bonds created a sense of loss and worry that the community would never return to what it had been.

Bundy militia supporters outside the federal court building in Portland, Oregon (February 28, 2017).

In September 2017, almost two years after the occupation of Harney County had begun, Harney County judge Pete Runnels (who took office in January 2017) described the effects of the occupation on the community:

> People are a little more suspecting than they used to be. Everybody used to be very easygoing and trusting. That trust level has come down. Whether it's your neighbor, or someone you walk by in a store, there's more keenness, awareness. That's one of the biggest changes. It broke some bonds. But time is healing those. The night of the [Finicum] shooting was probably the darkest, gloomiest night ever. Nobody knew what was going on. There was a cloud over us, you could feel it in the air, how people felt. That's just not us. That's stuck with a lot of us. But, still, overall we're resilient. We're moving on. The fabric is torn, but it can be mended.[27]

The goal of moving on inspired deliberate efforts to weave back together the frayed threads of the community. It would not be easy. An early effort to reinforce community bonds became entangled in the still-raw emotions between pro- and anti-Bundy community members. On the afternoon of Saturday, February 6, 2016, several dozen people—many outside militia groups, and some local—gathered at the side of Highway 395 where LaVoy Finicum had been shot on January 26. Prayers and angry

Sheriff Dave Ward (left) at a law enforcement appreciation dinner organized by the community (February 6, 2016).

expressions of grief were voiced, including an armed man who vowed, "This is the shot that will be heard around the world."[28] In the evening of the same day, several hundred community members joined in the festively lit and decorated Harney County Fairgrounds Memorial Building. The purpose of the event was to express appreciation to local, state, and federal law enforcement officers who had (in the view of most in attendance) protected the community under extraordinary duress. Although four "holdouts" still occupied the Malheur Refuge at the time, the sense of siege was lifted, and many urgently needed to reassert normalcy. Some danced, including Sheriff Ward.

The juxtaposition of the two events that day—the angry, grieving gathering at Highway 395 in honor of LaVoy Finicum, and the law enforcement appreciation dinner at the fairgrounds in Burns—had unanticipated consequences. Someone video-recorded local people dancing at the fairgrounds and posted on social media that the event was a celebration of the killing of LaVoy Finicum. The video became explosive. The false characterization of the dinner at the fairgrounds as a celebration of the killing of LaVoy Finicum sank deep roots locally and on militia web pages nationally. Two months later, on April 7, 2016, Oregon Public Broadcasting's *Think Out Loud* radio program organized a community meeting in the very same Harney County Fairgrounds Memorial Building to discuss "healing" in Harney County.[29] Some local and outside individuals made the event into an opportunity to publicly air grievances heard during the occupation, including harsh accusations against county officials. One Burns resident stated, "The sheriff said he was really upset and really down, but then I seen a video where [Sheriff Ward] was out dancing after the killing" (of LaVoy Finicum). Sheriff Ward replied, "I wasn't celebrating anyone's death, that death was tragic." Those who knew Ward personally knew he felt deep and genuine pain at Finicum's death. The public, very personal accusation felt like tearing a scab. "Healing," it appeared, would take time.

Other special efforts were made to reinforce community cohesion, with better success. One event occurred on March 24, 2016, when ranchers who hold permits to graze on the Malheur National Wildlife Refuge held a barbecue for refuge employees. Some of the refuge's sixteen employees were originally from Harney County, and others had come to feel very much part of the community, until the Bundy occupation. During the occupation, all of the refuge employees were relocated, in some cases to distant undisclosed locations because of credible militia threats against them. When refuge employees returned to temporary trailer offices while the main refuge buildings were being repaired in March 2016, they were uncertain where they stood in a community that was painfully divided. Serving up sliced beef, cheesy potatoes, broccoli, and fruit salad, the ranchers who graze the refuge and work closely with the refuge staff made it clear: refuge employees are neighbors and friends, part of the community. The event was private and members of the media were not admitted. Malheur Refuge fish biologist Linda Beck described the barbecue as "wonderful," "because we had that support.... It made it better."[30]

In addition to supporting federal employees, some members of the community saw a need to use science and education to counter what they perceived as misinformation spread by Ammon Bundy about management practices on public lands.[31] A core group of about a dozen local ranchers, farmers, and agricultural scientists formed the Western Working Lands Initiative, a 501(c)(3) nonprofit. The group's goals are to serve as a clearinghouse for peer-reviewed science that supports multiple-use management on public lands, and to demonstrate how science-based and collaborative management has been put to constructive use locally and in resource-dependent communities across the West. The initiative predated the occupation of Harney County, but Ammon Bundy's unsubstantiated claims of mismanagement at the Malheur Refuge enhanced local interest and participation.[32] Some local Bundy supporters interpreted the initiative as a counterpoint to the creation (at Bundy's urging) of the Harney County Committee of Safety. (Initially the group was to be called the Western Working Lands Resource Center—similar to Bundy's renaming of the Malheur Refuge headquarters as the "Harney County Resource Center."[33])

Although the idea of the Western Working Lands Initiative was not originally formed in response to the Bundy occupation, it did provide those in the community who rejected the Bundy message an opportunity to respond in a manner characteristic of Harney County: by supporting a community-based problem-solving group. On May 23, 2016, with support from the Harney County Cattlewomen and local shopkeepers, the initiative was launched in a characteristic Harney County way: with a barbecue (and local craft brew).

Harney County judge Pete Runnels, who campaigned for office in 2016 during the difficult adjustment period after the end of the Malheur Refuge takeover, pledged to travel to remote areas of the county (which is the size of Massachusetts) to listen and convey a sense that the county government cares about remote rural communities. While there is a great deal of discussion in Oregon and other states with large rural areas about the rural-urban divide, Harney County[34] has its own divide, with much of the support for the Bundy occupation coming from the remote areas outside Burns and Hines. Reflecting a general commitment to inclusive governance as well as some specific concern about the legacy of the Bundy occupation, Judge Runnels stated,

> Part of my campaign pledge was to meet out in our rural communities. We take the county [government] out there for a meeting twice a year. I began

those in the spring of 2017. We've gone to Crane, Drewsey, Riley, Fields, Frenchglen and Diamond. . . . We're not going out with an agenda. We're asking the people what we're missing that the county should be taking care of. We might squelch a rumor. That's a big thing. Sometimes people have heard part of the story but not all of the story. . . . It's been a great outreach. It's helped bond the community together. We send postcards to every mailbox [announcing the meetings]. It's part of the healing.[35]

By reaffirming ties between the community and federal employees, building new community groups such as the Western Working Lands Initiative, and establishing greater outreach and communication between the county government and remote population centers, Harney County deliberately built the walls of resilience to future political disruptions a bit higher, and tried to return to life as normal.

To a considerable extent, the community recognized that reestablishing normalcy required a conscious resolve to move on—and to some degree that required simply not talking about the Bundy occupation. In private, when asked by an outsider about the Bundy occupation, even two years later some individuals showed they could talk for hours—they almost seemed to need to do so. In public, however, many residents insisted on putting those disruptions in the past. When public conversations seemed to steer too close to that topic, some would half-jokingly remind others that it is not an appropriate topic. On the one-year anniversary of the takeover of the Malheur Refuge, former Harney County judge Steve Grasty insisted to out-of-town reporters, "We're fine. . . . We're going about business like we always have, like nothing happened last year."[36] In September 2017, former Harney County commissioner Dan Nichols was asked about the Bundy occupation during an interview with professors and students from the University of Oregon. Nichols replied, "It isn't making that much difference—it's things like this [interview] that keep bringing it up."[37]

Similarly, Harney County judge Pete Runnels observed:

The fallout has filtered out. You can relate it to the explosion of a volcano. The big particles have to come back to earth. There are still a few blowing around, but the focus of the community is mostly positive. "Let's move on. . . . Let's just not talk about that [the occupation]." Just don't talk about it. It's over. It'll always be a huge part of our history, but it's over.[38]

Local middle school math teacher Son Burns agreed:

I don't think it will ever go away, . . . but it's not something I hear talked about openly. It's still going on in social media. . . . For example when they're talking about the [Bundy] trials and stuff like that. In public, people are keeping their cards close, keeping [discussion of the Bundy occupation] in their own private circles. . . . The one thing that did raise some eyebrows and got people talking was the [2017] fair parade, where there were some local people in the parade with signs in favor of pardoning the Hammonds. . . . Other than that, it's just not something you casually talk about anymore.[39]

Rancher and retired journalist Pauline Braymen, like others, observed that, given the county's small population, there is often little choice but to "pull together as a whole." There are too few people in the community to avoid everyone who took an opposing view of the Bundy occupation:

We don't have an unlimited number of venues in which to seek social involvement. [For example,] if you become alienated with the Chamber Music Society because your political beliefs don't stack up with other members, there are few other opportunities to take part in musical activity with others who play the French horn, for instance.[40]

In this sense, the choice to "pull together as a whole" regardless of differing views about the Bundy occupation was viewed as the only viable choice if Harney County wished to resume something like the community life it previously had. On that, there seemed near-unanimous agreement: Harney County greatly values its community and invests extraordinary efforts in building and maintaining its social bonds. Although the Bundy occupation of Harney County unquestionably drove wedges into the fissures of social life, it also provided an opportunity to take stock of and celebrate the community's unique qualities. The possibility of losing the truly remarkable qualities of its community drove many in the county to work harder than ever to strengthen social bonds.

Probably no one had a greater appreciation of the special qualities of Harney County's community or was a greater proponent for maintaining

and strengthening social bonds than Sheriff Dave Ward. Ward was born and
raised in rural Douglas County, in western Oregon. In the 1980s, Douglas
County was hit hard by a changing timber economy. The population grew
and the culture changed as migrants arrived from California and other states
(Brown 1995). Many in-migrants were not raised in rural communities and
did not understand the rural lifestyle and culture Ward grew up in. After
serving in the US Army as a combat medic in Somalia and Afghanistan,
Ward moved his family to Eastern Oregon specifically because he wanted
to raise his children in a place that still had the kind of rural community he
grew up in. When Harney County's sense of community was threatened by
discord and division during the Bundy occupation, Ward had an outside
perspective on the uniqueness and value of a healthy community:

> The good things you're talking about, like the High Desert Partnership, that's
> people from every walk sitting down at the table trying to come to the best
> decision for everybody in the region. Those positive things were happening
> long before the Bundys showed up. Those things were disrupted for a while.
> There was more gas poured on the fire, so to speak, as far as negativity or
> people planting their feet on both sides. But this community is unique in
> the fact that those folks, while they're mad right now, they will come back
> together—to work together for the greater good. You'll see that.
>
> Go to the high school sporting events. You'll see families who supported
> the Bundys sitting in the same set of bleachers as families who were ada-
> mantly against [the Bundys]. They're cheering for the same team. This com-
> munity has always come out to support youth. If you look at the 4-H and
> [the Future Farmers of America] kids, the way people come out to support
> those kids, it's the same scenario. People from both sides are supporting
> those kids. They'll come together for the common good of the community.
>
> There are a lot of positive things about this community that a lot of folks
> don't know. Even in 2016 when we were going through such a turbulent time
> for our community, Oregon's first national commander of the American
> Legion was elected. That was Charlie Schmidt, out of Harney County. In
> our little American Legion chapter, we have the national commander. . . .
> The American Legion works very hard for veterans. . . . In running for the
> position of national commander, Charlie visited every state and territory in

the union, and ten different countries. . . . We're a very isolated community, but only geographically.

Like many in Harney County, Sheriff Ward places a great deal of confidence in the community's youth. Harney County, where the demographic and economic future is precarious, invests a great deal of its community life in nurturing the next generation and building a spirit of achievement and community cohesion. Ward suggests that, even after a major disruption, Harney County will always come back together for its children, and that the values of community carried on by and for its children will heal the Bundy wounds:

> And the work ethic that you see in this community—you know, you hear a lot of complaints about millennials. One of the positive things is that ours aren't "there" yet because we're thirty years behind! People raise their kids with the expectation that they have to make their own way. Go to our high schools and walk down the halls and look at all the pictures of state champions. . . . We've had ten straight back-to-back team championships in wrestling. We've had back-to-back baseball state championships. Volleyball state championships. These kids work hard. They go places around the state. They're noted not only as good athletes but also as good citizens. Because that's what our community expects from them. We don't accept less than that.
>
> That comes from the work ethic and character of generations before them. . . . They're not out goofing around in the summer, they're baling hay, they're working on ranches. It's a positive atmosphere. If you look at this community wherever you go, it looks like Norman Rockwell paintings. This is a community where, if something bad happens, people who don't know you will show up and offer to help. People will make food and bring it because they know that you don't have time for that. I myself have experienced that. People that I don't know have shown up and done chores for me because I was dealing with something that was overwhelming. I have a neighbor—everybody here is my neighbor—who drove his tractor from twenty miles away to come and set hay out for my cows while I was dealing with things that were going on here. That's not because I'm the sheriff that he did that, he'd do it for anybody. That's the kind of community we have here.
>
> These folks [the Bundys and militia] came from elsewhere, and they

created dissention in the community. But when the chips are down, this community will go back to taking care of their own because that's what people do here. That's not something you see elsewhere. . . . There was a gentleman last winter [during the Bundy occupation] and at first I didn't know who it was. He just showed up and snow-plowed my driveway. Why? Because he knew I had other things I was doing. . . . That's just how people are here. That's the way things will get back to. . . . Not this year, maybe not next year, but in a few years things will come around and get back to normal. There are some friendships that are never going to be repaired. But the fact is, this community—the character of the community itself—will rise above what happened. . . .

This is probably one of the most active citizenries anywhere in maintaining the good things about the community. That's going to continue to happen. Whatever wedges some people tried to drive through the community are simply going to fall away. This community is going to be here a long time after those [Bundy militia] people are gone.[41]

Sheriff Ward is far from alone in his appreciation of the qualities of life in Harney County. Despite (or because of) its geographic isolation and sometimes difficult circumstances, many Harney County residents came from more populous areas intentionally seeking a different way of life. Among those born and raised in Harney County, some leave as young adults and never permanently return; but others do return, and settle down—for similar reasons as their urban-refugee neighbors. Those native to the county and those who came from other places know that Harney County is *different*. Cultural traditions such as the County Fair are revered—*everyone* goes. When going to town, not only will residents know many of the people they meet at local stores—they will also know the names of each other's children, and ask how the kids are doing. If residents meet someone they've never seen before, by the next time they see them that person is considered a friend—"How are you, how have you been? Good to see you again." Residents passing each other on remote county roads wave. A honking horn is more often a greeting than an expression of anger. If a driver has a mechanical problem not only will someone bring help, but someone else will wait to keep the stranded motorist company. If a UPS package has the wrong address, it will still be delivered to the right person because the driver knows where almost everyone is. Residents joke that if you dial a wrong number, the chances are you will know the person you accidentally called.[42]

This closeness within the community was in some ways actually enhanced by the Bundy occupation (which the outside media had almost uniformly called "divisive"). While it was true that some divisions were created, many new friendships were created as well. The occupation was an experience so extraordinary and intense it may not be unreasonable to compare it to a war (Harney County sheriff Dave Ward said he was never as stressed even in his US Army combat service in Somalia or Afghanistan). Not unlike a war, the Bundy occupation brought together people who might have never met under ordinary circumstances, welded together in the kind of friendship forged only through shared adversity.[43] In significant ways, the shared adversity made a community of strong personal bonds stronger still.

Outsiders passing through Harney County—whether travelers going to other destinations or press crews monitoring an uninvited armed insurrection—will often see only desert, the tattered remnants of bygone industries, and probably a gas station. They frequently miss—or dismiss—the proud and determined community around them. They will typically fail to get off the main road and look more closely into the subtler spaces that make up a community. Harney County's citizens know their lives are invisible to many outsiders, and they tend to accept that so long as their community is not disrupted. If disruption occurs, the community will push back in defense of a way of life they prize.

Hardening

Inevitably, however, an event of the magnitude of the occupation of Harney County and the armed takeover of the Malheur National Wildlife Refuge could not leave the community's way of life unchanged. During the occupation of the refuge, Ammon Bundy was asked by British journalist Henry Langston how the takeover actually occurred, and Bundy replied, "We just walked down in here, the doors were open. That's what happened, it was that easy."[44] Bundy smiled and laughed slightly when speaking the words: "It was that easy." What Bundy described was characteristic of Harney

County. Being isolated and ignored by most of the world, Harney County was the kind of place where doors often remained unlocked and nothing would come of it. Ironically, after Bundy's takeover of the Malheur Refuge, the way of life in Harney County would never be quite as "easy" again.

When entering Burns from the west by Highway 20 (the most-traveled route from more populous Central and Western Oregon), one immediately sees an unmistakable manifestation of the more hardened, less innocent way of life that resulted from the Bundy occupation. Thirty miles away at the Malheur National Wildlife Refuge, Ammon Bundy railed against the Bureau of Land Management and its alleged "tyranny" against the people of Harney County (even though the Malheur Refuge is operated by the US Fish and Wildlife Service, not the BLM). Yet, when entering Burns on Highway 20, the Burns District Bureau of Land Management office is literally the first major building one sees, directly along the highway. The building had been almost completely accessible to the public, exposed. The district manager, Jeff Rose, recalled how visitors would come into the building and simply walk to his office without security restrictions.[45] The Bundy occupation changed that.

In the period before the takeover of the Malheur National Wildlife Refuge on January 2, 2016, there was concern that Ammon Bundy and his militia supporters might try to seize the Burns District BLM office, since the Bundy family was well known for its grievances against the BLM (almost everyone was surprised that he instead seized the Malheur Refuge, operated by the US Fish and Wildlife Service). Federal employees described an atmosphere of intimidation by the out-of-town militia, and some individual employees received explicit threats. In response, federal agencies including the US Forest Service and Bureau of Land Management sent more than 150 employees home beginning on December 30, 2015—three days before the Malheur Refuge takeover.[46] The expectation that the BLM office might be a target was not misplaced: on January 9, 2016, Ryan Bundy, with occupier Ken Medenbach and two others, made their views clearly known by nailing a sign on the BLM office stating that the office was "CLOSED PERMANENTLY."[47]

When the Burns District BLM office reopened on February 9, 2016, major security upgrades followed, including a seven-foot steel fence surrounding the facility and a three-inch clear acrylic barrier at the receptionist's desk. District manager Jeff Rose considered the acrylic barrier a slightly less intimidating compromise than the alternative—noting that, "Nothing says public service like 'mmphh mmffph mm mhhff mfffh?'" (imitating sound of the words "How can I help you?" spoken through bulletproof glass).[48] With sadness in his voice, Rose observed that the new security precautions were only a partial solution, and he could not fully protect his staff from someone intent on doing something truly "crazy."

One member of a federal employee family in a neighboring county with ties to Harney County observed a sense of despair that harassment of federal employees had already gone on for years, and the Bundy occupation would only make it worse:

> There are refuge, BLM, USFS men and women who are now suffering from PTSD as a result of this [Bundy] business. Finally, they are broken emotionally and physically. After years of shrugging it off as just another part of the job, many are really broken. How can one not take everything personally? Because it is personal. Very personal. They [federal employees] are just as vested in their community as anyone else is. They put their lives on the line fighting fires and now they [put their lives on the line] just going to work. They have a big target across their backs, and over their hearts. It says BLM, USFS, Malheur Wildlife Refuge. . . . They [militia] could follow you and your fellow employees or your family members in the store. Sit outside your home to intimidate you and your fellow employees. They could terrify your children, send you threatening emails and letters, make threatening phone calls. . . . Unfortunately, that's not the worst of it. The worst is knowing that it's far from over. That was just the tip of the iceberg. The cancer is spreading.[49]

With Harney County still prominent in the memories of anti-federal-government activist groups, the sense of being singled out and targeted simply for doing their jobs is a cold reality that federal land management employees and the community would have to live with. The way of life in Harney County, which Ammon Bundy described with a smile as "easy," would never be quite so at-ease again.

For some members of the community, the reality of living with the sense of being a potential target was too much. One employee of the Malheur

National Wildlife Refuge recalled making a decision to leave the refuge after receiving specialized security training to respond to a potential "sovereign citizen" attack.[50] After the emotional trauma of being harassed and intimidated by outside militia groups during the Bundy occupation, the prospect of living indefinitely with the fear of being attacked again was unbearable. With a staff of only sixteen, four key employees of the Malheur Refuge left as a direct or partial result of the occupation. In 2017, Deputy Manager Jeff Mackay explained that the employees "had a difficult time functioning here because of the impact the occupation had on [them[51]] emotionally and mentally, that's why [they] departed—the occupation ruined this county, their home, for [them]."[52] Decades of accumulated knowledge and relationships nurtured between the community and refuge staff were lost. While Mackay described the loss of continuity, he also noted that transition and turnover is not new at the refuge, and hopefully the "knowledge base" would be rebuilt and the loss would be only short term.[53] Like the BLM office in Burns, the Malheur Refuge headquarters buildings also received costly security upgrades, in some cases creating literal, physical barriers between the public and the refuge staff.

The physical hardening of federal facilities in Harney County both symbolized and reinforced a kind of social hardening of the community. Two years after the Bundy occupation, residents observed that while in most outward ways community life had returned to a semblance of pre-occupation normalcy, the "feel" of the community was different, and not as friendly and easygoing as it had been. There was a widespread sense that the community was less trusting, warier. The Bundy occupation was such a major social trauma, it was impossible for anyone to forget—as county judge Pete Runnels observed in 2017, "It will always be a huge part of our history."[54] Yet there was little opportunity for a constructive conversation that might bring the community closer to mutual understanding of the events.

During the occupation itself, several community-wide meetings were held that allowed different points of view to be aired, but in the atmosphere of extraordinary anger and anxiety at the time there was little clear movement toward mutual understanding. After the Malheur takeover ended, there were no comparable community-wide meetings about the Bundy occupation, with the exception of a single meeting called by Oregon Public Broadcasting in April 2016, which merely seemed to dredge hard feelings back to the surface, including bitter personal accusations. It was not clear how or if a community-wide conversation about the occupation ever could, or should, take place. In November 2017, two years after the Bundy occupation of Harney County started, when one lifelong resident was asked whether, under the surface, local people were "still sore," the answer was, "They sure are."[55]

Much about community life in Harney County returned to at least a semblance of normality, but some significant divisions remained. Even though the majority of the community seemed more committed to collaborative problem-solving than ever, the occupation and the divisions that it created appeared to push the strongest supporters of the Bundy ideology further to the sidelines of the county's many collaborative groups. Gretchen Bates, the chair of the Harney County Republicans and project manager for the Community-Based Water Planning Group, observed,

> In some senses it's harder to bring people in to the collaborative process because they may have some interpretation about sitting down at the table with somebody they don't agree with because of what fell out of the [Malheur] takeover. . . . If you think that there's going to be more difficulty sitting across the table from someone that has a different opinion because of what happened last year [the Bundy occupation], they're not going to take the time to get involved. . . . I haven't seen anybody who was involved with the Committee of Safety come to any of our [collaborative] meetings.[56]

Like much of American society in the second decade of the twenty-first century, some social divisions in Harney County also seemed to be created, expressed, and reinforced on the internet (Klein 2017). During the Bundy occupation, much of the community self-segregated into social media communities (especially on Facebook) populated by pro-Bundy or anti-Bundy community members. Long after the occupation, the online separation persisted, with certain pages populated mostly by individuals with particular viewpoints on issues such as the long-running Bundy trials in Portland and Las Vegas and support for figures associated with the Bundy occupation such as deceased Bundy spokesman LaVoy Finicum.

On November 11, 2017, the Mohave County, Arizona, board of supervisors voted to rename a section of road in honor of Finicum,[57] predictably eliciting "likes" on the Bundy-leaning "Harney County United!" Facebook page, and equally predictable scorn on the anti-Bundy-leaning "WE are Harney County" Facebook page. Public support for the Bundy ideology—including from supporters of the Harney County Committee of Safety[58]—did not disappear, but settled and hardened into an almost separate community existing largely in the realm of social media, with few opportunities to expand mutual understanding. Something like "normal" community life resumed, but often with angry divisions covered over by a thin skin of determined civility.

Inoculated

On July 14, 2016, fifth-generation Harney County rancher Gary Marshall stood on his family's ranch property near Drewsey, Oregon, inspecting a cattle trough and proudly showing the riparian rehabilitation work he had done. Native willows, grasses, and sedges thickly lined the restored streambanks, possibly resembling the way it looked when Marshall's ancestors and other early Euro-American settlers first came to Harney County in the nineteenth century. The Marshall family had faced tough opponents in the past—his family had prevailed at the United States Supreme Court against none other than Harney County's most powerful cattle baron, Pete French (in a legal decision that validated his family's homestead claim against French's land claims based on riparian doctrine[59]). Six months after the takeover of the Malheur National Wildlife Refuge had ended, Marshall reflected on overcoming another strong-willed adversary:

> With the High Desert Partnership, I think just where we were at that point in time helped inoculate the community against the Bundy disease. Our immune system was much higher than it would have been had we not had the High Desert Partnership in place.
>
> It's not that we didn't get some sniffles and a cough during that time [the Bundy occupation], but we weren't down in bed and close to death, at any time. I know that a lot of that was due to the High Desert Partnership because

there were people in our county leadership like [Judge Steve] Grasty and [Commissioner Dan] Nichols that were able to turn and say, "Look, here's what we've got going on in the community right now." Without that, Grasty would have had nothing to hold onto. He would have had to respond in a lot of different ways. That was his rock that he was able to hang on to. He was able to say, "We've got this working, we've got a proved track record of what Harney County has been able to do." . . . Through the whole Bundy thing, [the High Desert Partnership] was his rock to hang on to, it truly was. Not just the High Desert Partnership, but these other [collaboratives] too.[60]

The Bundy occupation made the value of Harney County's decades of investment in collaborative approaches to problem-solving apparent to federal land managers as well as local leaders. The US Bureau of Land Management Burns District manager, Jeff Rose, concurred with rancher Gary Marshall's view that collaboration had "inoculated" the community from the Bundy's revolutionary approach:

> We invested a lot of time a lot of time and effort [in collaboration].[61] The occupation happened, and it could have happened anywhere but it happened here. Because of our investment, the outcome was not as bad as it could have been. But it could have been really bad. I think a lot of that [avoiding a bad outcome] was driven by the community and the BLM and the [other federal] agencies from what they've done [in collaboration].[62]

Public officials, however, were not the only members of the community who specifically observed that the county's history of collaborative problem-solving helped it to choose a different path than armed rebellion. On January 6, 2016, at the first Harney County community meeting following the Malheur takeover, Gary Marshall's wife, Georgia Marshall (who had no formal role in the High Desert Partnership), gave by far the most impassioned speech of the evening, imploring the community to not give up on the collaborative process in favor of armed revolt:

> Let's not destroy what we are doing because we think we have to make a stand for everything that's happened in the goddamned past. This is our time now, and not a hundred years ago or sixty years ago or thirty years ago. . . . We don't know our future but I'll tell you what, it's better than what we had.

So, let's try to keep going. Let's not get caught up—like I'm pissed as hell right now. . . . I'm proud of who I am . . . and I'm not going to let some other people be my face.

Georgia Marshall's defiance against the "other people" (the Bundy occupiers) trying to be the community's "face" and her celebration of the county's achievements in finding cooperative solutions went hand in hand, and set much of the tone for the majority of the community who opposed the Malheur takeover.

When the Bundy occupation leaders met with local ranchers at the Crystal Crane Hot Springs resort on January 18, 2016, several ranchers expressed skepticism or outright dismissal of the revolutionary goals of the occupiers and specifically cited the improved relationships between ranchers and the Malheur National Wildlife Refuge as a reason. Directly confronting Ammon Bundy, fourth-generation Harney County rancher Scott Franklin objected:

I'm not going to fight an uphill battle that's not going to be won. . . . If you guys wanted to change something, if you really wanted to change something, I would say let's bring a body in here and we'll change how our federal government works with Harney County. It would be structured like a school board. We'll have a BLM board. We'll have a refuge board. The BLM is going to answer to that board. But what you guys are asking, to take over that refuge, that will never, never happen. You can try to fight this by driving around without a driver's license, but they're going to haul you to jail and they're going to fine you, and that's what's going to happen. . . . You're asking us to give up everything by this rebel cause. Actually, as far as the refuge goes, they're easy to work with. They're good to work with. The refuge isn't a problem.

Another Harney County rancher, Buck Taylor (who supported much of the Bundy constitutional argument) responded to Franklin's praise for Malheur Refuge by noting that the refuge had not been a problem to work with "recently"—emphasizing past contentious relations with the refuge but also acknowledging the efforts by the Malheur Refuge in recent years to work more cooperatively with refuge permittees like himself. Taylor also

Harney County rancher Scott Franklin told Ammon and Ryan Bundy that their "rebel cause" would fail (January 18, 2016).

observed that "if the Hammond's place wasn't right alongside the refuge this wouldn't even be an issue." The tone in Ammon and Ryan Bundy's voices changed, becoming angry and argumentative—accusing some ranchers in the room of displaying a "slave" mind-set.

That moment at the meeting in Crane was pivotal. It was the moment the Bundy occupiers chose to explicitly invite Harney County ranchers to join their revolution and provide them with armed "protection." The mood in the room ranged from hesitant embrace of some of the Bundys' political goals to open hostility. Rancher Scott Franklin's explicit rejection of the Bundy's allegations of "tyranny" at the Malheur Refuge, backed up by Bundy-sympathizer Buck Taylor's acknowledgment that working with the Malheur Refuge was not a problem "recently," seemed to douse the spark of revolutionary fire before it could fully ignite. The Bundys' chosen symbol of alleged government "tyranny"—Harney County ranchers—had failed to produce the angry, radical response the occupiers hoped for. If the

Ammon Bundy reacts angrily against dissent by Harney County rancher Scott
Franklin (January 18, 2016).

Malheur Refuge had not recently made significant efforts to work cooperatively with local ranchers, the mood and the outcome of the meeting might
have been different.

Other ranchers in other forums continued to make a similar case against
the Bundy revolution. On January 19, 2016, standing directly in front of
Ammon Bundy (a few rows of bleachers away) in the Burns High School
gym, local rancher Tom Sharp took a microphone and denounced Bundy's
disruptions and appealed directly to the community to resume working
together as it had in the past. Sharp had chaired the local steering committee that crafted a landmark 2015 agreement with the US Fish and Wildlife
Service to protect sage grouse habitat and avoid an Endangered Species
Act listing of the bird[63]—the kind of cooperative win-win problem-solving
between a community and the federal government that Bundy dismissed:

> The refuge occupiers just yesterday came to the Crystal Crane Hot Springs
> and lectured our local ranchers to stop paying their BLM grazing fees, and

tear up their grazing permits. Such advice is terribly destructive. It would impact our livelihood, it would destroy our cattle industry here in this country. Over the last three weeks Harney County has been gripped by a paralysis of disruption and dysfunction. Our government offices have been closed, we've lost productivity, people have felt fearful and intimidated, our personal relationships have been damaged, outside groups of uncertain intent have arrived. . . . Harney County is a community that needs to work. We need to continue to work together. We need to be able to work with our government agencies. Our ability to do that has been disrupted, stopped, and compromised. It's time for many to go home. It's time to begin healing and restoring out great community.

Harney County ranchers Tom Sharp, Scott Franklin, and even Bundy-leaning Buck Taylor—along with many others—displayed resistance to the radical changes in social and political relations that the Bundy occupiers offered. Ammon Bundy seemed to believe that Harney County's population was "on the verge," ready to transform their social and political system. In doing so Bundy overestimated the precariousness of the current social order, and underestimated the degree to which the community had successfully adapted to the existing order in ways that did not throw out the existing system but had made it work reasonably well for them. Bundy, who knew almost nothing of the community other than what he had apparently been told by a few angry local individuals, may have also overestimated the degree to which the influence of larger-scale political identity and ideology might trigger the kinds of local social reactions he hoped for.[64] Harney County is one of the most conservative and reliably Republican counties in Oregon, but it is not radical—and it does not strongly align with larger-scale political movements. Harney County was not, as Bundy seemed to assume and hope, "on the verge"; it was, and remained, in many respects, almost rock-steady.

The local political and social character of Harney County was not, however, the only force that came into play during the Bundy occupation. Harney County residents emphasize that while the community is geographically isolated, it is not culturally isolated. In fact, in many respects Harney County has stronger ties to the cosmopolitan world than many other thinly populated "frontier"[65] counties. Among the most important

ties between Harney County and many other more populous and urban-
ized areas is the Malheur National Wildlife Refuge itself. In the early twentieth century, Malheur Lake became an icon for conservationists nationally.
Among the most important ambassadors for Malheur Lake and its surrounding bird habitats was wildlife photographer and friend of President
Theodore Roosevelt, William Finley, who was instrumental in persuading
the president to designate Malheur as one of the nation's first wildlife ref-
uges in 1908. Finley was also president of the Portland Audubon Society,
which up to today considers Malheur sacred ground.[66] The Bundy takeover
of the Malheur National Wildlife Refuge in 2016 was cause for profound
alarm at Portland Audubon,[67] as well as many other conservation groups.
This alarm among outsiders presented the potential to draw in still more
destabilizing forces into an already highly volatile situation. Once again,
however, many years of investments in collaboration appeared to have the
unintended but welcome consequence of providing a source of stability at
a time of crisis.

Bob Sallinger, the conservation director for the Portland Audubon
Society, describes how social relationships built through the High Desert
Partnership and the collaborative Malheur Comprehensive Conservation
Plan became critical in defusing a potentially explosive situation.
Immediately after the takeover of the Malheur National Wildlife Refuge,
Sallinger and the Portland Audubon Society were deluged with demands by
thousands of angry birders for Audubon to take action in Harney County.
Sallinger chose instead to hold back the birders, in the belief that their pres-
ence in Harney County would further destabilize the situation and possibly
precipitate violent conflicts with the Bundy occupiers. Sallinger describes
how his group's involvement in the Malheur Comprehensive Conservation
Plan provided him with access to local contacts and—most importantly—
confidence that the Harney County community would stand against the
Bundys.

In Sallinger's view, the community's rejection of the Bundy occupation
would send a far more powerful message against militant seizures than a
battle between outside birders and militia. Sallinger's ability to contain his
membership's intense desires to intervene was built through his own direct
involvement in local collaborative efforts:

Did I anticipate the Bundys? No! [laughs] I wish I could tell you I said, "Yeah, we're going to be occupied within a few years, so we better . . . " [but] when we contacted people in Harney County and we asked "What do you want us to do?"—you know, our first urge was to go out there [to Harney County] to confront it, as some [environmentalists] did. But the message we got was very clear, it was "Please don't do that." Having environmentalists come shooting in from the sidelines to defend the refuge is not the outcome you want. What you want is the community to reject this. If you want a sustainable outcome, that's not going to happen with a clash between outsiders coming in and fighting over this place. So, we got in many conversations with local people and we were told, "Don't come here now." We ended up in the position of holding people back, us and other groups. We decided to do a rally [in Portland]. There was a lot of discussion, and a lot of debate, and we got many, many phone calls a day from people who said we need to go [to Malheur]. . . . There was an overwhelming desire to be on the ground out there. . . .

[Yet] I still feel that for the most part the fact that the community rejected them was the most important thing that could happen. What happened out there [in Harney County] was actually very powerful. The fact that [the militia] went to this place [Harney County] and [the militia] said to everybody, "Come and help us," and instead the community turned their backs on them for the most part is really, really powerful. The enduring image is of the community turning its backs on them. If there had been 5,500 environmentalists there, it would have just blown up, and it would have been a different image.

We were told by law enforcement in Harney County to have faith in the community—this community that we've gotten to know to some degree [through collaboration]—that [the occupation] is not what they want. They agree with some of the things—I've heard this from people in the community: "We're glad [the Bundys] raised some of these issues, but we do not agree with [the Malheur takeover]." Over and over we heard that from people we knew and trusted. We were told [Harney County] is absolutely not going with them. It might take a while—it took longer than anybody expected—but based on the relationships we had formed, we trusted that. If we hadn't had those relationships, I think we would have gone there and it would have been a very different dynamic, and I think it might have turned out a lot worse. It was very much a respect thing: people we trust . . . told us they want to handle it themselves. I realized, "Yeah!" If the local community turns their backs on the Bundys, that makes it a whole lot harder [for the militia] to come back . . . [and] the relationships developed through the collaborative efforts are stronger than ever.[68]

When Bob Sallinger of the Portland Audubon Society spoke of the hope for a "sustainable" outcome in Harney County, he was speaking not only of resolving the Malheur takeover: he had in mind a "long game" of building and sustaining local support—"hearts and minds"—and social relationships that would help sustain and build resilience for conservation at the Malheur Refuge generations into the future.

In thinking about a long game, Sallinger was not alone. Whether coping with local disturbances or potential destabilization from outside, a resilient community must think about the future. In a remote and geographically isolated frontier economy that has been losing population and high-quality jobs for decades, sustaining a strong, cohesive community into the future is a major concern for many local residents. Harney County's young people often leave and never permanently return. For those who remain at home, limited economic opportunities are a very real obstacle. Many local residents recognized that the ability of the community to achieve desired societal goals—whether conservation at the Malheur Refuge or anything else—depends on maintaining a sound economic footing and the capacity to work together effectively as a community.

With an eye to long-term social, economic, and ecological sustainability, local leaders have sought ways to retain young people in the community and prepare for the future by engaging those community members who will lead in the future. In August 2016, just six months after the end of the takeover at the Malheur National Wildlife Refuge, Harney County's High Desert Partnership launched a project that took the group in a new direction, creating a new line of activity different from its previous focus on conservation planning and forest management: the group launched a new Youth Initiative (later renamed the Youth Changing the Community initiative). In its first official act, the Youth Initiative, at the request of youth leaders, worked together to refurbish a skateboard park in the center of Hines. Christy

Cheyne, the head of the US Forest Service's local Emigrant Creek District, who was a leader in developing the Youth Initiative, explained that this initial project was seen as a first step toward a more ambitious set of goals:

> Some youth from the high school wanted to show that they could be creative and come up with a solution that the youth are concerned about. The thing that they chose, with a survey at the high school, was this skate park down here. So, they're redesigning the skate park. Even though not all youth use the skate park, it's a symbol that this collaborative group is energetic and behind improvements in the community, and that's just a starting point.[69]

As described by High Desert Partnership executive director Brenda Smith, the skateboard park was a first expression of a desire by the HDP to build "a closer connection to the community and the schools" in order to build community and collaborative skills both through and among youth. Smith explained:

> The main driver [behind the creation of the Youth Initiative] was, even in such a small community, to engage different sectors of the community. Pretty much everybody has some sort of interaction with youth. The concern was to get some cross-linking, so people know what other people are doing through youth activities.[70]

Engaging with youth would not only build community and collaborative skills but also provide an opportunity to address one of the key forces that have destabilized the community and threatened to continue to do so: the out-migration of young people. Brenda Smith of the HDP explained that the group wanted "to make sure the youth understand what opportunities are here," and "we want them to realize the good things about the community, and maybe come back."[71] Christy Cheyne elaborated,

> We are looking at everything from early childhood to having Harney County youth prepared to leave Harney County but in hopes they will want to come back some day. Just the opportunities, skills, and education that can get them out, getting more education, but then coming back, and being part of the community. Retention is a really big deal. A lot of youth do leave and not return. . . . We're talking a lot about internships, and working through all the

different government agencies to see if there are ways to mentor kids, and have them "job shadow" so they know the opportunities.[72]

The goal of providing more opportunities for local youth to remain at home and help build and sustain vibrant rural economies and communities is a key concern for state leaders in places such as Oregon that have a very pronounced rural versus urban divide. On April 12, 2017, Oregon governor Kate Brown visited Harney County for the first time since the Bundy occupation, and she focused much of her visit on two themes: economic development and youth—specifically citing her desire to help enable Harney County youth who choose to do so to find careers in the community where they grew up.[73] On Brown's official Facebook page, her main comments about her visit to Harney County focused on the Youth Initiative, citing concerns similar to the reasons that the High Desert Partnership formed the group:

> The Burns community in Harney County is resilient and working together to grow a thriving, frontier economy. The High Desert Partnership is integral to this collaborative effort, and I was thrilled to be on hand for the launch of their new youth initiative.[74] I appreciate all those I met, including students and faculty at Burns High School who are focused on hands-on learning to prepare students for careers after graduation. I also sincerely thank members of the Burns-Paiute tribe who shared their stories and progress toward improving educational outcomes for native youth.[75]

The Youth Initiative pre-dated the Bundy occupation of Harney County and there was no direct relationship between the two (although funding for the HDP and the Youth Initiative was boosted by the occupation because of funders seeking ways to help the community[76]). However, the Youth Initiative illustrated one of the core aspects of the social and cultural character of Harney County that ultimately led to the failure of the Bundy occupation: by the time of the Bundy occupation in 2016, Harney County had cultivated a deliberate commitment to problem-solving through collaboration. The Bundy occupation itself illustrated the value of collaboration for building resilience (a word explicitly used in the youth group). The Youth Initiative—an embodiment of the commitment to community-building and collaboration—not only survived the Bundy occupation (and was perhaps even boosted by it), but in moving forward aggressively after the Bundy occupation, the initiative illustrated that the community, while still nursing wounds, reaffirmed its commitment to problem-solving through community dialogue.

The US Forest Service's Christy Cheyne observes that, in the period immediately after the end of the Malheur takeover, some who supported the confrontational Bundy approach attempted to get their message out in meetings of the High Desert Partnership's Harney County Restoration Collaborative (a group dedicated to problem-solving for stakeholders in the Malheur National Forest) but their confrontational style was defused by the collaborative approach:

> We've had some of the more active anti-government-type John Day[77] folks come down to be on our collaborative. They're all about road closures [in the national forest]. They were here, and we let them talk. Jack [Southworth, the collaborative's facilitator] always lets everybody talk as long as they want to talk, so everybody gets heard. But they don't come anymore. They just couldn't get the emotional reaction, the energy that they wanted I guess. Maybe they can get it in John Day, I don't know. But they just stopped coming after a while.[78]

Resilience implies the ability to withstand and recover from disturbances, whether predictable events (fire, flood, drought) or unpredictable events that cannot even be imagined. The Bundy occupation of Harney County fell squarely into the category of disturbances that could not possibly have been predicted (even after the Bundy militia arrived in Harney County, almost no one locally expected that they would take over the Malheur National Wildlife Refuge). However, many years of investment in building social relationships through conservation collaboratives had the unintended effect of enabling the community to prevent the disturbance from escalating to something even more catastrophic, and to continue building community resilience into the future.

Awake

On the morning of January 20, 2016, de facto Bundy occupation spokesman LaVoy Finicum stood outside one of the Depression-era stone buildings that make up the headquarters of the Malheur National Wildlife Refuge and spoke with me. Finicum, wearing a denim jacket, cream-colored cowboy hat, and a holstered Colt .45 revolver, was in a jovial mood, chatting about his self-published book (Finicum 2015) and autographing a copy of the famous "pocket Constitution" for me.

When I asked about the previous evening, Finicum became serious, with an edge of defensiveness. Most of the leaders of the Malheur takeover had abruptly entered a community meeting in Burns and the majority of local people in the auditorium had risen to their feet and chanted "Go home! Go home! Go home!" I asked if the apparent anger by the community toward the occupation leaders changed his thinking. Finicum responded emphatically, comparing the state of mind of the community to a person asleep. Finicum rhetorically asked if I like being woken up. Maybe the community needed to be woken up, Finicum suggested, and it was to be expected that some would not like it.

The analogy would not sit well with many in the community. Two nights earlier in Crane, Finicum had literally begged Harney County ranchers to attend a ceremony on January 23, 2016, to repudiate their federal grazing contracts, but none agreed to do so. Some ranchers at the meeting openly stated that the approach Bundy and Finicum and others were taking was unnecessarily extreme, and that the situation was not so dire as the occupiers believed. Many in the community would insist that if anyone was not fully awake and aware, it was the occupation leaders.

The occupation did, however, give some community members a renewed awareness of the importance of participating in collaborative processes. The Bundys provided a reminder that if local people do not speak up for themselves, someone else will—and they may not like what is said on their behalf. As rancher Kenny Bentz observed,

> I hesitate to ever say something positive about those knotheads [the Bundys]
> being here, because I don't like to give them any credit for doing anything

other than causing a lot of problems. . . . [But] it encouraged action in a variety of different people, probably myself included. If you don't want Bundy and those kind of folks speaking for you, then you better get off your butt and go do it yourself, otherwise that's what happens. Somebody is always going to fill that position [of speaking for the community]. . . . You always sit and [wonder] "Lord, why is that idiot up there?" . . . This isn't the only time someone is going to show up and presume to speak for us. . . . Since then, we have gotten up and said "Listen, if someone is going to go out and do the talking for us, we're going to do it ourselves." And that's what should have been happening all along. I think that's one of the very positive things that's probably come out of [the occupation]. It drives people out of the shadows. If you don't want idiots representing you, you better do it yourself.[79]

Brenda Smith, the executive director of the High Desert Partnership, confirmed that the Bundy occupation seemed to stiffen the resolve of Harney County citizens to solve their own problems in their own way without being told what to do by outsiders claiming to represent them. The occupation also raised the profile of the High Desert Partnership and other collaboratives in beneficial ways:

I think collaboration is going as well as always, and probably better. The attention has helped us, really. People are a lot more interested, and they kind of want to understand better what we do. It's made for particularly busy times for us. We haven't been taking many breaks! It was kind of like, here's our opening, let's work on making it go. It's brought more financial support, and more people interested in potentially funding us. . . . People who were already part of the collaborative process at least feel as committed, if not more committed to collaborating. Maybe just to prove a point. . . . One thing I've noticed about Harney County, and I really appreciate about it, is [the attitude of] "get out of our business, and let us figure out our own deal." I think that's just foundational to Harney County. I don't think that's because they've been collaborating, and it may actually be why they've embraced collaboration. It's like, "Stay out of our business, and let us figure it out."[80]

The Bundy occupation appeared to stiffen the resolve of Harney County citizens to do things their own way, but this was not new. For many years,

Harney County citizens had been speaking for themselves in a variety of collaborative venues, using community-based collaborative problem-solving methods to address many of the very same issues that the occupiers spoke of (to the extent the occupiers were ever specific in explaining their claims about government "tyranny"). The collaborative problem-solving approaches for which Harney County had become known nationwide could be seen as almost the diametric opposite of the confrontational, armed, politically radical approach of the occupiers.

The innovative, collaborative approaches widely used in Harney County could also be seen as having significantly helped the community to withstand and recover from the disruption caused by the Bundy occupation. In ecological science, the capacity of a system (whether social, ecological, or social-ecological) to withstand disturbance has long been a central theme and, in recent years, has focused on the concept of resilience (Holling 1973), defined as the capacity of a system to absorb disturbance and retain its essential structure and identity, avoiding transformation to a fundamentally different and less desirable state (Walker et al. 2004).

If Harney County rancher Gary Marshall was correct that collaborative problem-solving methods helped to inoculate the community from the revolutionary fever brought by the Bundy occupiers, then collaboration helped make Harney County more resilient. What the Bundys offered was nothing less than a transformation to a fundamentally new, "federal-free" social order. Collaborative approaches had given local residents a means to minimize problems associated with use of federal lands without resorting to such radical transformations. Though the community as a whole declined the offer of revolution, it was not unaffected by the disturbance, and will never be exactly the same (including memories of division and lasting enmities).

The essential functions, structure, and identity of the community, however, remained largely unchanged. In fact, to the extent that collaboration itself is part of Harney County's function and identity, the occupation seemed, if anything, to have redoubled local commitment to problem-solving through collaborative approaches—whether by investing in the community's future collaborative capacity and social and economic stability through the High Desert Partnership's Youth Initiative, or in the Harney County Watershed Council's newly invigorated commitment to "getting ahead" of state regulation for water users.

6

Conclusions

On October 21, 2017, former chief White House strategist Stephen K. Bannon gave a speech to California Republicans in Anaheim that should have profoundly alarmed Ammon Bundy and other leaders of the 2014 Bunkerville standoff, who were at the time awaiting trial in Las Vegas (delayed for two weeks by a horrific spasm of killing on the Las Vegas strip). Describing himself as President Donald Trump's "wingman outside," Bannon—widely considered the intellectual architect of a new, more nationalist Republican Party—urged California Republicans to avoid losing hope of regaining political traction in the heavily Democratic-leaning state.

The most remarkable part of the speech was that Bannon expressed concern that—unless brought back into the Republican fold—California might secede from the United States. The fact that a man who had sat at the right hand of the president of United States spoke seriously about the nation's richest and most populous state possibly declaring sovereignty from the union illustrated the seemingly fraying national political fabric of the time. For the Bundy family, who saw states as sovereign political entities under the Constitution, the notion of state secession might have seemed encouraging. From that view, what Bannon said next might have felt chilling. Using Civil War–era analogies, Bannon hinted at the validity of using armed force, if needed, to maintain federal government control:

> California is to Donald Trump as South Carolina was to Andrew Jackson. Back in the 1830s the folks in South Carolina didn't like the fact that Jackson,

a populist, and Congress had put on tariffs, federal tariffs, on products. And they decided that in South Carolina they weren't going to have those tariffs, and they were independent and they could do what they want. They could choose what federal laws they wanted to have and not have.

And General Jackson said that if they can pick and choose what laws they want, eventually they are going to split off and try to form a Southern Confederacy. He said this like in 1832. So Jackson passed another law and powered the US Army. He was going to send the Army into South Carolina. And he told somebody, "And if I have to, I'm going to hang John C. Calhoun from a lamppost, but we are going to enforce federal law."

[Bannon continued] ... Trust me, if you do not roll this back [California's leftward shift]—and I'm talking about people in this room—10 or 15 years from now the folks in Silicon Valley and the progressive left in this state are going to *try to secede* from the union. Now my hometown is Richmond, Virginia. My hometown was burned to the ground in April 1865. And in hindsight, it was burned to the ground for a pretty good reason.[1]

In April 2014, in Bunkerville, Cliven Bundy, with his sons Ammon and Ryan, led what amounted to a secession movement against the federal government. To the Bundy family's surprise and delight, their effort appeared to work—President Barack Obama chose not to burn "Richmond" (Bunkerville) to the ground. When Donald Trump won the presidency in 2016, some in the Bundy movement rejoiced, believing Trump would sympathize with their anti-federal-government stance. The Bundy Ranch website celebrated Trump's election by posting an image of a Christmas gift. Some Bundy supporters predicted Trump would pardon the Bundys.

Such a view seemed profoundly ignorant of the historical roots and contemporary mood of the Republican Party, especially in the Bundys' home state of Nevada. Although family patriarch Cliven Bundy stated, "I don't recognize the United States government as even existing," the Constitution of the State of Nevada contains one of the nation's strongest statements of "paramount allegiance" to the federal government: "No power exists in the people of this or any other State of the Federal Union to dissolve their connection therewith or perform any act tending to impair, subvert, or resist the Supreme Authority of the government of the United States." The strong pro-Union language was no accident: Nevada entered the Union while the Civil War was raging in the east, and in 1864 Republican president Abraham Lincoln authorized Nevada to convene a state constitutional convention led by overwhelmingly pro-Union state leaders.[2]

In 2017, Steve Bannon's "America First" nationalist speech in California echoed the anti-secessionist mood in which the Nevada state constitution was framed, including explicit references to pre–Civil War–era leaders and debates. Those who have studied the origins of the modern American "patriot" movement would recognize Bannon's reference to John C. Calhoun—a pro-slavery, secessionist South Carolina politician and one-time vice president of the United States. Calhoun was one of the originators of the ideology of nullification, the belief that states and counties can ignore laws they perceive to be unconstitutional (Levitas 2002). Nullification is a core principle in the Bundy and militia ideologies—that counties and states have higher authority than the federal government. Bannon, in stark contrast, stated that preserving federal supremacy over secessionists was a "pretty good reason" for burning his own hometown to the ground. While Bannon served as its executive chair, the alt-right online Breitbart News specifically disavowed any association between Trump and Bundy as a deliberate "smear," and indicated contempt for the almost cartoonish rural imaginary at the core of the Bundy worldview.[4]

Although Bannon was reported to have maintained a close personal relationship and a position of influence with President Trump even after Bannon had been removed from the White House, by early 2018 the two antiestablishment Republicans' friendship came to an extraordinarily bitter and public end over Bannon's statements to a reporter about his dim view of Trump and Trump's family.[5]

For the Bundy family, the fall of nationalist Steve Bannon offered little new hope. Accounts by White House insiders and journalists suggested that the president was detached from and incapable of absorbing information about public policy (Wolff 2018). With order inside the White House seemingly held together by a handful of retired generals, Trump's public lands policies appeared to be steered, to a large degree, to his interior secretary, Ryan Zinke, who had emphatically and repeatedly insisted since his nomination that, "I am absolutely against transfer or sale of public land."[6]

Zinke insisted that federal resources would remain under federal control to serve national objectives (Zinke spoke of promoting domestic "energy dominance"). Even when Zinke controversially proposed shrinking some national monuments created under the 1906 Antiquities Act to allow greater economic uses, he praised the act as an "overwhelming American success" that had protected almost two hundred of "America's greatest treasures."[7] The land remained federal.

The Trump administration's apparent disinterest in anti-federal politics was not lost on Ammon Bundy. On January 4, 2018, well after nationalist Steve Bannon left the White House, Bundy perceived Trump as continuing the nationalist approach:

> What I am worried about is that [Trump] is a nationalist. . . . My family has received more tyranny and more suffering under the Trump administration than we did as far as being prosecuted under the Obama administration. . . . Up to now there has been nothing done about the Gold Butte National Monument [near the Bundy Ranch]. . . . There may be a lot of people that want to drink the Trump Kool-Aid. To be honest with you I want to drink it. But I don't drink Kool-Aid unless the facts show that it's worth drinking. . . . Why hasn't Trump pardoned the Hammonds? . . . People want to say that maybe President Trump doesn't know, but I disagree.[8]

Recent history suggested that anti-federal militia members are most active and potentially dangerous when they feel ignored or dismissed in such a manner. Militia groups enjoyed a revival during the administration of Barack Obama (Sunshine 2016), who many militia groups expected to launch an aggressive gun control campaign. Militia groups appeared even more alarmed by the prospect of a Hillary Clinton presidency: in the run-up to the 2016 election, some militia openly prepared to battle a presumed Hillary Clinton administration.[9] As the initial celebratory mood among the militia following the surprise victory by Donald Trump dissipated, concerns about further violent extremist actions seemed warranted. For the Bundy family and like-minded militia, Trump was as favorably inclined a president as they were likely to get, yet they were still not getting anything close to the "federal-free" rural America they wanted.

There was every indication that Bundy supporters and other

radicalized militia groups would continue to gear up for a "second American Revolution" (MacNab forthcoming). During the 2016 presidential campaign, prominent militia leaders predicted unrest and violence on "both sides,"[10] no matter who won the election—a prediction that appeared prophetic after street battles between white nationalist marchers and counter-protesters left three dead in Charlottesville, Virginia, on August 12, 2017,[11] as well as less lethal clashes between extreme right and left groups across the country. Roger Stone, a one-time Trump adviser and veteran far-right political operative, warned that if Trump were impeached, "You will have a spasm of violence in this country, an insurrection like you've never seen."[12] By late 2017 and early 2018, a sense of the nation falling apart felt like the new normal.

Having walked free from charges of armed confrontation against the federal government not once but twice by early 2018, the Bundy family emerged as almost mythic folk heroes representing one of the most radical currents in this seemingly chaotic political mood.

The single event that dented the Bundy family's triumphant image was their rejection by the majority of citizens in Harney County. By the metric of Bundy's stated goals, his occupation of Harney County was an abject failure. Dwight and Steven Hammond remained in prison, and there was no indication that they would receive clemency; not one square inch of the Malheur National Wildlife Refuge was transferred to state, local, or private control; and in declining to tear up their government grazing contracts, Harney County citizens thwarted Bundy's explicitly stated goal to make Harney County the nation's first "federal-free," "constitutional" county.

The patience of law enforcement and stunning tactical errors by the Bundys helped make the end of the Malheur takeover less violent than many had predicted, but it was ultimately the refusal by the majority of the Harney County community to embrace the radical anti-federal agenda that led to Bundy's failure at Malheur (Walker 2016). Where federal courts failed to slow the Bundys, Harney County citizens succeeded—a fact worthy of reflection.

The occupation of Harney County in 2016, together with the standoff at Bunkerville, Nevada, in 2014, marked a major milestone in the history of the Sagebrush Rebellion in the American West—a movement often dated to the 1970s, but more accurately dated to the 1890s (McCarthy 1992; Makley 2017). Events at Bunkerville and Harney County represented a major escalation.[13] At the Malheur Refuge, Ammon Bundy called for "thousands" of like-minded individuals to come with their arms. In response, federal, state, and local law enforcement amassed an enormous arsenal of firepower, and the world's media descended into the frozen desert—all in a tiny community that was far more accustomed to being ignored by the outside world and that had never invited the armed visitors nor wished for the media spotlight. Most residents understood the danger: the mix of massive quantities of arms, passionate political views, and flamboyant and provocative personalities created a potential powder keg.

Although many of its citizens were not aware at the time, Harney County was arguably the first community to receive an explicit invitation to be the birthplace of a "second American Revolution." Ammon Bundy initially spoke of freeing Dwight and Steven Hammond, but after seizing the Malheur National Wildlife Refuge his publicly stated goals shifted to giving refuge land "back" to unidentified "rightful owners." Behind closed doors, Bundy revealed a far grander vision, calling Harney County the "tip of the spear" and pleading with ranchers to declare their sovereignty and lead a movement that would expel the federal government from rural America. "You guys will be an example of a federal-free county," Bundy pleaded.[14] Many accepted some parts of the Bundy message, especially the call to free Dwight and Steven Hammond.

Yet, in the end, few in the community embraced the Bundys' constitutional theories, and nearly all rejected the Bundys' radical, armed methods. The majority of Harney County's community just wanted the Bundys, the militia, outside law enforcement, and the media to leave them alone. Asked to lead a revolution, the majority in Harney County replied, "Go home."

Harney County's choice was made not because the community's ranchers, farmers, and loggers do not bridle at certain federal rules—they do. Harney County's choice was also made not because ranchers, farmers, and loggers do not see a form of property right in their federal lands contracts—some do. Rather, Harney County rejected the Bundy occupation in large part for reasons similar to the Bundys' own motivations: westerners on the whole dislike being told what to do by outsiders.

Harney County is no exception, and Ammon Bundy seemed unable to grasp that, for most Harney County citizens, his cowboy hat did not make him local. Bundy was far less of a member of the community than many of the employees who represented the federal agencies Bundy so strongly disparaged. Many local Bureau of Land Management, US Forest Service, and US Fish and Wildlife Service employees are themselves originally from Harney County. They are brothers and sisters, daughters and sons. Those not originally from Harney County are neighbors and friends. Bundy seemed oblivious to the fact that he was acting in exactly the way he claimed "arrogant" federal authorities act: he knew almost nothing of the community, he came uninvited from far away, and, without consulting with most in the community, he claimed he knew Harney County's problems and had the solutions. Worst of all, to the outside world Bundy claimed to speak for Harney County.

Harney County citizens make it clear they did not want outsiders claiming to speak for them (Highway 20, east of Burns, February 13, 2016).

The community's response to an outsider with little local knowledge coming in to Harney County, causing disruption, and claiming to speak for the community was predictable. Harney County rancher Tom Sharp asked, "What gives them the right to come and simply take over a facility in an armed confrontation, making demands that haven't been the demands of the local people?"[15] Harney County Republican Party chair Gretchen Bates, a twenty-year Harney County resident born into an Oregon farm family, observed, "You can't come into someone else's county and bring your own issues and decide you're going to take over part of their county. Go do it in your own county!"[16] There was no indication that Bundy, who complained bitterly about outsiders telling local people in Nevada what to do, ever saw the irony. Bundy never diluted his attitude of total self-certainty with a much-needed dose of humility.

Ammon Bundy might have benefited from a double dose. Certainly, he could have benefited from better research. When Bundy arrived in Harney County, he spent hours and days listening to the views and beliefs of a single distressed ranching family who reaffirmed many of Bundy's own views. Although liked and respected by many in the county, Bundy's informants were not originally from Harney County and were known as outliers in their stance toward the federal government. Those views were not in sync with the majority in the county—and most local people had no need or interest in being "educated" by Ammon Bundy, whose press conference pronouncements about Harney County's problems were often profoundly disconnected from the realities most residents knew.

Ammon Bundy appeared incapable of grasping that much of his information was, at best, misguided. Immediately after seizing the Malheur National Wildlife Refuge, Bundy declared his intention of "getting the ranchers back to ranching, . . . loggers back to logging, . . . miners back to mining." In reality, in Harney County agriculture was doing reasonably well; there had never been significant mining; and, as rancher Keith Baltzor points out, the glory days of the big sawmills "wasn't even close to sustainable."[17] Bundy repeatedly claimed that the entire Malheur National Wildlife Refuge was created by taking land from more than a hundred ranches. Locals like rancher Kenny Bentz knew that was simply not true: "There were tiny little pieces of the refuge that Teddy Roosevelt's administration condemned and took and that was wrong, but the vast majority of it the government bought—my Great-uncle Will sold it to them, for the Swift Company. The government did *not* take it."[18]

As for Bundy's claim that the federal government was putting Harney County "into poverty," most understood, as former local mill operator and hospital executive Jim Bishop observed, that without federal employment and payments the county's economy would be in "*big* trouble."[19] As former county commissioner Dan Nichols noted, financially speaking, the prospect of a "federal-free" Harney County was a nonstarter. Bundy's lack of basic understanding of the county's history and economy hurt his credibility and reinforced a familiar sense of yet another poorly informed outsider attempting to tell Harney County what to do.

The gap between Ammon Bundy's views and the views of the majority in Harney County was widest in regard to solutions. There was probably no one in Harney County who did not see real challenges in working with federal management agencies. In the 1970s, 1980s, and 1990s, frictions among federal agencies and local land users were intense and bitter. Yet, local people including farmers and ranchers, local government, the Burns Paiute Tribe, environmentalists, and federal employees invested many years and countless meetings in building the social capacity to work together to find, at a minimum, mutually acceptable solutions—and, often, innovative win-win solutions that left all parties better off. It is precisely because these users of federally managed public lands typically *do* resent faraway politicians deciding their fate that Harney County has, time and again, turned to collaboration so they can have a voice in deciding their own future.

Ammon Bundy seemed entirely unaware of the creative and effective collaborations that the community had invested so much time and effort in building—including the 2013 Malheur Comprehensive Conservation Plan for the very place where Bundy stood and condemned in sweeping terms government "tyranny."[20] When ranchers who actually held permits at the Malheur National Wildlife Refuge attempted to explain that the situation was not so dire, Bundy dismissed their views as merely proof that ranchers had been intimidated and were living in fear of the government—what Bundy called a "slave" mind-set. To many in the community, this dismissiveness appeared nothing short of uninformed arrogance. Thus, when

Ammon Bundy spoke of federal government "overreach" and implored local ranchers to join him in establishing a "federal-free" county through armed force, the view of many was that the questions he posed were not necessarily entirely off the mark, but his solutions were completely wrong for Harney County. Had Bundy truly listened to the community as a whole, and not just to a few distressed individuals, he might not have been surprised on January 23, 2016, when no locals heeded his call to declare sovereignty from the United States.

In the same sense that an individual such as Ammon Bundy would have been well advised to listen more carefully and understand local ways of viewing and solving land use problems, society broadly would do well to take such lessons to heart. Had Harney County's citizens flocked to Ammon Bundy's side at the Malheur National Wildlife Refuge, the consequences could have been dire. The occupiers had enough weapons and ammunition for a small war. If the "thousands" Bundy had called to the refuge had come with their arms, the odds of the occupation ending with a minimum of bloodshed would have greatly decreased.

By turning their backs against an armed, radicalized sagebrush rebellion, Harney County defused what could easily have become a violent tragedy in American history and a rallying event for anti-federal-government militia. Whether it ended in a symbolic victory for the Bundys, like Bunkerville, or in a bloody shootout, the takeover of the Malheur National Wildlife Refuge could easily have become the kind of motivating event that the federal siege in Waco, Texas, was for the militia movement of the 1990s. Some occupiers openly accepted the possibility of bloodshed, calling the Malheur takeover "Armageddon," and stating that the government "probably will kill us, but we're just a few and there are many more."[21]

No one in Harney County indicated interest in that outcome. Instead, almost as soon as the last refuge occupiers had been arrested peacefully and the militia, outside law enforcement, and journalists had left Harney County, the community resolutely resumed its *old* normal—intentionally reweaving the community fabric and working collaboratively to find practical solutions to tangible problems.

Many people in Harney County do believe that they are often ignored, and that their fate is too often decided by powerful people far away who do not understand their circumstances. It is for precisely this reason that Harney County invested decades in developing collaborative solutions: not because they do not resent outside control, but because collaboration at least provides a seat at the table and a voice. Harney County's land users want to do things their own way, and collaboration is seen as the most realistic way to achieve that goal. Rancher Kenny Bentz stated, "Waving AR-15s [assault rifles] around hasn't worked in the past—you've got to find another method."[22] Like most Westerners, few citizens of Harney County want to see ownership of public lands transferred to states or local control,[23] citing the expenses and risks involved.

Real concerns exist, but given the slowness and difficulty of legislative solutions and the prohibitive costs of litigation, the most realistic option is collaboration—which allows local people to "get ahead" of government restrictions, or at least to have a voice in the outcome. Rancher Stacy Davies—a staunch conservative Republican who was as sympathetic to the Bundys as anyone in Harney County yet played a key role in at least eight major local collaboratives—put it succinctly: "I prefer collaboration because we get more done on the ground."[24] Collaboration has not always been easy—as the chair of the Harney County Republican Party observed about sitting down with people with polar opposite views, "It's hard!"[25] Yet, decades of investment in multiple collaborative efforts have paid off. Building a community that works together takes work. Today, that effort has become part of the local culture: working together is what Harney County does.

As rural America continues to struggle with economic and social challenges that create fertile ground for those who advocate radical and violent solutions, society would be well advised to see investment in collaborative problem-solving in other communities as a way not only to manage natural resources, but also to build a more resilient society. In building its capacity to work together, Harney County built walls of resilience that enabled it to bounce back—if not immediately, if not completely—from a crisis unlike anything that almost any American community had faced before. Invited to take a radical path, Harney County instead followed a path that has repeatedly brought results that, if not perfect, were better than the alternatives.

Resilience in Harney County was all about Harney County: another community might have responded very differently, and there is no simple way to export a Harney County "model" to other communities that might be invited to walk down the radical path in the future. Harney County succeeded because its distinctive way of solving problems evolved organically, from the grassroots of the community over a long period of time. Other communities must evolve their own organic, grassroots solutions—*before* emergencies arise. Harney County cannot provide a model; but it can provide inspiration. Harney County proved that in a divided nation where rural communities often do face daunting challenges, and where radical activists believe they can find fertile ground for rebellion, there are alternatives to radicalization.

In a nation staggering to find its center of gravity, Harney County proved the power of a community that knows how to work together. With a new, more dangerous sagebrush rebellion[26] seeking platforms to launch its radical vision, Harney County was the first community asked to host a second American Revolution. It almost certainly will not be the last. The nation should breathe a sigh of relief that, by chance, the revolutionaries picked perhaps one of the least likely places to accept a radical message. Through lack of research and planning, they chose a community that had invested heavily for decades in non-radical problem-solving and had intentionally built up its community in ways that provided strength and resilience at a time of crisis, enabling the community to reject a glittering mirage of revolution.

Instead of glamorous revolution, Harney County returned to the unglamorous, time-consuming, sometimes tedious but often effective work of sitting across the table with people of different viewpoints to find mutually beneficial, practical solutions to shared problems. At a time when the nation felt in many ways like it was coming apart at the seams, it was worth noting and understanding how Harney County turned away a radicalized sagebrush rebellion in favor of sagebrush collaboration.

Notes

Preface

1 With a distinctive history, its own city government, and a population of 1,565 in the 2010 US Census, the City of Hines has its own identity. In Harney County, "Burns" is generally used to describe Hines and the adjoining larger City of Burns, together. This book uses "Burns" in the same way.

2 Amelia Templeton, "Militia Occupying Federal Land: 'We Are Not Hurting Anybody,'" Oregon Public Broadcasting, January 3, 2016, https://www.opb.org/news/article/militia-oregon-wildlife-refuge-burns-bundy-hammond/.

3 Maxine Bernstein, "Cliven Bundy Standoff Case Thrown Out in Another Stunning Blow to Government," *Oregonian*, January 8, 2018, http://www.oregonlive.com/oregon-standoff/2018/01/cliven_bundy_standoff_case_thr.html.

Chapter 1

1 United States Census estimate as of May 2017.

2 Audio recording of Sheriff David Ward interview with Sheriff Ozzie Knezovich, April 19, 2016. http://www.spokanetalksonline.com/category/podcasts/sheriffs-report/.

3 Interview with author, Sheriff Ward, May 19, 2016.

4 In Harney County, the word "militia" is widely used to describe groups that make up a self-described "patriot" community. Their goals and methods vary widely, but these groups generally consist of citizens organized and armed to protect communities against real or perceived crises, either natural or human-made. The groups that occupied Harney County in late 2015 and early 2016 do not necessarily fit the historic definition of the word "militia"

in the American context. However, this book uses the term "militia" because it is the word most commonly used locally.

5   Carli Brosseau, "Refuge Occupation's Co-leader Disillusioned by Iraq Finds Purpose in Bundys' Cause," *Oregonian*, January 22, 2016; updated February 22, 2016, http://www.oregonlive.com/oregon-standoff/2016/01/oregon_ occupation_leader_ryan.html.

6   Audio recording of Sheriff David Ward interview with Sheriff Ozzie Knezovich, April 19, 2016, http://www.spokanetalksonline.com/category/ podcasts/sheriffs-report/.

7   Interview with author, Sheriff Ward, May 19, 2016.

8   This book avoids the often-used term "Oregon standoff." Except for the arrests of the occupation leaders on January 26, 2016, and in the final hours of the occupation of the Malheur refuge on February 10–11, there was no direct confrontation between law enforcement and the Bundy militia.

9   Interview with author, Sheriff Ward, May 19, 2016.

10   The Bundy group, Pacific Patriots Network, Oath Keepers, Bearded Bastards, Idaho III% (Three Percenters), and the Central Oregon Guard.

11   Federal prosecutors, cited in the *Oregonian*, "Ammon Bundy Had Intended Refuge Occupation to End Up in Federal Court, Lawyers Say," by Maxine Bernstein, May 9, 2016, http://www.oregonlive.com/oregon-stand-off/2016/05/ammon_bundy_had_intended_refug.html. The warning about "extreme civil unrest" was also stated almost verbatim on the Bundy Ranch blog, bundyranch.blogspot.com: "We further warn that the incarceration of the Hammond family will spawn serious civil unrest," posted November 3, 2015, http://bundyranch.blogspot.com/search?updated-max=2015-11-27T10:27:00-08:00&max-results=7&reverse-paginate=true.

12   Grasty was apparently omitted from the "Redress of Grievance" because Ammon Bundy did not understand that, in some rural Oregon counties, the chair of the county commission has the title "judge" despite having no formal judicial role.

13   Personal communication with author, March 13, 2017.

14   Audio recording of Sheriff David Ward interview with Sheriff Ozzie Knezovich, April 19, 2016, http://www.spokanetalksonline.com/category/ podcasts/sheriffs-report/.

15   "November 12, 2015, Hammond Family Declared as Terrorist and Sentenced to Five Years in Federal Prison," http://bundyranch.blog-spot.com/search?updated-max=2015-11-12T05:45:00-08:00&max-re-sults=7&start=41&by-date=false.

16 http://bundyranch.blogspot.com/search?updated-max=2015-11-27T10:30:00-08:00&max-results=7&reverse-paginate=true.

17 *The Pete Santilli Show*, episode no. 1101, Ammon Bundy, "BLM Terrorizes Oregon Family," https://www.youtube.com/watch?v=v1BYIPFcrwI.

18 http://bundyranch.blogspot.com/2015/11/hammond-family-declared-as-terrorist.html.

19 Les Zaitz, "Oregon Ranchers' Fight with Feds Sparks Militias' Interest," *Oregonian*, December 31, 2015, http://www.oregonlive.com/pacific-northwest-news/index.ssf/2015/12/ranchers_fight_with_feds_spark.html.

20 Audio recording of Sheriff David Ward interview with Sheriff Ozzie Knezovich, April 19, 2016, http://www.spokanetalksonline.com/category/podcasts/sheriffs-report/.

21 Audio recording of Sheriff David Ward interview with Sheriff Ozzie Knezovich, April 19, 2016.

22 Harney County Sheriff's Office, "Malheur Wildlife Refuge Occupation" handout.

23 https://www.youtube.com/watch?v=PEvbIbxrj3Y; some YouTube channels have been removed in connection with the lawsuit, but this video can also be found at https://www.youtube.com/watch?v=ttnT4rQUbPc.

24 Interview with author, May 19, 2016.

25 https://www.youtube.com/watch?v=2zvrrQbjepc.

26 Interview with author, June 2016, name withheld by request.

27 https://www.youtube.com/watch?v=Aeeclad8G3E.

28 Maxine Bernstein, "Ammon Bundy's Facebook Posts Revealed: 'I Would Never Show Up at a Rally without My Arms,'" *Oregonian*, September 16, 2016, http://www.oregonlive.com/portland/index.ssf/2016/09/ammon_bundys_facebook_posts_re.html.

29 Interview with author, October 26, 2017.

30 Ibid., May 13, 2016, name withheld by request.

31 Interview by author with the resident, June 2016.

32 Interview with author, Burns Paiute Tribe then chair Charlotte Rodrique, November 14, 2017.

33 Interview with author, May 2016, name withheld by request.

34 Some estimated a higher number, but a careful count based on panoramic video taken at the meeting indicates thirty-five to forty persons in attendance.

35   Harney County Town Hall, no. 2, December 15, 2015, http://www.youtube.
      com/watch?v=JF2c6UYRdE0.

36   Les Zaitz, "Militiamen, Ranchers in Showdown for the Soul of Burns,"
      Oregonian, December 30, 2015; updated February 22, 2016, http://www.ore-
      gonlive.com/pacific-northwest-news/index.ssf/2015/12/militiamen_ranch-
      ers_in_showdow.html.

37   Members of the Committee of Safety declined repeated invitations to be
      interviewed for this book, citing scheduling conflicts.

38   Harney County Committee of Safety, "Comments on Events in Burns on
      January 2, 2016, Surrounding the Hammond Support Rally" (undated); later
      trial testimony provided conflicting accounts of whether any Committee of
      Safety members were aware of or involved with discussions about a possible
      takeover.

39   Luke Hammill, "Oregon Standoff: Harney County Group Asks Bundy to
      Leave but Takes on His Cause," *Oregonian*, January 8, 2016, http://www.
      oregonlive.com/pacific-northwest-news/index.ssf/2016/01/oregon_stand-
      off_harney_county.html.

40   Interview with author, Sheriff Ward, May 19, 2016.

41   Les Zaitz, "Ranchers Heading for Prison but Will Seek Clemency
      from Obama," *Oregonian*, January 4, 2016, http://www.ore-
      gonlive.com/pacific-northwest-news/index.ssf/2016/01/
      ranchers_heading_for_prison_to.html.

42   Idaho III% (Three Percenter) militia leader Brooke Agresta speaking at a
      rally for the Hammonds in Burns, Oregon, January 2, 2016; see "Hammonds
      Rally Burns OR Jan 2nd, 2016 part 1," 5:31, https://www.youtube.com/
      watch?v=QOEl53g4srE.

43   Pete Santilli, "Live Feed Hammond Ranch" (1:06:00, 1:09:00), streamed
      January 2, 2016, https://www.youtube.com/watch?v=jBBJe7FmRXI.

44   KOIN TV's Jennifer Dowling, January 2, 2016, reporting from Burns,
      Oregon.

45   The word "takeover" is used here to emphasize that the headquarters of the
      Malheur National Wildlife Refuge was not passively occupied; rather, it was
      seized with force of arms.

46   Jeremy P. Jacobs, "Jury Hears from the Accidental Occupier," *E&E News*,
      September 15, 2016, http://www.eenews.net/stories/1060042882/print.
      Butch Eaton, the "accidental occupier," was a strong local supporter of the
      Bundys. He claimed in court testimony that he went with the Bundys to
      the refuge not knowing what they intended to do. He claimed that when

he realized they were seizing and occupying the refuge, he didn't want to participate and walked several miles back on the road until his wife picked him up. For more, see https://www.opb.org/news/series/election-2016/oregon-standoff-trial-day-3-ammon-bundy-walter-eaton/.

47 *Oregonian*, "Militia Members Outline Their Plan," video, courtesy of Sarah Dee Spurlock, published January 2, 2016, http://videos.oregonlive.com/oregonian/2016/01/militia_men_outline_their_plan.html.

48 The Bundy occupiers became icons in both positive and less-positive ways, being mocked by some as "Vanilla ISIS" and "Y'all Qaeda" (referring to the Islamic State and Al Qaeda terrorist groups, respectively).

49 Les Zaitz, "Militant Leader Explains Intentions on Oregon Refuge Takeover," video, for the *Oregonian*, January 3, 2016, http://www.oregonlive.com/pacific-northwest-news/index.ssf/2016/01/ammon_bundy_plans_news_confere.html.

50 Personal communication with author, Sheriff Dave Ward, February 28, 2017.

51 Conrad Wilson, "2nd Malheur Trial Goes to Jury, Tempers Flare Outside Courtroom," *Oregonian*, March 7, 2017, http://www.opb.org/news/series/burns-oregon-standoff-bundy-militia-news-updates/closing-argument-apology-jason-patrick-jarvis-kennedy/.

52 Interview with author, November 14, 2017.

53 The Malheur National Wildlife Refuge was established in 1908 by President Theodore Roosevelt on 81,786 acres of federal land. In the following decades, the refuge grew to 187,756.54 acres, mostly through purchases from willing sellers, donations, and exchanges. Only 5,070.39 acres were acquired through condemnation (US Fish and Wildlife Service, Malheur National Wildlife Refuge Comprehensive Conservation Plan, 2013, pp. 1–13). Ammon Bundy's often-stated claim that "hundreds" of ranchers were forced off the land that is now the refuge is simply false. However, federal leases were increasingly restrictive because of new environmental regulations in the 1970s and 1980s, which appears to be the source of Bundy's claim that the land was "taken" from ranchers.

54 Interview with author, May 19, 2016.

55 Les Zaitz, "Militia Takes Over Malheur National Wildlife Refuge Headquarters," *Oregonian*, January 2, 2016, http://www.oregonlive.com/pacific-northwest-news/index.ssf/2016/01/drama_in_burns_ends_with_quiet.html.

56 United States of America v. Steven Dwight Hammond and Dwight Lincoln Hammond Case No. 6:10-CR-60066-HO June 12, 2012, Transcript of Proceedings.

57 United States Department of Justice, "Eastern Oregon Ranchers Convicted of Arson Resentenced to Five Years in Prison," US District Attorney's Office, District of Oregon, October 7, 2015.

58 Interview with author, June 10, 2016, name withheld by request.

59 Kathie Durbin, "Ranchers Arrested at Wildlife Refuge," *High Country News*, October 3, 1994.

60 Personal communication with author, Les Zaitz , June 26, 2016; Les Zaitz, "Militia Takes Over Malheur National Wildlife Refuge Headquarters," *Herald and News*, January 3, 2016, http://www.heraldandnews.com/news/ oregon/militia-takes-over-malheur-national-wildlife-refuge-headquarters/ article_8c23e4be-006f-5686-a3c3-809a486e596b.html.

61 Kathie Durbin, "Ranchers Arrested at Wildlife Refuge," *High Country News*, October 3, 1994.

62 Ibid.

63 CNN Television, 1994.

64 Denis C. Theriault, "Oregon Militants: Death Threats from Ranchers Reported Years before Standoff," *Oregonian*, January 6, 2016, http://www. oregonlive.com/politics/index.ssf/2016/01/oregon_militants_years_ before.html; Steve Lundgren, "Harney Fence Feud Nets Rancher's Arrest," *Burns Times-Herald* August 10, 1994, p. 1.

65 Richard Cockle, "Federal Agents Arrest Rancher in Water Dispute," *Oregonian*, August 10, 1994.

66 Personal communication with author, former Malheur National Wildlife Refuge law enforcement officer Daniel Schiell, June 24, 2016.

67 Malheur National Wildlife Refuge, correspondence file for the Hammonds.

68 Mr. Cameron confirmed these statements with the author by telephone on April 2, 2017, based on an interview reported by Arun Agrawal, "Oregon Ranchers Who Sparked Standoff Threatened to Wrap Official's Son in Barbed Wire and Drown Him," January 21, 2016, http://www.rawstory. com/2016/01/oregon-ranchers-who-sparked-standoff-threatened-to-wrap- officials-son-in-barbed-wire-and-drown-him/.

69 David Lewis, *War in the West*, CNN video documentary, 1994.

70 Interview with author, April 8, 2016, name withheld by request.

71 Interview with author, Sheriff Ward, May 19, 2016.

72 Harney County Sheriff's Office, "Dusty Hammond Docs_00022," investiga- tion report on case no. 0403055, 2004.

73 Conor Friedersdorf, "Oregon and the Injustice of Mandatory Minimums: America's Political Left Shares Far More in Common with the Armed

Protestors Than Many Apparently Realize," *Atlantic* magazine, January 5, 2016, http://www.theatlantic.com/politics/archive/2016/01/oregon-mandatory-minimums/422433/.

74 Transcript of Proceedings: United States of America, Plaintiff, v. Steven Dwight Hammond and Dwight Lincoln Hammond, Jr., Defendants. Case No. 6:10-CR-60066-HO June 12, 2012, Portland, Oregon; personal communication with author, Assistant US Attorney Frank Papagni Jr., November 20, 2017.

75 United States District Court, District of Oregon, United States of America v. Steven Dwight Hammond and Dwight Lincoln Hammond, Jr., CR No. 10-60066-HD Indictment.

76 Document titled, "United States v. Hammond, Et Al. (Dwight, Steven and Susan) Harney County Arsons Investigation 1982 through 2006," December 28, 2009.

77 United States District Court, District of Oregon, Eugene Division, United States of America v. Steven Dwight Hammond and Dwight Lincoln Hammond 6:10-CR-60066-HO Superseding Indictment; personal communication with author, November 20, 2017, Assistant US Attorney Frank Papagni Jr., who led the Hammond prosecution.

78 United States District Court, District of Oregon, United States of America v. Dwight Lincoln Hammond, Jr., No. 10-cr-60066-2-HO Verdict.

79 United States District Court, District of Oregon, United States of America v. Steven Dwight Hammond, No. 10-cr-60066-2-HO Verdict.

80 United States Court of Appeals, Ninth Circuit, United States of America, Plaintiff–Appellant, v. Steven Dwight Hammond, Defendant–Appellee. United States of America, Plaintiff–Appellant, v. Dwight Lincoln Hammond, Jr., Defendant–Appellee. Nos. 12–30337, 12–30339. Decided: February 07, 2014.

81 The agreement also allowed Steven Hammond's two five-year sentences to run concurrently, effectively cutting each sentence in half. Kimberley Frieda and John Sepulvado, "Court Papers: Hammonds Enter Plea Deals Knowing Mandated Sentences Loomed," Oregon Public Broadcasting, January 19, 2016, http://www.opb.org/news/series/burns-oregon-standoff-bundy-militia-news-updates/hammonds-entered-plea-knowing-sentences-loomed/.

82 Community meeting in Crane, January 18, 2016.

83 Ammon Bundy interview from the Multnomah County jail, by Kyle Iboshi, KGW TV News, March 3, 2016, http://www.kgw.com/news/local/watch-ammon-bundy-interview-from-jail/66722905.

84   Ibid.

85   Amanda Peacher, "Burns Meeting Grows Tense when Militants Arrive," Oregon Public Broadcasting, January 19, 2016, http://www.opb.org/news/series/burns-oregon-standoff-bundy-militia-news-updates/burns-meeting-grows-tense-with-bundy-presence/.

86   Amanda Peacher, "Harney County Voters Weigh Candidates on Refuge Occupation," Oregon Public Broadcasting, May 10, 2016, http://www.opb.org/news/series/burns-oregon-standoff-bundy-militia-news-updates/harney-county-malheur-bundy-refuge-occupation-voting/.

87   Interview with author, May 2016, name withheld by request.

88   Conrad Wilson, "Harney County Sheriff: Who Wants the Bundys To Go?" *Oregonian*, January 8, 2016, https://www.opb.org/news/series/burns-oregon-standoff-bundy-militia-news-updates/harney-county-residents-speak-out-on-occupation/.

89   "Harney County Resident May Want Militia to Remain," *Oregonian*, January 6, 2016, https://www.youtube.com/watch?v=t_nis1Ddov0.

90   "Rancher Georgia Marshall Speaks Out at Burns Community Meeting," *Oregonian*, October 27, 2016, https://www.youtube.com/watch?v=dn-6tEgaNkXs. In this video, Georgia Marshall sums it up in about four eloquent and passionate minutes.

91   Samantha White, "Seeing Harney County for What It Is," *Burns Times-Herald*, January 6, 2016, http://btimesherald.com/2016/01/06/seeing-harney-county-for-what-it-is/.

92   Personal communication with author, May 22, 2017.

93   Samantha Swindler, "A Rural Paper's Decision on the Voice of Harney County," *Oregonian*, April 27, 2016, http://www.oregonlive.com/oregon-standoff/2016/04/who_can_speak_for_harney_count.html.

94   "Oregon Standoff: Who Are the 'Rightful Owners' of the Land?" RT America interview with Burns Paiute tribal chair Charlotte Rodrique, January 15, 2016, https://www.youtube.com/watch?v=9VMtvZEkLsM.

95   Ian Kullgren, "Burns Paiute Tribe: Militants Need to Get Off 'Our Land,'" *Oregonian*, January 6, 2016, http://www.oregonlive.com/pacific-northwest-news/index.ssf/2016/01/burns_piaute_tribe_militants_s.html.

96   Interview with author, November 14, 2017.

97   Jim Urquhart, "Oregon Town Tense amid Dueling Protests after Wildlife Refuge Takeover," Reuters, February 1, 2016, http://www.reuters.com/article/us-oregon-militia-protests-idUSKCN0VA3EG.

Chapter 2

1   United States District Court District of Nevada, United States of America, Plaintiff, v. Cliven Bundy, Defendant, Case No. 2:12-cv-0804-LDG-GWF July 9, 2013.

2   United States of America, Plaintiff, v. Cliven Bundy, Defendant. CV-S-98-531-JBR (RJJ). United States District Court for the District of Nevada. 1998 U.S. Dist. LEXIS 23835.

3   United States District Court District of Nevada, United States of America, Plaintiff, v. Cliven Bundy, Defendant. 02:98-CV-00531-LRH-VCF ORDER October 8, 2013.

4   Michael Flynn, "Interview with Sniper in Bundy Standoff," The Independent (on YouTube), April 14, 2014, https://www.youtube.com/watch?v=AhNFqaLioD4.

5   Jim Urquhart, "Nevada Showdown," Reuters, April 23, 2017, http://blogs.reuters.com/photographers-blog/2014/04/23/nevada-showdown/.

6   Tom Ragan and Annalise Porter, "BLM Releases Bundy Cattle after Protesters Block Southbound I-15," *Las Vegas Review-Journal*, April 21, 2017, https://www.reviewjournal.com/news/bundy-blm/blm-releases-bundy-cattle-after-protesters-block-southbound-i-15/.

7   Adam Nagourney, "A Defiant Rancher Savors the Audience That Rallied to His Side," New York Times, April 23, 2014, https://www.nytimes.com/2014/04/24/us/politics/rancher-proudly-breaks-the-law-becoming-a-hero-in-the-west.html.

8   Jasonpatrick11/bambuser, "Bundy Ranch FULL Interview. Uncut/Unedited," April 19, 2014, http://bambuser.com/v/4549915.

9   Interviewed on InfoWars, *The Alex Jones Radio Show*, April 11, 2014, https://www.infowars.com/rancher-cliven-bundy-speaks-i-dont-recognize-them-having-any-jurisdiction-or-authority-over-this-land-video/.

10   Replayed on *The Dana* [Loesch] *Show*, April 10, 2014, http://danaloeschradio.com/the-western-war-last-remaining-rancher-vs-the-federal-govt/.

11   Meeting in Crane, Oregon, January 18, 2016.

12   Rebecca Boone, "4,000 Artifacts Stored at Oregon Refuge Held by Armed Group," Associated Press, January 16, 2016, https://apnews.com/amp/7e0b0a391bd3425ab5ddb65d2ee7b04f.

13   Interview with author, Harney County Sheriff Dave Ward, September 23, 2017.

14   Personal communication with author, Spencer Sunshine, October 31, 2017.

15   A term that somewhat confusingly replaced the older term "anti-federalist."

16   JJ MacNab, "Context Matters: The Cliven Bundy Standoff—Part III," *Forbes*, May 6, 2014, https://www.forbes.com/sites/jjmacnab/2014/05/06/context-matters-the-cliven-bundy-standoff-part-3/#1f4a5fa76599.

17   Ibid.; Southern Poverty Law Center, "What Is a 'Sovereign Citizen'?" November 30, 2008, https://www.splcenter.org/fighting-hate/intelligence-report/2015/what-sovereign-citizen.

18   Southern Poverty Law Center, "Sovereign Citizens Movement," https://www.splcenter.org/fighting-hate/extremist-files/ideology/sovereign-citizens-movement.

19   JJ MacNab, "Anti-Government Extremist Violence and Plots as of February 2017," www.jjmac.net.

20   Federal Bureau of Investigation, "FBI Law Enforcement Bulletin: Sovereign Citizens a Growing Domestic Threat to Law Enforcement," September 2012.

21   CSPOA, "About Us," http://cspoa.org/about/.

22   Fox News, "The Real Story: Feds Release Seized Cattle after Showdown with NV Rancher," April 14, 2014.

23   Richard Mack meeting at the Harney County Fairgrounds, February 12, 2016.

24   In Waco, Texas, in 1993, the Bureau of Alcohol, Tobacco, and Firearms attempted to arrest the leader of a religious sect suspected of having illegal guns and sexually abusing minors, resulting in events that caused the deaths of eighty members of the sect (twenty-one of them children) and four federal agents. A year earlier in Ruby Ridge, Idaho, when FBI agents attempted to arrest white supremacist Randy Weaver on gun charges, Weaver's wife and son and a federal agent were killed in a gun battle.

25   Named according to the belief that only 3 percent of American colonists successfully fought off colonial oppression during the American Revolution.

26   Brandon Smith, "Oregon Standoff a Terrible Plan That We Might Be Stuck With," January 4, 2016, https://www.oathkeepers.org/oregon-standoff-a-terrible-plan-that-we-might-be-stuck-with/.

27   Video recorded in "Operation Hammond Freedom," by the *Pete Santilli Show*, https://www.youtube.com/watch?v=jBBJe7FmRXI.

28   John Sepulvado, "GOP Politicians Planned and Participated in Key Aspects of Refuge Occupation," March 16, 2016, http://www.opb.org/news/series/burns-oregon-standoff-bundy-militia-news-updates/republican-gop-politicians-coalition-western-states/.

29   Coalition of Western States, http://cowstates.com/.

30 John Sepulvado, "GOP Politicians Planned and Participated in Key Aspects of Refuge Occupation," March 16, 2016, http://www.opb.org/news/series/burns-oregon-standoff-bundy-militia-news-updates/republican-gop-politicians-coalition-western-states/.

31 Coalition of Western States Facebook page, February 29, 2016, https://www.facebook.com/CoaltionofWesternStates/.

32 Lee Davidson, "FBI Files Shed Light on Ezra Taft Benson, Ike and the John Birch Society," *Salt Lake Tribune*, November 16, 2010, http://archive.sltrib.com/article.php?id=50349153&itype=CMSID.

33 Henderson State University history professor Matthew Bowman, cited by Leah Sottile, "Cliven Bundy's Fight against the Feds Has Roots in Interpretations of Mormon Scripture," *Washington Post*, December 7, 2017, https://www.washingtonpost.com/national/cliven-bundys-fight-against-the-feds-has-roots-in-interpretation-of-mormon-scripture/2017/12/07/0ef-8fea6-d93b-11e7-a841-2066faf731ef_story.html?utm_term=.008f97ef10f1.

34 Chris Zinda, "The 50-Year Leap: Of Theo-Constitutionalists and Theme Parks," *The Independent*, April 18, 2016, http://suindependent.com/theo-constitutional/.

35 Alexander Zaitchik, cited by Amanda Marcotte in, "Behind the Western Land War: How the Fringe Ideology of Anti-Government Cranks Is Becoming the GOP Mainstream," *Salon*, March 17, 2017, http://www.salon.com/2017/03/17/behind-the-western-land-war-how-the-fringe-ideology-of-anti-government-cranks-is-becoming-the-gop-mainstream/.

36 Leah Sottile, "Cliven Bundy's Fight against the Feds Has Roots in Interpretation of Mormon Scripture," *Washington Post*, December 7, 2017, https://www.washingtonpost.com/national/cliven-bundys-fight-against-the-feds-has-roots-in-interpretation-of-mormon-scripture/2017/12/07/0ef-8fea6-d93b-11e7-a841-2066faf731ef_story.html?utm_term=.008f97ef10f1.

37 The Church of Jesus Christ Latter Day Saints' official statement was that, "While the disagreement occurring in Oregon about the use of federal lands is not a Church matter, Church leaders strongly condemn the armed seizure of the facility and are deeply troubled by the reports that those who have seized the facility suggest that they are doing so based on scriptural principles. This armed occupation can in no way be justified on a scriptural basis," http://www.mormonnewsroom.org/article/church-responds-to-inquiries-regarding-oregon-armed-occupation.

38 The author thanks LDS Bishop Kevin Johnson for sharing his views on Mormon faith, interview with author, July 13, 2016. The author's interpretations here are his own.

39   Personal communication with author, Spencer Sunshine, April 10, 2017.

40   Phil Taylor, "'Mr. Sagebrush Rebellion' Bankrolls Push to Seize Federal Land," *E&E News*, March 18, 2016, https://www.eenews.net/stories/1060034277.

41   Personal communication with author, Kieran Suckling, executive director of the Center for Biological Diversity, April 25, 2017.

42   Michael McCarthy, "The First Sagebrush Rebellion: Forest Reserves and States Rights in Colorado and the West, 1891–1907," Forest History Society, The Origins of the National Forests: A Centennial Symposium 1992, http://www.foresthistory.org/Publications/Books/Origins_National_Forests/sec13.htm.

43   See United States v. Grimaud, 220 U.S. 506 (1911).

44   Oregon Public Broadcasting, *Think Out Loud*, "History of Public Land," political scientist Phil Brick interviewed on how the Bundy occupation fits into the history of conflicts over public lands in the West.

45   In particular, anger arose when the 1976 Federal Land Policy Management Act halted the disposal of federal lands and ordered the Bureau of Land Management to identify areas for wilderness and other environmental protections.

46   Bill Prochnau, "Sagebrush Rebellion Is Over, Interior Secretary Says," *Washington Post*, September 12, 1981, p. A9.

47   Sean Whaley, "US Supreme Court Closes Book on Wayne Hage, Sagebrush Rebellion Court Case," *Las Vegas Review-Journal*, October 26, 2016, https://www.reviewjournal.com/news/politics-and-government/nevada/us-supreme-court-closes-book-on-wayne-hage-sagebrush-rebellion-court-case/.

48   Jonathan Thompson, "A New and More Dangerous Sagebrush Rebellion," *High Country News*, February 10, 2016, http://www.hcn.org/articles/a-new-and-more-dangerous-sagebrush-rebellion.

49   Conrad Wilson and Amelia Templeton, "Bundys Urge Oregon Ranchers to Tear Up Grazing Contracts," Oregon Public Broadcasting, January 18, 2016, http://www.opb.org/news/series/burns-oregon-standoff-bundy-militia-news-updates/ammon-bundy-oregon-grazing-blm-finicum-crane/.

50   CNN report by Sara Sidner, "Protester: We'll Stay until We Secure Land," January 2, 2016, http://www.cnn.com/videos/us/2016/01/04/oregon-wildlife-refuge-protest-sidner-lklv.cnn.

51   Some critics concluded incorrectly that the "pocket Constitutions" carried by the occupiers must be "fake," or modified to fit their ideologies. In fact,

these documents were verbatim reproductions of the US Constitution (along with the Bill of Rights and the Declaration of Independence). What distinguished the "pocket Constitutions" was the preface, which included selected quotes from the Founders intended to suggest that the United States government must be guided by religion.

52 For example, a January 22, 2016, response to the constitutional views of Bundy-supporter KrisAnne Hall, authored by law professor Susan Lea Smith ("Federal Ownership of Land in Oregon and Other States West of the Mississippi"), was posted on the Harney County government's web page and circulated widely.

53 Interview with author, August 22, 2016. The interview was private and off-record until the end of the Bundys' Bundy occupation trial.

54 Ryan Bundy at meeting in Crane, Oregon, January 18, 2016, from author's recording.

55 Bundy made no mention of the Paiute people, who indisputably "got there first" in Harney County and the Malheur National Wildlife Refuge.

56 "The Congress shall have Power to dispose of and make all needful Rules and Regulations respecting the Territory or other Property belonging to the United States; and nothing in this Constitution shall be so construed as to Prejudice any Claims of the United States, or of any particular State."

57 "To exercise exclusive Legislation in all Cases whatsoever, over such District (not exceeding ten Miles square) as may, by Cession of Particular States, and the Acceptance of Congress, become the Seat of the Government of the United States, and to exercise like Authority over all Places purchased by the Consent of the Legislature of the State in which the Same shall be, for the Erection of Forts, Magazines, Arsenals, dock-Yards, and other needful Buildings"

58 The correct wording is "10 miles square," meaning 100 square miles.

59 The name given by the occupiers to the headquarters of the Malheur National Wildlife Refuge.

60 Finicum claimed a Harney County rancher would participate, which did not occur.

61 For example, Kimberly Paxton, "Militias Are On Route: Is the 2nd American Revolution Starting in Bunkerville, Nevada?" *Daily Sheeple*, April 10, 2014, http://www.thedailysheeple.com/militias-are-on-route-is-the-2nd-american-revolution-starting-in-bunkerville-nevada_042014; also Administrator Ryan, "The Second American Revolution—A Definitive Guide," January 28, 2016, https://uscrow.org/2016/01/28/the-second-american-revolution-a-definitive-guide/.

62   Bundy used the word "stand" to mean illegal seizure of land while taking an armed stance to prevent government intervention.

63   Author's conversation with Ammon Bundy in Crane, Oregon, January 18, 2016.

64   Interview in video documentary, *American Standoff*, by Josh Turnbow, an AT&T production for DirectTV, first aired May 3, 2017.

65   "Town Hall Meeting Regarding Hammond Family—Burns, OR—12-15-2015, 2 of 3," December 15, 2017, 11:28–13:01, https://www.youtube.com/watch?v=OPTLXg1fKZ8.

66   Payne repeated this at the January 18, 2016, meeting with ranchers in Crane, Oregon.

67   "Occupiers Fire Rifles from Malheur National Wildlife Refuge Boat Ramp" (filmed January 25, 2016), *Oregonian*, November 5, 2016, https://www.youtube.com/watch?v=x61x1-iw3CE.

68   Maxine Bernstein, "Feds Present Dramatic Display of 22 Long Guns, 12 Handguns Recovered from Refuge," *Oregonian*, September 27, 2016, http://www.oregonlive.com/oregon-standoff/2016/09/feds_present_dramatic_display.html.

69   Maxine Bernstein, "Michael Emry, Facing Federal Gun Charges, Traveled to Oregon in Van Loaned to Him by Ammon Bundy, Prosecutors Say," *Oregonian*, July 14, 2016, http://www.oregonlive.com/portland/index.ssf/2016/07/michael_emry_facing_federal_gu.html; Maxine Bernstein, "Michael Emry Pleads Guilty in Federal Court to Possession of a Machine Gun," *Oregonian*, January 23, 2017, http://www.oregonlive.com/oregon-standoff/2017/01/michael_emry_pleads_guilty_in.html.

70   Interview with MSNBC reporter Tony Dokoupil, January 26, 2016.

71   Les Zaitz, "Militia Takes Over Malheur National Wildlife Refuge Headquarters," January 2, 2016, *Oregonian*, http://www.oregonlive.com/pacific-northwest-news/index.ssf/2016/01/drama_in_burns_ends_with_quiet.html.

72   Audience Network, "American Standoff Trailer" (1:28), https://www.youtube.com/watch?v=lmJFd35099w.

73   Interview with MSNBC reporter Tony Dokoupil, January 26, 2016.

74   Dan Zak, "I Listened to Live Audio of the Oregon Standoff. This Is How Riveting and Ridiculous It Was," *Washington Post*, February 11, 2016, https://www.washingtonpost.com/news/arts-and-entertainment/wp/2016/02/11/thousands-listened-to-the-surreal-oregon-standoff-livestream-heres-what-it-sounded-like/?utm_term=.1ac0692c9690.

75   Maxine Bernstein, "Video Shows Chaos as Refuge Occupiers Debate Whether to Leave after LaVoy Finicum Died," *Oregonian*, February 23, 2017, http://www.oregonlive.com/oregon-standoff/2017/02/video_shows_chaos_anger_on_ref.html.

76   Maxine Bernstein, "Judge Orders Release of Holdout Sean Anderson Despite Inflammatory Videos," *Oregonian*, http://www.oregonlive.com/oregon-standoff/2016/05/judge_orders_release_of_refuge.html.

77   Personal communication with author at the Malheur National Wildlife Refuge, January 20, 2016.

78   Outpost of Freedom, "About Gary Hunt," http://outpost-of-freedom.com/blog/?page_id=6.

79   Outpost of Freedom, "Burns Chronicles No. 4: Stand Up Stand Down," http://outpost-of-freedom.com/blog/?p=1338.

80   Hour of the Time, "Oklahoma City Bombing: The Plot Thickens," http://www.hourofthetime.com/plot.htm?276,34.

81   http://outpost-of-freedom.com/blog/?p=1188.

82   Personal communication with author, May 19, 2016.

83   On June 8, 2014, married couple Jerad and Amanda Miller murdered two police officers, apparently selected at random, in a Las Vegas pizza restaurant, then covered the bodies with a yellow Gadsden flag and swastika, and pinned a note on one declaring "This is the beginning of the revolution." "Anti-Government Killers Put Swastika, Flag on Metro Police Officer's Body," *Las Vegas Sun*, June 9, 2014, https://lasvegassun.com/news/2014/jun/09/police-describe-bloodbath-created-neo-nazi-couple-/.

84   Personal communication with author, Center for Biological Diversity executive director Kieran Suckling, January 23, 2016.

85   John W. Whitehead, "Why a Violent End in Oregon Standoff Would Be a Loss for Us All," *The Blaze*, January 5, 2016, http://www.theblaze.com/contributions/why-a-violent-end-in-oregon-standoff-would-be-a-loss-for-us-all/.

86   Maxine Bernstein, "Ammon Bundy's Facebook Posts Revealed: 'I Would Never Show Up to a Rally without My Arms,'" *Oregonian*, September 16, 2016, http://www.oregonlive.com/portland/index.ssf/2016/09/ammon_bundys_facebook_posts_re.html.

87   Interview in video documentary, *American Standoff*, by Josh Turnbow, an AT&T production for DirectTV, first aired May 3, 2017.

88   Recorded on cell phone video during the arrest by co-occupier Shawna Cox inside LaVoy Finicum's pickup.

89   Interview in video documentary, *American Standoff*, by Josh Turnbow, an AT&T production for Direct TV, first aired May 3, 2017.

90   Press conference, January 5, 2016.

91   Interview with author, May 19, 2016.

Chapter 3

1   Video recording, January 23, 2016, provided by Candy Henderson.

2   Ibid.

3   Ibid.

4   Brian Maffly, "Utah Ranchers Renounce Federal Control of Their Lands at Gathering with Ties to Oregon Occupation," *Salt Lake Tribune*, January 27, 2016, http://www.sltrib.com/news/3467639-155/ utah-ranchers-renounce-federal-control-of.

5   Sam Levin, "Utah Ranchers Vow to Stand Up to Government Despite Oregon Arrests," *The Guardian*, April 4, 2016, https://www.theguardian.com/us-news/2016/apr/04/ utah-ranchers-oregon-standoff-federal-government-cliven-bundy.

6   Tay Wiles, "Malheur Occupation Impacts Linger throughout the West," *High Country News*, October 4, 2016, http://www.hcn.org/articles/ ammon-bundy-malheur-standoff-effects-sagebrush-rebellion.

7   Les Zaitz, "Oregon Standoff: Ranchers, Including Ex-Con, Renounce Grazing Permits," *Oregonian*, January 24, 2016, http://www.oregonlive.com/ oregon-standoff/2016/01/post_1.html; "Ax-Swinging Former OSU Student Gets Five Years' Probation," May 10, 2002, http://www.tulsaworld.com/ archives/ax-swinging-former-osu-student-gets-five-years-probation/arti- cle_2494589e-1b6f-56c0-a081-bf426cd6a4cf.html.

8   Silver City Ranger District Gila National Forest, "Annual Operating Instructions 2016 Walnut Creek Allotment #720 Bear Mountain Cattle Company"; Greta Anderson, "Forest Service Increases Rogue Rancher's Use by 70% for 2016," *Wildlife News*, March 28, 2016, http://www.thewild- lifenews.com/2016/03/28/forest-service-increases-rogue-ranchers-use-by- 70-for-2016/; Tay Wiles, "Malheur Occupation Impacts Linger throughout the West," *High Country News*, October 4, 2016, http://www.hcn.org/ articles/ammon-bundy-malheur-standoff-effects-sagebrush-rebellion.

9   Video interview posted to Bundy Ranch Facebook page, January 2, 2016, https://www.facebook.com/bundyranch/videos/938588846217924/.

10   First video statement by Ammon Bundy from occupied Malheur National Wildlife Refuge, January 2, 2016, posted to Facebook by Sarah Dee Spurlock.

11   US Census Bureau Small Area Income and Poverty Estimates, accessed through http://www.countyhealthrankings.org/app/oregon/2016/measure/factors/63/datasource?sort=desc-2.

12   US Census Bureau American FactFinder, 2011–2015 American Community Survey, https://factfinder.census.gov/faces/tableservices/jsf/pages/pro-ductview.xhtml?pid=ACS_13_5YR_DP03&prodType=table.

13   US Census Bureau Small Area Income and Poverty Estimates: All Ages in Poverty for Harney County, Oregon in 2015, https://www.census.gov/did/www/saipe/data/interactive/saipe.html?s_appName=saipe&-map_yearSelector=2015&map_geoSelector=aa_c&s_state=41&s_coun-ty=41025&menu=grid_proxy.

14   American Community Survey data for 2015 reported by the US Department of Agriculture Economic Research Service, in "Poverty Overview," https://www.ers.usda.gov/topics/rural-economy-population/rural-poverty-well-being/poverty-overview/.

15   US Census Bureau Small Area Income and Poverty Estimates: All Ages in Poverty (1997–2015) for Harney County, Oregon, https://www.census.gov/did/www/saipe/data/interactive/saipe.html?s_appName=saipe&-map_yearSelector=2015&map_geoSelector=aa_c&s_state=41&s_coun-ty=41025&menu=trends.

16   US Bureau of Economic Analysis, Regional Interactive Data for all counties in Oregon, 1969–2015, https://www.bea.gov/.

17   US Bureau of Economic Analysis Interactive Regional Data CA25: Total Full-Time and Part-Time Employment by SIC Industry; and CA25N: Total Full-Time and Part-Time Employment by NAICS Industry, https://www.bea.gov/.

18   Oregon Office of Economic Analysis, "Harney County, A Brief Historical Perspective," January 6, 2016, https://oregoneconomicanalysis.com/2016/01/06/harney-county-a-brief-historical-perspective/.

19   City of Hines, Oregon, "Hines Mill History," http://ci.hines.or.us/history.

20   Oregon Historical Society, "Hines and the Edward Hines Lumber Company," https://oregonencyclopedia.org/articles/hines_and_the_edward_hines_lumber_company/#.WVCx5RPyvMU.

21   Although the northern spotted owl does not inhabit the drier forests of Eastern Oregon, it was widely believed within the timber industry that the owl had become a proxy for environmentalists' interest in protecting old-growth forests throughout the Pacific Northwest region. Facing weak market demand, new supply options overseas and in the southeastern US states, as well as high investment costs for modernizing mills and infrastructure,

litigation surrounding the spotted owl undermined business confidence in long-term access to old growth timber in the Pacific Northwest region as a whole and was perceived as contributing to the migration of the industry to other sources of supply.

22   Interview with author, June 16, 2017.

23   Interview with author, October 16, 2016.

24   Gaps in the graph represent US Bureau of Economic Analysis data: "Not shown to avoid disclosure of confidential information, but the estimates for this item are included in the totals."

25   Averaged for the decade of 1969 to 1979, just before the closing of the Hines mill in 1980. US Bureau of Economic Analysis.

26   In 2002. US Bureau of Economic Analysis.

27   US Bureau of Economic Analysis Regional Interactive Data, CA25N Total Full-Time and Part-Time Employment by NAICS Industry, https://www.bea.gov/.

28   2016 interview with Harney County resident Chris Briels, in video documentary American Standoff, by AT&T/DirectTV 2017.

29   Interview with author, June 3, 2017.

30   Interview with author, June 3, 2017.

31   Personal communication with author, former Harney County judge Steve Grasty, June 28, 2017.

32   Nichols interview with author, September 16, 2016.

33   Interview with author, June 16, 2017.

34   Utah H.B.148, Transfer of Public Lands Act and Related Study (Chief Sponsor: Ken Ivory), required the United States to extinguish title to public lands and transfer title of those public lands to the state on or before December 31, 2014.

35   Kindra McQuillan, "State Bills to Study Federal-To-State Land Transfers," High Country News, April 30, 2015, http://www.hcn.org/articles/state-bills-to-study-federal-to-state-land-transfers.

36   Jan Stambro et al., "An Analysis of a Transfer of Federal Lands to the State of Utah," November 2014, http://publiclands.utah.gov/wp-content/uploads/2014/11/1.%20Land%20Transfer%20Analysis%20Final%20Report.pdf.

37   Brenda Younkin et al., Y2 Consultants, LLC, "Study on Management of Public Land in Wyoming," p. xxi, August 31, 2016, http://slf-web.state.wy.us/osli/News/FinalStudyFedLand.pdf.

38 Bailey Bischoff, "Ten States with the Fastest Job Growth in 2016," *Christian Science Monitor,* June 15, 2016, https://www.csmonitor.com/Business/2016/0615/Ten-states-with-the-fastest-job-growth-in-2016/.

39 KATU interview, January 20, 2016 (7:33), https://www.youtube.com/watch?v=pl3USUqkzf4.

40 Gavin Seim, documentary video, *Bundy, the True Story—Official,* December 10, 2016, https://www.youtube.com/watch?time_continue=1325&v=nNPNRmEHBbo.

41 57,898.48 acres from the public domain; 55,929.86 from the US Department of Agriculture.

42 US Fish and Wildlife Service, 2015 Annual Report of Lands as of 9/30/2015, p. 24.

43 US Fish and Wildlife Service, 2013 Malheur National Wildlife Refuge Comprehensive Conservation Plan, chapter 1, "Introduction and Background," pp. 1–31.

44 Possibly the oldest positively dated evidence of human occupation in North America was found in the Paisley Caves, about a hundred miles west of Malheur Lake. Reasoning that the way of life at the time required roaming wide areas, it can be surmised that human occupation of the Harney Basin occurred at about the same time; communication with author, archaeologist Melvin Aikens, August 30, 2017, and archaeologist Dennis Jenkins, August 31, 2017.

45 Burns Paiute Tribe home page, https://www.burnspaiute-nsn.gov.

46 United States v. Oregon 295 U.S. 1 (1935).

47 United States Fish and Wildlife Service, 2013 Malheur National Wildlife Refuge Comprehensive Conservation Plan, chapter 1, "Introduction and Background," pp. 1–8.

48 Executive Order 929, signed by President Theodore Roosevelt on August 18, 1908, ordered that "all smallest legal subdivisions which touch the shoreline of Lakes Malheur and Harney . . . are hereby reserved, subject to valid existing rights, and set aside for the use of the Department of Agriculture as a preserve and breeding-ground for native birds."

49 US Fish and Wildlife Service, 2013 Malheur National Wildlife Refuge Comprehensive Conservation Plan, chapter 1, "Introduction and Background," pp. 1–9.

50 US Fish and Wildlife Service, 2013 Malheur National Wildlife Refuge Comprehensive Conservation Plan, chapter 1, "Introduction and Background," pp. 1–12.

51 Interview with author, October 16, 2016, rancher Kenny Bentz, a descendant of the Swift's representative in the sale.

52 Book 36, p. 437, Deed Records of Harney County, Oregon, February 21, 1935.

53 Interview with author, former Malheur National Wildlife Refuge manager Forrest Cameron, August 28, 2017.

54 Interview with author, Harney County rancher and local historian Pauline Braymen, August 27, 2017.

55 US Fish and Wildlife Service, 2013 Malheur National Wildlife Refuge Comprehensive Conservation Plan, chapter 1, "Introduction and Background," pp. 1–12.

56 Interview with author, former Malheur National Wildlife Refuge manager Forrest Cameron, August 28, 2017.

57 US Fish and Wildlife Service, 2013 Malheur National Wildlife Refuge Comprehensive Conservation Plan, chapter 1, "Introduction and Background," pp. 1–9.

58 Ibid., pp. 1–10.

59 Braymen's research was verified by the author's own visits to the Harney County records office.

60 The US Fish and Wildlife Service's 2013 Malheur Comprehensive Conservation Plan reported 5,070 condemned acres (pp. 1–13). Braymen's research was not yet complete at the time of this publication, and Braymen expected that her completed work would resolve the seeming discrepancy.

61 Interview with author, April 8, 2016.

62 Interview with author, former Malheur National Wildlife Refuge manager Forrest Cameron, July 26, 2017.

63 Communication with author, Malheur National Wildlife Refuge deputy manager Jeff Mackay, July 19, 2017; interview with author, Harney County Recorder Dag Robinson, July 18, 2017.

64 US Fish and Wildlife Service, Malheur National Wildlife Refuge 1978 Annual Narrative Report, p. 3; McEwen co-owned the property with several members of the Hill family.

65 US Fish and Wildlife Service, 2013 Malheur Comprehensive Conservation Plan, pp. 1–11; another 2,462-acre inholding on Mud Lake was acquired from Larry and Allene Dunn in 1984 in exchange for 1,042 acres of refuge land near Diamond, but was not controversial since the Dunn family had lost everything on their Mud Lake ranch because of severe flooding in the early 1980s. Various small exchanges, purchases, and donations to the refuge have also taken place. 2013 Malheur Comprehensive Conservation Plan, pp. 1–11.

66 Malheur National Wildlife Refuge 1978 Annual Report, p. 3.

67 United States of America v. Stella Hill et al., United States District Court for the District of Oregon Civil No. 78-1119 H-5155 Judgment in Condemnation and Order of Distribution February 17, 1981.

68 Oregon State University Agricultural Experiment Station, "An Economic Analysis of Land Prices of Mountainous Grazing Land in Eastern Oregon," Special Report 560, September 1979; for example, the only sale of comparable ranchland inholdings found in the Harney County Records Office for 1978 shows that Weigand Ranches, Inc., sold 960 acres in the Silver Creek Valley west of Burns for $417 per acre.

69 County of Harney v. United States No. 79-526BU (D. Or. November 10, 1982). Harney County, Ranchers for Conservation, Harney County Stockgrowers Association, and the National Association of Property Owners, Plaintiffs.

70 The dramatic Bundy family standoff with law enforcement officers in Bunkerville, Nevada, in 2014 traces back to patriarch Cliven Bundy's claim that new restrictions on his grazing permits for the protection of the desert tortoise were an unconstitutional taking of his "right" to the grass on federal land.

71 An AUM is the amount of forage required per month for an "animal unit," often defined as a mature 1,000-pound cow and her suckling calf; the author is grateful for data provided by the Malheur National Wildlife Refuge staff—Chad Karges, Ed Sparks, and Jeff MacKay, on September 20, 2017.

72 Wallace Turner, "Rising Lakes Are Drowning Oregonians' Dreams," New York Times, September 29, 1984, http://www.nytimes.com/1984/09/29/us/rising-lakes-are-drowning-oregonians-dreams.html?mcubz=0.

73 The Fifth Amendment of the US Constitution states, "Nor shall private property be taken for public use, without just compensation." The US Supreme Court has upheld that federal or state governments may "take" private property to serve a valid public use as long as the owner is compensated fairly. This principle was upheld, controversially, under a broad interpretation of "public use" in Kelo v. City of New London, 2005.

74 "Headwaters Economics 2017: A Profile of Land Use, Harney County, Oregon," from US Geological Survey Gap Analysis Program Protected Areas Database of the United States, Version 1.4.

75 Interview with author, September 9, 2016.

76 Ibid., October 16, 2016.

77 Ibid.

78 Interview with author, October 15, 2016.

79 Oregon Natural Desert Association Annual Desert Conference, Bend, Oregon, October 14, 2016.

80 Interview with author, June 3, 2016.

81 Ibid., September 17, 2016.

82 Ibid., June 3, 2016.

83 Interview by *Seattle Times*, January 9, 2016, http://www.seattletimes.com/seattle-news/politics/occupied-oregon-wildlife-refuge-known-for-listening-to-ranchers/.

Chapter 4

1   USDA Forest Service, "Environmental Assessment for the Dairy Project, Emigrant Creek Ranger District, Malheur National Forest," October 2011.

2   Personal communication with author, Brenda Smith, executive director of the High Desert Partnership, December 6, 2017.

3   Much of the information presented here was gathered from a group interview by the author with members of the Steens Interest Group (a temporary designation while the SMAC and other resource advisory councils were temporarily suspended for review by the Department of Interior in 2017) on June 15, 2017. Those present were David Bilyeu (state environmental representative), Stacy Davies (grazing permittee), Fred Otley (private landowner), Leon Pielstick (chair, and wild horse management representative), Owyhee Weikel-Magden (local environmental representative), Kali Wilson (grazing permittee), John Helmer (dispersed recreation representative), Karl Findling (mechanized or consumptive recreation representative), and Rod Klus (state liaison, nonvoting). Not present were Cecil Dick (Burns Paiute Tribe), Nathan Hovekamp (no financial interest), Mark Bagett (fish and recreational fishing representative), and the recreational permittee representative because of a vacancy in that position.

4   Personal communication with author, Steens Act coauthor Stacy Davies, December 11, 2017.

5   Michelle Nijhuis and Oakley Brooks, "Congress Moves on Local Proposals," *High Country News*, November 6, 2000.

6   114 Stat. 1666 Public Law 106-399 Oct. 30, 200: Steens Mountain Cooperative Management and Protection Act of 2000.

7   114 Stat. 1666 Public Law 106-399 Oct. 30, 2000 Sec. 132 (1), (2)(b).

8   This history is recorded in the unpublished document, History of the High Desert Partnership, by Gary Marshall and Chad Karges, provided to the

author by High Desert Partnership executive director Brenda Smith.

9   High Desert Partnership website, "Our Success," http://highdesertpartner-ship.org/who-we-are/our-success.html.

10   Personal communication with author, December 4, 2017.

11   Interview with author, July 14, 2016.

12   Jack Southworth, "History of Harney County Restoration Collaborative," unpublished document provided to author by HDP executive director Brenda Smith.

13   Flood irrigation allows water to flow over land surfaces creating broad, shallowly submerged landscapes rich in grasses and invertebrates that feed migrating birds. This practice can be beneficial to both wildlife and live-stock. See, Harney Basin Wetlands Initiative, https://www.youtube.com/watch?v=XfdoIWn7le8.

14   As of 2017, much of ODWR's decision-making in the Harney Basins relies on the only comprehensive groundwater study available, which dates to 1968.

15   Kelly House, "Valley Caught in the Middle," *Oregonian*, Draining Oregon series, August 26, 2016, http://www.oregonlive.com/environment/index.ssf/page/draining_oregon_day_2.html.

16   Originally called the Governor's Watershed Enhancement Board.

17   State of Oregon Water Resources Department, "Place-Based Integrated Water Planning," http://www.oregon.gov/owrd/docs/Place/20160415_PBP_Handout_FINAL.pdf.

18   Harney County Community-Based Water Planning Quarterly, Full Collaborative Summary Notes, July 19, 2017 meeting, http://hcwater-shedcouncil.com/wp-content/uploads/2016/12/Summary-HC-CBWP-July-19-2017.pdf.

19   Author notes from the Harney County Community-Based Water Planning Domestic Well/Municipal Water sub-workgroup meeting, December 13, 2017.

20   A definitive list of Harney County–based collaboratives would be difficult to establish since many have been very informal, and others would be open to question as to whether they fit a reasonable definition of a collaborative group. A partial list, in addition to the ones described in this book, would likely include Harney County Sage Grouse CCAA Steering Committee; Sage-Grouse Conservation Partnership (SageCon); Harney County Weed Management Partnership; Beatys Butte Working Group.

21   At the time the Malheur CCP was published, Karges was deputy project manager under refuge manager Tim Bodeen.

22   Interview with author, March 17, 2017.

23   Ibid., July 18, 2017.

24   Ibid., March 17, 2017.

25   Ibid.

26   Interview with author, September 20, 2016.

27   Also, Samantha White, "Local BLM Employees Aim to Enhance Communication with Community," *Burns Times-Herald*, March 23, 2016, http://btimesherald.com/2016/03/23/local-blm-employees-aim-to-enhance-communication-with-community/.

28   Interview with author, BLM district manager Jeff Rose, October 26, 2017.

29   Marshall Swearingen, "The BLM Has Armed Up since 1978, but It Is Still Outgunned," *High Country News*, January 7, 2016, http://www.hcn.org/articles/bureau-of-land-management-outgunned-bundy-malheur-blm-sheriff.

30   Interview with author, October 16, 2016.

31   Ibid.

32   Interview with author, September 17, 2016.

33   Personal communication with author, refuge manager Chad Karges, December 4, 2017; also, personal communication with author, Malheur Comprehensive Conservation Plan leader Bruce Taylor, December 4, 2017.

34   Interview with author, June 3, 2017; emphasis from interviewee's intonation.

35   Steens Mountain Cooperative Management and Protection Act of 2000 Sec. 132(2)(b).

36   Group interview with author and the Steens Mountain Advisory Committee, June 15, 2017.

37   Interview with author, October 27, 2017.

38   Ibid., July 14, 2016.

39   Ibid., July 18, 2017.

40   Ibid., March 17, 2017.

41   Ibid., September 20, 2016, name withheld by request.

42   Interview with author, July 15, 2016.

43   Ibid., July 14, 2016.

44   Ibid., March 17, 2017.

45   Ibid., October 5, 2017.

46   Ibid., October 27, 2017.

47   Ibid., October 26, 2017.

48 Ibid., with Bruce Taylor, July 18, 2017.

49 Interview with author, July 14, 2016.

50 Ibid., October 13, 2017.

51 Finicum acknowledged that his main income came from government payments for foster children in his family's care.

52 Interviewed in video documentary, No Man's Land, by David Byars, 2017 (33:06, 35:10).

53 Interview with author, July 18, 2017.

54 Ibid., July 14, 2016.

55   Ibid., August 2, 2016.

56 National Wildlife Association, "Chad Karges Honored with Lifetime Achievement Award at Department of Interior," December 2, 2016, https://www.prnewswire.com/news-releases/chad-karges-honored-with-lifetime-achievement-award-at-department-of-the-interior-300372180.html.

57 Interview with author, December 13, 2017.

58 Group interview by author with Steens Mountain Advisory Committee, June 15, 2016.

59 Interview with author, October 27, 2017.

Chapter 5

1 Gary Hunt, "Beirut, Waco, or Oklahoma City," April 19, 1995, posted to Hunt's Outpost of Freedom blog. Hunt wrote of the bombing, "If you truly believe that whatever is necessary to achieve the goal of restoration of the Constitution must be done, then you must learn to accept the reality of what may be necessary to achieve that goal. If an act such as this occurs, whether it be committed by neighbor or foreigner, if the cause for the event has, as it's [sic] object, the same enemy that we perceive, then the acts must never be condemned, nor the results discouraged," http://www.outpost-of-freedom.com/okc0419.htm.

2 Les Zaitz, "Oregon Standoff Spokesman Robert 'LaVoy' Finicum Killed, Bundys in Custody after Shooting near Burns," Oregonian, January 26, 2016, at 6:50 p.m., updated January 28, 2017, at 9:58 p.m., http://www.oregonlive.com/oregon-standoff/2016/01/bundys_in_custody_one_militant.html; Tierney Sneed, "Oregon Occupiers Put Out Call to Arms after Arrests of Militia Leaders," TPM Livewire, http://talkingpointsmemo.com/livewire/oregon-occupiers-call-to-arms.

3 Gavin Seim, "Burns, Oregon—Today Is the Edge of Revolution!"

YouTube video, posted January 27, 2016, https://www.youtube.com/watch?v=xZJQtiCMg1I.

4   Carissa Wolf and Kevin Sullivan, "'Rolling Rally' in Oregon Marks Killing of Wildlife Refuge Occupier LaVoy Finicum," *Washington Post*, January 30, 2016.

5   Video documentary by David Byars, *No Man's Land*, 2017.

6   A symbol of Finicum, who famously gave TV interviews sitting under a blue tarp.

7   Interview with author, camper-protester William C. Fisher at the USFS Joaquin Miller Horse Camp Campground near Burns, Oregon, June 13, 2016.

8   Images of the Hammonds were on the main CSPOA homepage from 2016 to at least September 30, 2017, http://cspoa.org/.

9   Hall spoke in Burns on January 18, 2016, and her associates spoke in Burns on February 11 and February 15.

10   McIntosh spoke in Fields (southern Harney County) on February 20, 2016, and in Burns on February 22, 2016.

11   Interview with author, January 3, 2016.

12   Ibid.

13   The shootings occurred in Las Vegas on June 8, 2014, after the Millers had participated in the Bunkerville standoff with the Bundy family.

14   Interview with author, January 3, 2017.

15   Travis Gettys, "Phony Judge May Have Illegally Impersonated a Cop to Bring Militants' Children to Occupied Oregon Refuge," January 26, 2016. https://www.rawstory.com/2016/01/phony-judge-may-have-illegally-im-personated-a-cop-to-bring-militants-kids-to-occupied-oregon-refuge/.

16   Language characteristic of the "sovereign citizen" movement.

17   Shawna Cox v. United States of America, Harney County Circuit Court, State of Oregon, Case # 16CV31361, filed September 26, 2016.

18   Shawna Cox and those similarly situated and those real parties to be joined as their names become known, Plaintiffs, v. United States Of America and John Does 1-100, Defendants Case No. 2:17-ev-00121-SU Findings And Recommendations, page 9 Findings and Recommendations.

19   These included the primary election for county judge and county commissioner in March 2016; the recall election against county judge in June 2016; and the election for sheriff in November 2016. The only election in which candidates perceived by some to be sympathetic to the Bundy ideology succeeded was the election of the Harney County Soil and Water Conservation District board.

20 Interview with author, October 27, 2017.

21 Ibid., October 27, 2017.

22 Ibid., October 13, 2017.

23 As expressed to the author by Committee of Safety member Melodi Molt in a phone call on Monday, October 23, 2017.

24 "Harney County Fair Gets Its Start in 1900," Harney County Historical Society Newsletter 19, no. 7 (September 1998): 1.

25 Facebook Oregon: Harney County United! September 7, 2017, post by Katie Batie.

26 Personal communication to author, August 28, 2017, name withheld by request.

27 Interview with author, September 22, 2017.

28 Personal communication to author while attending an impromptu memorial for LaVoy Finicum on Highway 395, February 6, 2016, source anonymous.

29 Phoebe Flanigan, "Healing in Harney County," Oregon Public Broadcasting, April 11, 2016 (noon), updated April 12, 2016 (2:10 p.m.), http://www.opb.org/radio/programs/thinkoutloud/segment/harney-county-discussion-healing-future/.

30 Jimmy Tobias, "Return to Malheur: A Battle-Scarred Community Where Cowboys and Conservationists Are Working . . . ," Pacific Standard, November 29, 2016, https://psmag.com/news/return-to-malheur-a-battle-scarred-community-where-cowboys-and-conservationists-are-working.

31 Interview with author, Harney County ranchers Keith and Katie Baltzor, members of the initiative, October 16, 2016.

32 Interview with author, Harney County rancher Kenny Bentz, considered the driving force of the group, October 13, 2017.

33 The Fizzle Flat, "Western Lands Resource Center . . . What?" January 6, 2016, http://www.fizzleflat.com/index.php/7-news/1119-western-lands-resource-center-what.

34 Harney County is often called a rural county, but it is more accurately described as a frontier county because of its isolation and extremely low population density.

35 Interview with author, September 22, 2017.

36 Dani Fried, "Back to Harney County, a Year after Refuge Takeover," Channel 21 News, January 2, 2017, http://www.ktvz.com/news/back-to-harney-county-one-year-after-the-takeover/243932901.

37   Interview with University of Oregon associate professor Marsha Weisiger, University of Oregon Public Lands Field School, September 7, 2017, attended and recorded by author.

38   Interview with author, September 22, 2017.

39   Ibid., October 12, 2017.

40   Personal communication with author, October 5, 2017.

41   Interview with author, September 23, 2017.

42   Some examples cited here were contributed by Harney County rancher Pauline Braymen, and by local residents in a Facebook ("True Harney County United!") conversation initiated by Harney County rancher Georgia Marshall, July 7, 2017. Most local phone numbers have a distinctive "573" prefix.

43   Interview with author, Hipolito Medrano, January 2, 2017.

44   VICE News, "The Oregon Standoff: A Community Divided," January 11, 2016, https://www.youtube.com/watch?v=3NeHPgF_9E0.

45   Interview with author, Thursday, October 12, 2017.

46   Lisa Rein, "The Government Closed Its Offices in Oregon Days before the Armed Takeover due to Fears of Violence," *Washington Post*, January 8, 2016, https://www.washingtonpost.com/news/federal-eye/wp/2016/01/08/the-government-closed-its-offices-in-oregon-days-before-the-armed-takeover-due-to-fears-of-violence/?utm_term=.b2c62fdc4b0c.

47   Maxine Bernstein, "Prosecutors: Oregon Standoff Defendants Broke into Safes, Stole Federal Documents, Called Refuge Takeover 'Another Bunkerville,'" July 30, 2016, http://www.oregonlive.com/oregon-standoff/2016/07/prosecutors_oregon_standoff_de.html; also see Amelia Templeton, "Judge Denies Motion by Ammon Bundy's Lawyer for Mistrial," September 16, 2016, http://www.opb.org/news/series/burns-oregon-standoff-bundy-militia-news-updates/malheur-national-wildlife-refuge-trial-facebook-evidence/.

48   Interview with author, October 12, 2016.

49   This excerpt is cited with permission by personal communication on December 2, 2017, based on a Facebook post dated June 2, 2016, name withheld by request.

50   Interview with author, June 28, 2016, name withheld by request.

51   Names omitted.

52   Interview with University of Oregon Associate Professor Marsha Weisiger, the University of Oregon Malheur Field School, in response to a question by the author, September 7, 2017, recorded by author.

53 Mackay also noted that his own position as deputy manager would not have been authorized had the manager's time not been so fully monopolized by trial testimony and other tasks associated with the occupation.

54 Interview with author, September 22, 2017.

55 Personal communication with author, November 4, 2017, name withheld by request.

56 Interview with author, October 27, 2017.

57 Mohave Valley Daily News, "Supervisors Rename Road for Militia Member," November 11, 2017, http://www.mohavedailynews.com/news/supervisors-rename-road-for-militia-member/article_5ca6b264-c771-11e7-ac0a-ff2670baea2b.html.

58 Members of the Harney County Committee of Safety repeatedly declined telephone and email requests for interviews for this book, citing scheduling problems.

59 Marshall v. French 1901, cited in US Fish and Wildlife Service, 2013 *Malheur National Wildlife Refuge Comprehensive Conservation Plan*, pp. 1–8.

60 Interview with author, July 14, 2016.

61 Rose noted that he and the local BLM office are involved in the Youth Changing the Community Initiative, place-based water planning, the Steens Mountain Cooperative Management and Protection Area, the High Desert Partnership, and the Harney County Restoration Collaborative.

62 Interview with author, October 26, 2017.

63 Eric Mortenson, "Harney County Ranchers Sign on to Sage Grouse Pact," May 27, 2014, http://www.capitalpress.com/Oregon/20140527/harney-county-ranchers-sign-on-to-sage-grouse-pact.

64 Walker et al. (2004) refer to these cross-scale interactions as "panarchy."

65 "Frontier" is a technical term, defined by the National Center for Frontier Communities as "the most remote and geographically isolated areas in the United States. These areas are usually sparsely populated and face extreme distances and travel time to services of any kind," http://frontierus.org/defining-frontier/.

66 Portland Audubon Society conservation director Bob Sallinger speaking at the Oregon Natural Desert Association Desert Conference, October 14, 2016.

67 Bob Sallinger, "Audubon Society of Portland Statement on the Occupation of the Malheur National Wildlife Refuge," January 3, 2016, http://audubon-portland.org/news/audubon-society-of-portland-statement-on-the-occupation-of-malheur-national-wildlife-refuge/?searchterm=malheur%20occupation.

68 Interview with author, October 5, 2017.

69 Ibid., October 27, 2017.

70 Ibid., November 11, 2017.

71 Ibid., October 27, 2017.

72 Ibid., October 27, 2017.

73 Amanda Peacher and Kate Davidson, "Gov. Kate Brown Makes Her First Post-Occupation Visit to Burns," Oregon Public Broadcasting, April 12, 2017, http://www.opb.org/news/ series/burns-oregon-standoff-bundy-militia-news-updates/ oregon-governor-kate-brown-first-post-occupation-visit-burns/.

74 The initiative was actually launched in August 2016, but was still in its formative stage when Governor Brown visited.

75 Governor Kate Brown Facebook page, posted April 13, 2017, https://www. facebook.com/oregongovernor/posts/1855815168010358.

76 Interview with author, High Desert Partnership executive director Brenda Smith, November 21, 2017.

77 John Day is the name of the largest town in Grant County, north of Harney County.

78 Interview with author, October 27, 2017.

79 Ibid., October 16, 2016.

80 Ibid., October 13, 2017.

Chapter 6

1 Los Angeles Times Staff, "This Is What Steve Bannon Told the California Republican Party Convention," http://www.latimes.com/politics/ la-pol-ca-steve-bannon-california-republicans-transcript-20171021-htmlstory. html.

2 Matt Ford, "The Irony of Cliven Bundy's Unconstitutional Stand," *Atlantic*, April 14, 2017, https://www.theatlantic.com/politics/archive/2014/04/ the-irony-of-cliven-bundys-unconstitutional-stand/360587/.

3 John Nolte, "Bogus Cliven Bundy Lawsuit: BuzzFeed Busted Fabricating Trump Smear," *Breitbart News*, January 4, 2016, http://www.breitbart.com/big-journalism/2016/01/04/ bogus-bundy-lawsuit-buzzfeed-busted-fabricating-trump-smear/.

4 Brandon Darby and Logan Churchwell, "The Bundy Family and Armed Resistance to 'Government Land Grabs': Know the Facts," *Breitbart News*, January 3, 2016, http://www.breitbart.com/big-government/2016/01/03/

the-bundy-family-and-armed-resistance-to-government-land-grabs-know-the-facts/.

5   Chris Cirillo, "Trump and Bannon: From Bromance to Breakup," *New York Times*, January 5, 2018, https://www.nytimes.com/video/us/politics/100000005646457/bannon-and-trump-from-bromance-to-breakup.html.

6   US Senate Committee on Energy and Natural Resources, Nomination Hearing of the Honorable Ryan Zinke to be The Secretary of the Interior, S. HRG. 115-10 January 17, 2017, p. 19.

7   Ryan K. Zinke, Memorandum for the President: Final Report Summarizing Findings of the Review of Designations Under the Antiquities Act, August 24, 2017.

8   Excerpts from interview with "patriot" internet activist Kelli Stewart, January 4, 2018, https://www.youtube.com/watch?v=W23J351Kclw.

9   David Zucchino, "A Militia Gets Battle Ready for a 'Gun-Grabbing' Clinton Presidency," *Washington Post*, November 4, 2016, https://www.nytimes.com/2016/11/05/us/a-militia-gets-battle-ready-for-a-gun-grabbing-clinton-presidency.html.?_r=0.

10   Ibid.

11   Deaths included counter-protester Heather Heyer and two state troopers killed in a helicopter crash while monitoring street battles. See Sheryl Gay Stolberg and Brian M. Rosenthal, "Man Charged after White Nationalist Rally in Charlottesville Ends in Deadly Violence," *New York Times*, August 12, 2017, https://www.nytimes.com/2017/08/12/us/charlottesville-protest-white-nationalist.html.

12   Paul A. Djupe et al., "Roger Stone Says There Would Be an 'Insurrection' If Trump Were Impeached. Is He Right?" *Washington Post*, September 15, 2017, https://www.washingtonpost.com/news/monkey-cage/wp/2017/09/15/a-new-survey-finds-trump-opponents-are-more-passionate-and-motivated-than-trump-supporters-by-a-lot/?utm_term=.6ba62e96913e.

13   Jonathan Thompson, "A New and More Dangerous Sagebrush Rebellion," *High Country News*, February 10, 2016, http://www.hcn.org/articles/a-new-and-more-dangerous-sagebrush-rebellion.

14   Bundy meeting with local ranchers in Crane, Oregon, January 18, 2016, attended by author.

15   VICE News, "The Oregon Standoff: A Community Divided," January 11, 2016, https://www.youtube.com/watch?v=3NeHPgF_9E0.

16   Interview with author, October 27, 2017.

17 Ibid., October 16, 2016.

18 Ibid. Because of legal uncertainties, the takings Bentz spoke of were not carried out until after a US Supreme Court decision in 1935 (during the Franklin D. Roosevelt administration) that reaffirmed the federal government's ownership of the refuge.

19 Personal communication with author, June 1, 2017.

20 Bundy spoke of Bureau of Land Management "tyranny" at the Malheur Refuge, apparently unaware that the refuge is managed by the US Fish and Wildlife Service.

21 Sean Anderson, in video documentary, *No Man's Land*, by David Byars, 2017 (02:52).

22 Interview with author, October 16, 2016.

23 Colorado College 2017 Conservation in the West Poll: Seventh Annual Survey of Voters in Seven Western States, January 2017, https://www.coloradocollege.edu/other/stateoftherockies/conservationinthewest/index.html.

24 Personal communication with author, September 10, 2017.

25 Interview with author, October 27, 2017.

26 Jonathan Thompson, "A New and More Dangerous Sagebrush Rebellion," *High Country News*, February 10, 2016, http://www.hcn.org/articles/a-new-and-more-dangerous-sagebrush-rebellion.

Bibliography

Author's note: In researching this book, I conducted more than one hundred original interviews; I also attended dozens of public meetings between January of 2016 and December of 2017. I recorded and transcribed these interviews and meetings into the text that makes up many of the extended quotations in this book. Because of the extraordinary nature of the events in Harney County associated with the Bundy occupation, I was able to find video recordings of other major events and meetings that I was unable to attend, which I also transcribed and transferred into this book. Sources for my interviews and outside sources are cited in the notes; all uncited quotes are sourced from my own transcriptions and notes from meetings I attended.

Aho, J. A. 2016. *Far-Right Fantasy: A Sociology of American Religion and Politics*. New York/London: Routledge/Taylor and Francis.

Aikens, C. M., and R. L. Greenspan. 1988. "Ancient Lakeside Culture in the Northern Great Basin: Malheur Lake, Oregon." *Journal of California and Great Basin Archaeology* 10 (1): 32–61.

Benson, R. D. 1996. "A Watershed Issue: The Role of Streamflow Protection in Northwest River Basin Management." *Environmental Law* 26 (1): 175–224.

Brimlow, G. F. 1951. *Harney County, Oregon, and Its Range Land*. Portland: Binford and Mort.

Brown, B. A. 1995. *In Timber Country: Working People's Stories of Environmental Conflict and Urban Flight*. Philadelphia: Temple University Press.

Charnley, S., T. E. Sheridan, and G. P. Nabhan. 2014. *Stitching the West Back Together: Conservation of Working Landscapes*. Chicago: University of Chicago Press.

Conger, R., and G. H. Elder. 1994. *Families in Troubled Times: Adapting to Change in Rural America*. New York: A. de Gruyter.

Couture, M. D. 1978. Recent and Contemporary Foraging Practices of the Harney Valley Paiute. Master's thesis, Anthropology, Portland State University, Oregon.

Ferguson, D., and N. Ferguson. 1983. *Sacred Cows at the Public Trough*. 1st ed. Bend, OR: Maverick Publications.

Finicum, L. 2015. *Only by Blood and Suffering: Regaining Lost Freedom*. Rochester, NY: Legends Library.

Gray, E. 1995. *Life and Death of Oregon "Cattle King" Peter French 1849–1897*. Eugene, OR: Your Town Press.

Griffiths, D. 1902. "Forage Conditions on the Northern Border of the Great Basin." Washington, DC: United States Department of Agriculture. https://archive.org/details/forageconditions15grif.

Hage, W. 1989. *Storm Over Rangelands: Private Rights in Federal Lands*. 1st ed. Bellevue, WA: Free Enterprise/Merril Press.

Holling, C. S. 1973. "Resilience and Stability of Ecological Systems." *Annual Review of Ecological Systems* 4:1–23.

Holloway, C. 2015. *Hamilton versus Jefferson in the Washington Administration: Completing the Founding or Betraying the Founding?* New York: Cambridge University Press.

Jackman, E. R., and R. A. Long. 1964. *The Oregon Desert*. Caldwell, ID: Caxton Printers.

Jenkins, D., L. G. Davis, and T. W. Stafford Jr. 2012. "Clovis Age Western Stemmed Projectile Points and Human Coprolites at the Paisley Caves." *Science* 337 (6091): 223–228.

Jenkins, D. L., L. G. Davis, J. Thomas W. Stafford, P. F. Campos, T. J. Connolly, L. S. Cummings, M. Hofreiter, et al. 2013. "Geochronology, Archaeological Context, and DNA at the Paisley Caves." In *Paleoamerican Odyssey*, edited by K. E. Graf, C. V. Ketron, and M. R. Waters, 485–510. College Station, TX: Center for the Study of First Americans.

Klein, A. 2017. *Fanaticism, Racism, and Rage Online: Corrupting the Digital Sphere*. 1st ed. New York: Nature America.

Langston, N. 2003. *Where Land and Water Meet: A Western Landscape Transformed*. Seattle: University of Washington Press.

Levitas, D. 2002. *The Terrorist Next Door: The Militia Movement and the Radical Right*. 1st ed. New York: Thomas Dunne Books/St. Martin's Press.

MacNab, JJ. Forthcoming. *The Seditionists*. New York: St. Martin's Press.

Makley, M. J. 2017. *Open Spaces, Open Rebellions: The War over America's Public Lands*. Amherst: University of Massachusetts Press.

Mayer, J. 2016. *Dark Money: The Hidden History of the Billionaires behind the Rise of the Radical Right*. 1st ed. New York: Doubleday.

McCarthy, M. 1992. "The First Sagebrush Rebellion: Forest Reserves and States Rights in Colorado and the West, 1891–1907." In *The Origins of the National Forests: A Centennial Symposium*, edited by Harold K. Steen and the T. F. H. Society. Durham, NC: Duke University Press.

Mulloy, D. J. 2004. *American Extremism: History, Politics and the Militia Movement*. London: Routledge.

Neiwert, D. A. 1999. *In God's Country: The Patriot Movement and the Pacific Northwest.* Pullman: Washington State University Press.

Newman, T. M., R. Bogue, C. D. Carley, R. D. McGilvra, and D. Moretti. 1974. Archaeological Reconnaisance of the Malheur National Wildlife Refuge, Harney County, Oregon. Manuscript on file at the Oregon State Historic Preservation Office, Salem, Oregon.

Robbins, W. G. 2016. "The Malheur Occupation and the Problem with History." *Oregon Historical Quarterly* 117 (4): 574–603.

Skousen, W. C. 1985. *The Making of America: The Substance and Meaning of the Constitution.* Washington, DC: National Center for Constitutional Studies.

———. 2007. *The 5000 Year Leap: The 28 Great Ideas That Changed the World.* Malta, ID: National Center for Constitutional Studies.

Sunshine, S. 2016. *Up in Arms: A Guide to Oregon's Patriot Movement.* Scappoose, OR/ Somerville, MA: Rural Organizing Project/Political Research Associates.

US Department of Agriculture. 1911. *Report of the Chief of the Bureau of Biological Survey Henry W. Henshaw.* Washington DC: Government Printing Office. https:// sora.unm.edu/sites/default/files/journals/auk/v029n02/p0263-p0263.pdf.

Walker, B., C. S. Holling, S. R. Carpenter, and A. Kinzig. 2004. "Resilience, Adaptability and Transformability in Social-Ecological Systems." *Ecology And Society* 9 (2).

Walker, P. 2016. "Why the Court 'Victory' for Malheur Militants was Anything But." *The Conversation.* http://theconversation.com/ why-the-court-victory-for-malheur-militants-was-anything-but-67896.

Wolff, M. 2018. *Fire and Fury: Inside the Trump White House.* New York: Henry Holt.

Index